A Forager's Life

A
Forager's
Life

Finding my heart
and home in nature

Helen Lehndorf

HarperCollins*Publishers*

Important notice: before taking any natural remedy you should consult a health care professional if you have an existing medical condition or are taking any existing medication.

HarperCollins*Publishers*
Australia • Brazil • Canada • France • Germany • Holland • India
Italy • Japan • Mexico • New Zealand • Poland • Spain • Sweden
Switzerland • United Kingdom • United States of America

First published in 2023
by HarperCollins*Publishers* (New Zealand) Limited
Unit D1, 63 Apollo Drive, Rosedale, Auckland 0632, New Zealand
harpercollins.co.nz

A catalogue record for this book is available from the National Library of New Zealand

ISBN 978 1 7755 4220 9 (pbk)
ISBN 978 1 7754 9251 1 (ebook)

Cover design by Hazel Lam, HarperCollins Design Studio
Cover images: Manuka, Kawa kawa, Kūmarahou and Pohutukawa by Sarah Featon / Te Papa; Fruit of the Supplejack by Martha King, courtesy National Library of New Zealand; Nettle by istockphoto.com
Internal images by istockphoto.com
Typeset in Adobe Garamond Pro by Kirby Jones
Printed and bound in Australia by McPherson's Printing Group

MIX
Paper | Supporting responsible forestry
FSC
www.fsc.org
FSC® C001695

To the weeds

... romp on, green things!

AUTHOR'S NOTE

I have included the botanical names of plants in recipes and activities to avoid misidentification. Please take care never to eat any foraged foods that you aren't 100 per cent sure about.

Some names have been changed to protect privacy. Some sequences of events have been condensed for narrative flow.

I am a Pākehā New Zealander with German, English, Scottish and Danish ancestry. I write about ideas of ancestral exploration and reconnection from the perspective of a sixth-generation Pākehā New Zealander/tauiwi. I want to acknowledge that the experience of connection to place and ancestral knowledge is utterly different for tangata whenua, the first people of Aotearoa. I wish to offer respect and gratitude to all tangata whenua, who suffer many fractures to their intergenerational cultural transmission due to the actions of Aotearoa's early 'invasive species': the European ancestors of Pākehā New Zealanders, like my own, and Pākehā today.

CONTENTS

*If to forage is to seek, to hunt, to find and to gather
plants in wild places …
what is it called when the plants find you?*

PROLOGUE

Stone soup

A tired traveller arrives in a village. He asks the locals if they will share some food with him, but they all say they have nothing to share. Unfazed, he lights a fire in the village square anyway, puts a large cauldron of water on to boil, drops a stone in it and says, 'No problem, I will just sit here a while and eat my stone soup.'

One of the villagers feels bad about this poor man with his miserable stone soup and so goes home to rummage in her kitchen. She returns, saying she's found an onion he can have. Then another villager finds a spare potato, another some herbs, another some salt. These small contributions continue until eventually the boiling water has turned into a delicious, rich soup. The traveller offers to share his 'stone soup' with the villagers. A merry fireside feast ensues, shared by all.

*

The story of stone soup is a potent parable about 'enoughness' and how many humble offerings put together can make a feast, that lots of little gestures can add up to a lot, and that people are stronger together.

It also captures how I was raised: on a steady diet of stone soup, well fed by the contributions of many people in my small town. No one had a lot of money, but there were other riches to be found. Food was foraged and fished, hunted and harvested, grown and gathered and, invariably, shared. With everyone's contributions, there was always enough.

Seeds + Roots

CHAPTER 1

A bramble scrump

Blackberry

In rural north Taranaki, 1976, I have a new baby brother. Roy. He is fat and cute and I like him, but I'm also a bit annoyed at how distracted Mum has been since he arrived. Dad is taking me out on his motorbike for the day so that Mum and Roy can get some rest. I love going for rides on Dad's bike. He sits me in front of him on the petrol tank and cuddles me close. I feel both terrified and safe. Thrilled. I have my own small orange glittery helmet, and I'm very proud of it as we roar off, out of town and into the hills.

In Taranaki, we say that the mountain only appears to you when he's feeling happy. He is out in all his glory today, his usual cloak of cloud absent in the crisp autumn morning.

In a deep valley, Dad meets up with some friends. They are planning to ride off-road. Dad is the only one who has turned up with a kid in tow, and his friends tease him.

'Nah, she'll be all right,' he says. 'She's a sensible kid. There's nothing that can hurt her down here.'

He wants to ride up some hilly terrain that isn't suitable for a four-year-old, so he plonks me on to a large fallen log in a patch of sun at the bottom of the valley.

'You'll be all right, Rigs. We won't be long,' he says. 'You stay put. I'll be able to see you from up the top of the hill. You should be able to see us from here but, if you can't, you'll be able to hear us.'

I am a bit unsure, but I trust Dad, so I nod.

'Why don't you see what you can find with your magnifying glass?' he says.

I have a small, heavy magnifying glass on a cord around my neck. It has a black resin handle and a thick round lens. I got it in my Christmas stocking. It is one of my favourite things. It feels important to me, serious, not a toy but a tool. I love to peer through it at the hairs on my arm, at ladybirds and slaters in the back garden, at the centres of flowers and at cross-sections of carrot. I hold them up to the light to see the blazing suns in their centres. The magnifying glass has given me a new way of looking. I take it off my neck.

The men hoon off on their bikes in a flurry of noise and stinky exhaust, leaving a plume of black smoke. At first I stay put, staring up at the clear sky. The sound of motorbikes echoes through the valley. Dad was right. I can't see them but I can hear them.

After a while, though, the sound grows fainter and it begins to feel like they've been gone a long time. I slip off the log, bored of the moss and wood I've been looking at through my magnifying glass. It is hard to concentrate. I've never been left by myself before. I feel like I'm shrinking. The valley is so vast and overwhelming. I could dissolve into the cold air and never be seen again.

A large magpie is eating from a thick bush at the edge of a patch of trees where the sun is hitting the valley floor. I wander over to look more closely. It's a blackberry patch. I know about blackberries from when we went blackberrying on Aunty Trixie's farm. We spent a long time gathering enough berries to make pies.

The blackberries sat in flat cardboard boxes lined with newspaper on our kitchen bench, waiting for Mum to cook them into pies with apples, flaky pastry and a thick sprinkle of white sugar on top. I couldn't stop myself from pinching mouthfuls of the gleaming bounty.

'Who's been at the blackberries?' Mum said in annoyance. Because of my greed, our pies ended up being more apple than berry, pink-stained rather than brilliant crimson, but I was unrepentant. The shiny fresh blackberries were too hard to resist.

The magpie squawks at me, unwilling to share. I am scared. Dad told me that magpies love shiny things and sometimes attack people for their buttons, brooches and sparkly eyes. Dad tells me lots of tales, some scary, some true. I don't want the magpie to come for my shiny eyes. I keep to the opposite end of the thicket and peer into the brambles. Fat bunches of berries in every shade, from mottled green to dull red, purple to shiny black, hang from the branches. The blackberry bush feels friendly to me. I am in good company. She will extend her brambles to protect me as well as her fruit.

I pull the sleeve of my jersey over my hand so that only my fingertips are poking out and tentatively start plucking the darkest fruits. I get pricked and scratched, but it doesn't bother me too much. Dad always says that we have to pay the blackberry bush with a little of our blood. The berries are tart and the juice paints my fingertips a brilliant red. I keep one eye on the magpie while I pick and gobble.

When I've eaten all the berries I can, I pull my *Holly Hobbie* handkerchief out of my pocket and start to collect some for Dad. I peer at one through my magnifying glass. Up close it looks even blacker. I can see tiny red hairs sticking out of every berry sac. Everything looks better magnified: worlds within worlds.

When I've harvested a good mound of fruit, I screw up the open ends of the handkerchief and go back to the log where Dad left me.

I start to get cold. The patch of sun has moved on and the valley is beginning to feel gloomy. Eating so many berries has made me thirsty, and I need to pee. Can I still hear the motorbikes? I'm not sure. The memory of the sound is circling my mind. I pull my pants down and pee right where I'm standing, in the long grass beside the blackberry. I go as quickly as I can, scared the magpie will be attracted to my white bottom, and then yank my pants back up.

The magpie does seem to be getting bolder, coming in closer to me then flitting off. I throw a stone at it and make a sound from deep within me, a growling gut-cry. The blackberry bush has given me courage, reminded me that I am whole, too solid to be swallowed by the valley's vastness. The magpie takes off into the trees in a flurry.

I turn my back on it and focus on staring at the shiny berries, the ones higher up, out of my reach. I climb up on the log and listen hard for the bikes. I put my magnifying glass back on, make tight fists with my hands and thrust them into my pockets.

I resolve to hold my hands in fists until the men come back. If I can keep squeezing them tightly they will return faster.

For a long time there is nothing, only the sound of the wind in the trees, but just when my hands are beginning to go numb from clenching, I hear the faint whining of motors. I wave my arms and yell, 'Hello? I'm here! I'm down here!'

All at once, the bikes burst over the top of the hill and the valley fills with the engines' roaring. The riders pause, taking in the view. Dad sees me waving and waves back. He cups his hands to his mouth and lets out a yodel: '*Yoodelayeeeooooo!*'

I feel like I might cry with relief but I push the tears down. I don't want Dad to think I'm a sook. Part of going on adventures with Dad means showing that I am brave and can handle a challenge.

I watch the bikes wind and bump their way down the ridge, coming slowly towards me. I am weak with relief.

Dad pulls up alongside me. 'Ya right, love? You found some blackberries, I see.' He draws a circle in the air around his mouth. I hand him the handkerchief bundle. It's slowly turning purple as the berry juices leak through the white fabric. He throws his head back and tips the berries into his mouth. The fruit of my labours disappear in one swallow.

'Good on you, Rigs.' He ruffles my hair.

'You were gone a very long time and I'm thirsty,' I say. He grabs my helmet off the log and scoops me up on to the bike's petrol tank.

'Aw, I think you're okay. The blackberries kept you busy, eh? But let's get you a drink.'

Dad's friends have sprawled out with their lunch and broken out a flagon of beer. We leave them to it and bump across to a small creek on the other side of the valley.

'Where shall we get our drink?' he asks. A small test. He's been teaching me how to drink from streams and creeks, how to avoid stagnant pools and look for swift-moving waters. I point to a step in the creek where the water is tipping over the edge of some boulders, falling into a pool below.

'Yes! That's the trick!' He pulls his army-surplus woollen hat out of his jacket pocket and scoops up some water from the swift part of the creek. 'Drink it quick! Before it seeps out.'

I take the hat. I drink and drink the cold fresh water.

Dad dampens the end of his jersey sleeve and tries to wipe the blackberry juice off my face. 'Better not take you home to Mum looking like that, eh?'

We share a squashed ham sandwich that he pulls from his other pocket. Then he pushes my tight helmet down on my head, buckles the strap, and we start the long journey home. The magpie watches us depart from high up in a macrocarpa tree above the log. I wonder if it will try to chase me home.

I'm not the same kid who rode into the valley that morning. I look back at my blackberry friend and wave goodbye.

*

My family often ate foraged fruits and vegetables when I was growing up, although we didn't call it 'foraging'. We were more likely to say 'gathered' or maybe 'scrumped'. Foraging has connotations of randomness and chance, whereas to be a gatherer suggests a longer relationship with the land, a sense that food will be in the same place it was last season, year after year, in a long chain of harvesting from place. I grew up feeling held by the land because it endlessly provided for us.

We ate with the seasons. In late summer we'd go blackberrying along country roads, wearing long sleeves to avoid getting too scratched by the bushes. A wilding fruit tree on an isolated roadside was considered a free-for-all, and we'd jump out of the car to fill our boot with bags of fruit. When the market gardens in our area had pick-your-own days towards the end of the season, we'd go along for a Sunday family outing and pick buckets of peas or boxes of strawberries in the hot sun. We never ate tomatoes in July or leeks in January.

In autumn, we'd gather field mushrooms. I'd cut them from the ground with my pocketknife and inhale the musky perfume they released when first picked. Roy and I were charged with checking the mushrooms for wormholes. If a mushroom had them, we'd jump on it, grinding it into the ground with our gumboots and kicking it around to spread the mycelium for next year's season. Mum and Dad would cook the mushrooms in lots of butter and black pepper, and we'd eat them alongside beef steaks or with fried eggs for breakfast.

There was a squirrel-like approach to our gathering, garnering and storing food. It was important that there was an abundance in the cupboard in case of lean days. My parents were happy to eat leftovers, we called them 'scraps', for several nights in a row, always prioritising thrift over novelty; nothing was ever wasted.

In the comic strip *Garfield*, there's a running gag that whenever Jon, Garfield's owner, attempts to talk about his feelings, his mother responds by sliding a plate towards him and saying, 'Eat. Eat.' It makes me laugh because this is how my parents have always been, too. Talking can be difficult. Offering food is easy. Food as love.

*

When I'm around plants, I think of them as living beings, individuals with personalities – similar to the way I think of people. Plants give off vibes. They talk to me and I talk to them. Not out loud, of course, but the communication feels tangible nonetheless. It can be overwhelming at times, like my senses are merging with the plant's. Mostly, though, it's a positive thing, rich, illuminating and difficult to convey without sounding a bit eccentric.

The blackberry bush in the valley is the first plant I remember communicating with. As a bramble, blackberry is a plant of boundaries and edges. That day, the blackberry gifted me my own edges, a sense of self in a moment when I was overwhelmed. It offered me something secure to connect to.

A few years ago I learned about the world of plant-essence medicines. These healing potions are made by capturing the vibrational essence of a flower or plant. You immerse the plant in water and leave it to steep for a day or so, then preserve it with a little brandy or vinegar. Flower essences are not herbal tinctures, homeopathic remedies or essential oils. They're highly dilute substances believed to hold the energetic imprint of a plant, its consciousness and characteristics.

People take flower essences for psychological and emotional healing. The idea is that it will awaken in the person the qualities of the plant, helping to foster wellbeing. Scientists are highly sceptical about the efficacy of plant essences. To a scientist, any benefits claimed from using them land somewhere on a spectrum from placebo effect to deluded magical thinking. But plant essences are vibrational medicine – a difficult thing to measure and quantify. Some people report experiencing plant personalities or energies after taking hallucinogenic phytochemicals, like magic mushrooms, when the apertures of their perception have been widened.

I've tried commercial plant essences. Some seemed to have an effect on me and others not so much. What interests me most about them is how often a plant essence's description matches the personality, or characteristics, of a plant that I feel through my own synaesthetic perceptions. And it's not just me: plant essences might explain why some people feel compelled to hug trees. As big, old plants, they give off comforting and grounding vibrations. Experiencing a plant's essence is similar to the enchantment of getting to know a new person you feel drawn towards.

I don't believe it's necessary to take plant essences, though. I think the best way to receive healing and wisdom from a plant is to find it growing somewhere, alive and thriving, and to sit with it, tune in, see what comes.

Blackberry is said to be anchoring. It can put a scattered mind back together. It's a plant of vigour and tenacity, encouraging you to stand in your own power and find the courage to move forward.

Foraging for blackberries is a common New Zealand pastime: we go 'blackberrying'. For lots of folks, it is their main (and sometimes only) experience of foraging. Blackberry grows prolifically here, especially on marginal lands – beach and bush edges, railway lands and lower mountainous terrains – making it a burgundy jewel in memories of late-summer holidays.

Along with other brambles and plants with thorns or stingers, like rose, nettle and thistle, blackberry is a boundary plant. It asserts its strong personality by warning you to keep back. Brambles appear throughout folklore and myth as impenetrable borders, tests of strength and determination. While their fruits are delicious and highly nutritious, they can only be accessed by those willing to approach slowly and with respect.

Blackberry is also a voracious pest plant because of its rampant reproduction. It colonises through its creeping roots; its seed, spread wide and far by birds; and its questing canes, which can form roots wherever they meet the ground. Even tiny scraps of root can grow new canes, making it very difficult to control. If left untended, the new season's growth will grow on top of last year's brittle, dry plants, meaning they can soon form a prickly, impenetrable and highly flammable wall. It is vigorously sprayed by many local councils and farmers.

Wild blackberry is not fooling around. It can swallow human-hewn paths in one season, effortlessly winding over human markings on the land. On a recent walk, I saw thick ropes of creeping blackberry bramble growing atop the tar seal of the abandoned Manawatū Gorge road. It seemed to be doing just fine without soil to bed into.

Blackberry will always be an important ancestor plant to me. In a lifelong dance of reciprocity, every autumn I harvest its fruit and give it back a little of my blood. It is thorny and unforgiving, a blight on the landscape to some and the source of sunny memories for others. It's a plant that has taught me a lot about boundaries and the strength required to live on the margins, out on the edge.

Blackberry and thyme oxymel

Makes approximately 600 ml

The best thing to do with a blackberry is eat it, warm from the sun, while you're standing beside the bush. After that, it's hard to go past a blackberry and apple pie. But, third in line, I like to make the most of blackberry's many medicinal qualities with a tincture or oxymel – some autumnal armour for the cold winter months ahead.

If you've never made your own home remedies or medicines before, starting can be a little intimidating. A simple oxymel is great because you can use it as a preventative medicine or just add it to your food. Oxymels have been used as medicines since ancient times. The name comes from the Latin term *oxymeli*, meaning 'acid and honey'.

The honey and apple cider vinegar extract the healing components of the fruit and herbs. Blackberry (*Rubus fruticosus*) acts as an antimicrobial and anti-inflammatory. It's very high in vitamin C and the mineral manganese. Thyme (*Thymus vulgaris*) supports bronchial health, blood oxygenation and immunity. It's also very soothing for a sore throat. (When I feel a sore throat coming on, I put a large sprig of thyme in a cup with a teaspoon of honey and add boiling water. Just one cup seems to immediately reduce the discomfort.)

Take a spoonful of blackberry and thyme oxymel whenever you feel you need an immunity boost or if you have a cold. It can also be used in food as a dressing or marinade.

Ingredients
1 cup blackberries, tightly packed
½ cup sprigs of thyme, roughly chopped
1 ½ cups organic raw apple cider vinegar
1 cup honey

Method
Mash the blackberries in a bowl and then stir through the thyme. Tip the mixture into a large glass jar then cover it with the vinegar, ensuring the mix is totally submerged. Cover with a

non-metal lid (vinegar corrodes metal lids) and leave in a dark cupboard to steep for 2 to 4 weeks.

After the steeping is complete, strain the blackberry and thyme mix out of the vinegar. The vinegar will have turned a vibrant ruby red. Use a wooden spoon to slowly stir the honey into the vinegar, until it has completely dissolved. Label and store in the fridge for up to a year. (Don't forget to label your bottles with names, ingredients and dates. If I've learned anything in all my years of preserving, it's that any time I feel certain I will remember what's in a jar or bottle and when it was made, I never do. Sometimes I like to add a note about where I foraged the ingredients from, too.)

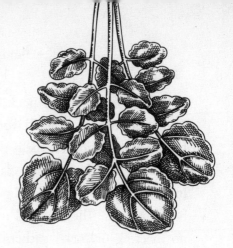

CHAPTER 2

Dead things swinging

Pūhā

I grew up on 1 Strange Street.

It's a distinctive address. When people asked where I lived, they would assume I was making a joke. But it's a real place and it was my childhood home: a 1960s white stucco house in the small coastal Taranaki town of Waitara. It's where I spent my first eighteen years.

Like a lot of streets in Waitara, Strange Street was named after a Pākehā soldier in the Taranaki land wars – just one of the many blood-soaked scraps of colonisation the wars have imprinted on the region.

The 1970s Taranaki of my childhood hadn't advanced much beyond the 1950s. The old men of the town still dressed in wool and tweed suits, leather brogues and work boots, and felt trilby hats. They smoked wooden pipes and hand-rolled cigarettes. They were gruff, nuggety and quick to give you a clip round the ear if you annoyed them, but they also carried bags

17

of boiled lollies in their pockets and would slip you one if you were well behaved. The old women wore pastel-coloured chiffon headscarves to cover their tight white perms, carried hard handbags with loud clicky clasps, and squeezed their bunions into shiny shoes. All the old people smelled like mothballs and boiled onions. They seemed to be constantly drinking tea and no meeting or social gathering happened without brewing a large pot. To this day the sight of a metal community teapot, the kind that needs two handles because it's so large, gives me a nostalgic boost of the spirits.

There was always dead things swinging around me. Certainly a lot down at Borthwicks, the freezing works where my father and many of our family and friends worked, but around our yard, too. On weekends, our car shed became an abattoir; animals were strung up from the rafters, waiting to be skinned, gutted, butchered. My father is a butcher, a hunter, a gatherer and a fine fly fisherman. His skills are often called on by his friends when they need help butchering their bounty. My brother, Roy, and I grew up seeing dead animals all around, so we weren't scared by them: sheep, pheasants, chickens, geese, wild goats and pigs, quails, fish of all kinds, seafood and whitebait.

Mum and Dad made a little go a long way. My mother is thrifty and hardworking. She taught us kitchen skills from a young age; it was my job to peel potatoes and prep vegetables for our tea from around the age of seven. Roy and I were on dishes from such a young age that my brother had to stand on a stool to put things away.

On weekends, Mum had a job as a clerk in the Waitara TAB, a sports-betting agency, so Dad looked after us. Without Mum's more sensible guiding hand around, we got up to all sorts of adventures. Dad would take us along to whatever he had planned: hunting for meat of various kinds, helping his mates, or on other missions – some more child-appropriate than others. He often did weekend moonlighting for extra cash or for land access to go hunting. He'd butcher bodies of beef for local farmers, and Roy and I would go along and play with the farmer's kids or the dogs. We'd look forward to a great morning or afternoon tea made by the farmer's wife. Used to feeding big shearing or mustering gangs, farmers seemed to effortlessly magic up piles of delicious food: scones with jam and cream, great wodges of cold bacon and egg pie topped with tomato relish, roasted lamb sandwiches on white bread with thick butter and hot English mustard.

*

Borthwicks was nicknamed 'the university' by locals, because it's where many of the town's young people went to work after leaving school and 'got an education in the school of life'. It stunk, a foul smoke emitting from large chimneys – the smell of burnt bones and offal. Pipes full of bleachy, bloody water polluted the Waitara River, which ran through the town. Roy and I knew it like our second home, especially the public-facing butcher shop where Dad worked. We'd often stop in after school in the hope Dad might cut a raw saveloy off a hanging link for us to munch on the way home.

In the bowels of the works was 'the chain'. Sheep and cows would come off transport trucks from farms into the open back end of the works, where they were electrically stunned and then had their throats slit – a literal death's door. The chain was the production line: the animals were butchered into cuts along a chain of workers, each doing the same repetitive cuts for their whole shift. Roy and I would watch the men – dressed in white from their hairnets, down long white plastic aprons, to their white gumboots with bright yellow soles – skinning, disembowelling and carving off different cuts of meat from the carcasses that swung past them in slow motion. They'd stand behind a shallow concrete drain that ran all day with bleachy, bloody water. It was a loud and overwhelming place. The men were both staunch and hilarious; they could veer between a hard glare and a belly laugh within seconds. I was always glad to pop out the chain's far end into the relative calm of the butcher shop.

*

We didn't have a lot of money but Mum and Dad were resourceful. They'd get food from the hills and the rivers, from the sea and the fields, and from friends and neighbours. We were wealthy in connection and sharing. We'd often get home from outings to find gifts of food sitting on our back step: vegetables, waxed cardboard cups of fresh cream, flat boxes of berries, bags of apples. Sometimes Mum and Dad knew who had dropped the gifts off and sometimes they'd never find out, but that wasn't seen as a big deal. Sharing was just what we all did when we had more than we needed.

Long before the revival of nose-to-tail eating, we were using every part of an animal. Mum would boil chicken carcasses to make fatty and nourishing chicken soups, a cure-all for colds and other illnesses. She'd cook ham bones with dried peas to make soup, or Dad would use them for boil-ups. Beef bones were brewed into dark stock. We ate all kinds of offal: cow's tongue was boiled with onions, weighted down between two plates then served in cold slices. Steak and kidney in gravy was a common weeknight dinner. Dad loved sheep's testicles, also known as 'mountain oysters'. Being willing to eat what we called 'gross stuff' would always win Dad's approval, so Roy and I gamely sampled all kinds of sinewy, chewy things, including huhu grubs. We'd hunt for them when we went camping, and Dad would cook them on a billy lid over the smouldering charcoals of the fire. They had crispy outers and creamy centres that tasted a bit like cheese sauce or peanut butter, depending on what the grub had been eating.

Most people had a huge vegetable garden, hidden away in the furthest corner of a section as though they were something to hide. We grew a few things at home – herbs and leafy greens, passionfruit, guavas and lemons – but for the most part we got our vegetables from neighbours. Mum and Dad would help with chores or give them meat, and they'd give us cardboard boxes of cauliflowers, cabbages and wonky, crinkly carrots.

All the grown-ups worked very hard. They'd work hard at their jobs and then carry on working hard on the weekends, when they'd fish, hunt, gather food for their families, garden, work on their houses, or help out at community events and working bees. Bigger working bees, like laying a driveway or a building job, ended with a Sunday night hāngī. Dad learned to cook hāngī from Māori friends at these gatherings and was soon in demand for his hāngī-prep services. Afterwards, he'd put the used hāngī baskets in the creek to attract eels and then stand on the bank shooting them.

Any rest was usually accompanied by alcohol. Beers by the crate for the men; large glass flasks of cheap sherry or cask wine for the women. There was lots of homemade alcohol, too – home-brew, hooches and fruit wines. The general rule was that you didn't start drinking until after 5 pm, so on Friday afternoons one of the aunties gathered at our place would hop up on a chair, cackling, and move the hands on the kitchen clock forward so that the sherry could be 'legitimately' uncorked.

Roy and I liked it when the adults were distracted by their own socialising. It meant we could do whatever we wanted. Once the adults got on the sauce, we'd tear around the neighbourhood with our rowdy gang of mates until eventually a parent would go to fetch a giant pile of fish and chips. Or Dad would bring home links of saveloys to be boiled up in a huge stock pot and served to us through the kitchen window on slices of bread and butter. No plates meant no washing up and, as a bonus, we could eat dinner without getting off our bikes.

Dad would often go bush, disappearing for the day and coming back with some manner of beast for the pot or freezer. Sometimes he'd take us, too. The main rules were 'no whining', 'don't do anything stupid', and 'always eat what you're given'. Even though we lived in town, the wilds, nature, was all around us: the beach, the bush, the mountain. 'Wild' was used to describe anger, too. My mother would complain to Dad about our antics: 'Oh, they made me so wild!'

Dad was a kind of bush superhero to me. He was strong, brave and loved eating off the land. He had a way of making everything seem like an adventure, and he spoke in salty aphorisms: chilly weather was 'cold as a witch's tit'; a speedy getaway was made 'as fast as a robber's dog'; a bad decision as 'dumb as eating yellow snow'. He dubbed coddled town dogs as 'turners', because 'all they're good for is turning good dog food into dog shit'. Anyone considered to be dishonest was dismissed as a 'total mongrel'.

He was a pragmatic teacher. While the bush, rivers and ocean were places of beauty, bounty and life, he made it clear that they were also places of threat. If we didn't learn some survival skills and stay vigilant, the forces of nature would have no qualms about swallowing us up. The stakes were high.

*

Up on the hill at Waitara's centre sits Ōwae Whaitara Marae, on the site of the historic Manukorihi Pā, home of local hapū Ngāti Te Whiti, Ngāti Rāhiri and Manukorihi of the Te Ātiawa iwi. On a clear day, you can see for miles from Manukorihi Hill – down the length of the Waitara River to the sea, and, to the south, Mount Taranaki.

When I was growing up, the marae was the social hub of Waitara and the phrase 'up the marae' was a common answer to the question, 'Where will the meeting/party/gathering be held?' We'd go there for school and community events. Dad would often drop meat parcels up the marae for tangihanga and other big events. He saw a lot of the back door of the whare kai, where he was well fed by the gaggle of whare kai nannies who wouldn't let him do a drop-off without stopping for a cup of tea and a treat.

Dad loved to terrify me and Roy, and he told us that the fierce carvings on the Te Ikaroa-a-Māui wharenui, with their flashing pāua-shell eyes and protruding pointy tongues, came alive after dark, climbing down off the boards and chasing naughty children. If we were misbehaving, he'd drive around the ring road of the marae, slowing down outside the wharenui and threatening to throw us out of the car to the taniwha. We'd cling to each other in the back seat, screaming, 'Sorry, Dad! We'll be good! We'll be good!' He'd watch us squirming in the rear-view mirror and have a good laugh before driving us home.

Dad told us the local eels were taniwha, too, so we were terrified of the fat, slow eels we'd see in the rivers and creeks. Sometimes he caught huge eels – as long and thick as his leg – but I was too scared to eat the meat, believing I'd be eating a taniwha. Dad kept us on our toes with his tales, all of which he'd finish by saying, 'Honestly, true story.'

*

We had close relationships with all our neighbours, but particularly the woman in the house behind us. We called her 'Nana Smith' although she wasn't our grandmother. Nana Smith was in her seventies and had snow-white hair in a bob that she kept off her face with a pearl hair clip. Her stories about farming life sounded like tales from an earlier century. She'd travelled in a horse and gig before cars were common, been cut off from the world by winter snow storms, seen gruesome farm accidents that her family had to attend to alone because the doctor was hours away by horse in New Plymouth.

I was obsessed with the Little House on the Prairie books and would read Nana Smith excerpts, asking, 'Have you ever done these things, too, Nana?' Often this invited a snort, followed by, 'I'm not *that* old,' but sometimes it was a yes, which gave me a thrill. I had first-hand contact with my very own 'pioneer' farm girl. No, she'd never tapped a maple tree for syrup. Yes, she had sewn clothing from sugar and flour sacks. No, she'd never made a doll from corn husks and wheat stalks. Yes, they had used giant blocks of ice to keep food cold before fridges were common.

I was tasked with running errands between our households – taking meals, jars of jam, cuts of meat – and I did them willingly because she'd press a jellybean into my palm to say thanks. She had an extensive vegetable garden and she saved her own seeds, made her own soil and used found materials for her garden beds.

Nana Smith was very strong and tough for a tiny, tottery woman. She would eat things even my thrifty parents baulked at. Whenever Dad shot a wild pig, he'd give me the head wrapped in muslin cloth to take over to her. She'd immediately plonk it on her chopping block and split it in two with a small axe so that she could make brawn, pig's-head meat set in aspic. Roy and I would shriek in horror at the sight of the cross-section of the pig's head, with its freakishly long nasal passage, its mouth with a purple-and-blue bisected tongue, and the small brown cloud of its brain.

She was our babysitter, and when we slept over she would put us to sleep in a bed with a huge feather mattress she'd handmade, during her farming days, from cotton ticking and goose down. It was fun to climb on, like crawling up a cloud, but not especially functional; by the morning we'd have sunk right through the middle, our bones cold and sore from the bed's wire base.

*

Roy and I were trusted with knives, needles, hammers and rifles from an early age. Dad gave both of us pocketknives on our sixth birthdays. He taught us how to load rifles and fire them, first at cardboard targets then at yard birds and possums. We'd earn pocket money by loading shot into bullet cases for duck-shooting season. On one weekend trip out to the Mokau estuary, Dad handed us floundering gaffs (broom handles with sharp barbs attached to one end) with the cheery warning, 'Just don't stab your foot!' It's a common floundering injury: someone mistakes their own pale foot for the white back of a flounder in the muddy shallows. I was much more cautious than Roy but Dad had little patience with my fretting. He'd pat me on the back and say cheerfully, 'Just don't do anything stupid and you'll be fine.'

He taught us how to sharpen knives, how to blow our noses without needing a handkerchief (by shooting the snot out at high pressure – a surprisingly useful life skill), how to find drinkable water in the wild, and how to cook a three-course camp dinner using one small billy.

Our growing bodies suffered the consequences of our adventures: sunburn, bee-stings, grazes, thistle scratches, small cuts, mosquito and sandfly bites. Dad would dig prickles or bits of gravel out of our grass-stained feet or shins with one of Mum's needles while we squealed and squirmed. I learned to be patient with small objects lodged in my skin. If I could tolerate the foreign object swelling up to a tight, hot knot, then a bit of pressure applied at just the right angle would see it come gushing out of the wound in a satisfying stream of yellow pus.

*

Across the road from our house there was an empty yard with a thick hedge at the back. Roy and I bashed a hole through the hedge as a shortcut to the nearby Karaka Flats and the creek behind it. Dad encouraged our explorations and built us a tree house with a rope swing in a large willow next to the creek.

After school, we'd go through the scrappy bushes into a greener, freer world. We'd wander along the creek, snacking on fruit from people's overhanging fruit trees and passionfruit vines. We'd try to catch kōura in the creek with nets we made from Mum's laddered stockings. When tea was ready, Mum would bang on a pot lid with a wooden spoon and we'd run out of the flats and across the road to home.

One afternoon when he was six, Roy didn't come back for the dinner bell. I'd had a piano lesson so we hadn't been playing together that day. Looking around, Dad noticed he'd taken his school bag and his slug gun with him. Mum and Dad flew into a panic and we all ran around the neighbourhood yelling his name.

After a while, we heard a shot. Dad found him down by the creek, hiding with his gun and a packed bag, waiting for dark to fall. He'd let off the shot by accident, giving himself away. He'd planned to run away from home after deciding going off to live in the hills was a much more attractive notion than school. Dad had instilled so much confidence in him that he'd figured he could fend for himself.

Mum and Dad yelled at him for a while for the big fright he'd given everyone, then he was sent to bed without dinner and banned from using his gun ... for a month.

*

I felt like my parents could do almost anything. They'd find useful things and change them or do them up so that they went from being junk to being an asset. Mum sewed and knitted most of our clothes. Dad hunted and fished his way through the different seasons. There was the roar (deer-hunting season), duck-shooting season, whitebait season. We went to wild-pig-hunting competitions where prizes were awarded for most pigs hunted, largest pig, and tallest hunting tale. Possums were hunted for the money for their fur.

Dad once 'shot' a Canada goose with his bare hands. We were kayaking down a river ravine in Tarata and a flock of Canada geese flew overhead. Dad, with no weapon to hand, raised his arms, mimicked holding a rifle and yelled, 'BOOM!' The sound echoed around the ravine and startled one of the geese. It flew into an overhanging tree branch, broke its neck and fell into the river. We paddled over and scooped it out of the water. Dad took this freak event as the ultimate compliment to his hunting skills. 'I don't even need a gun to get a goose!' he joked.

Roy took to hunting more than me. I didn't quite have the stomach for it. At first, I happily tagged along on possum-hunting sessions, excited to be allowed to stay up late. Then, one night in Karaka Flats when I was ten, Dad lined up a shot for me and I pulled the trigger and hit a possum.

'You got it!' Dad yelled. He clambered off into the dark bush and came back holding the possum by her tail. 'She's got a wee joey,' he said. He whipped his hunting knife off his belt, made a few quick nicks in the mother possum's belly, and then pulled the baby out of its pouch. Blinking in the harsh light of the torch, it was tiny and soft, its ears still small like a mouse's, its limbs circling out into the air, searching for its mother.

'Oh no! Dad, it's still alive!' I cried but, quick as a flash, Dad slit its throat and hurled it far into the bush. 'It's got no chance without its mother,' he said pragmatically.

I felt faint. I understood that we hunted possums to help the bush flourish but the image of that flailing baby marked the end of hunting animals for me.

I preferred hunting plants – blackberrying, picking fruit, learning the names of the wild plants I saw growing all around me. I knew that the flowers the bees loved best often had a tiny sip of nectar in their necks. I tasted everything, pinched and sniffed plants to see how they smelled and what seeped out when the petals were ripped up. I liked to pound heavily scented flowers – honeysuckle, jasmine, briar rose – and rub the mush all over my forearms, trying to coat myself in their scent. I was disappointed when it didn't last long on my skin.

Certain plants seemed to call me to sit beside them. I'd tuck their blooms behind my ears, study the flowers. If a plant was in flower, I could sense a density in its blooming. When a fruit tree was laden, the vitality of the swollen orbs would draw me in to its energetic orbit. I'd lean closer and feel the plants' supportive life force.

Compared to other local kids, I was cautious, watchful, thoughtful. I loved books and read myself myopic by the age of seven. My mother nicknamed me 'brown owl' because of the way I'd hang back and watch intently from a corner through my dark brown eyes.

*

In New Zealand, there are laws and then there are *local* laws. In any small town, there are accepted behaviours that can run contrary to the wider laws of the land. A feral quality. These can extend from road rules to land access, pub opening hours to hidden economies. People in small communities are often self-organising on lots of different levels because they have to be, to be strong and resilient.

There were downsides to living in such a close-knit community. I couldn't get into too much mischief without some aunty or uncle spotting me. In Waitara, calling someone 'aunty' or 'uncle' was a gesture of respect and affection. We had lots of aunties and uncles who weren't related to us. I'd get it in the neck when I got home from school because someone would have been on the phone to my parents about my exploits. Often I wouldn't find out who had dobbed me in, which added to the feeling there were eyes everywhere.

If it takes a village to raise a child, we had one with voluntary aunties and uncles around every corner. As I became a teenager, the feeling of being held and helped that I'd had as a kid began to turn into the feeling of being stifled and suffocated. I was growing into a strange flower, and not to everyone's taste.

Vegan boil-up (spiced miso with steamed pūhā)
Serves 4

Pūhā or, as it's known in the northern hemisphere, sow thistle, is one of New Zealand's most foraged greens because it's a key ingredient in boil-up, a salty soup from Māori cuisine made from slow-boiled bacon bones and root vegetables. Boil-up is a popular food in rural New Zealand, and in Māori communities everywhere, rural and urban. Pūhā's sharp flavour is a balancing counterpoint to boil-up's earthier, saltier ingredients.

There are a few varieties found in New Zealand, all called pūhā, including the native *Sonchus kirkii*, but common sow thistle (*Sonchus oleraceus*) is the easiest to find. It's a generous plant that grows almost everywhere, usually in marginal places like railway lands and ditches. When young, it looks like a green rosette, then it grows a central stalk with leaves coming out of the centre.

Pūhā is a great plant to look for if you're camping or tramping and want some pungent greens to mix up the colours and textures of starchy camp cooking. Pick the younger, more tender greens. It can be a little bitter but rubbing the stalks together while washing will remove the sap, which seems to reduce the bitterness.

Like many wild weedy greens, pūhā is a superfood, full of vitamins, minerals and antioxidants. It's also good in pesto or as a steamed-green side dish. Use it anytime you might use spinach or silver beet. In Greek and Italian cuisines, young sow thistle is quickly blanched then served with a drizzle of olive oil, a squeeze of lemon and a dash of salt. Another Italian dish is very similar to boil-up: a soup of pork bones and sow thistle, but large borlotti beans are added for starch in place of potatoes or dumplings.

Sharing a boil-up recipe can invite strong opinions. Some people make it with pūhā, others watercress, still others silver beet, and some even – controversially – cabbage. Some people add potatoes and pumpkin, others doughboys (simple flour dumplings), and opinions differ as to when it's best to add them.

Boil-up has a reputation for being a cure-all. My father tells me that drinking a pint of cold boil-up juice straight out of the fridge first thing in the morning is the ultimate hangover cure.

Rather than risk controversy by sharing my recipe for boil-up, here's a pūhā dish of my own invention. It's a great way to serve the nutritional power of pūhā to vegetarian or vegan friends – a kind of vegan boil-up. Miso provides the salty umami of the original recipe's meat broth, coconut oil provides a bit of richness and a silky mouth feel, and the spices give complexity to the salty and bitter combination of miso and pūhā.

Ingredients

1 heaped tablespoon coconut oil
1 small white onion, halved and sliced into crescent moons
1 teaspoon ground ginger
½ teaspoon cumin
½ teaspoon ground cardamom (or 1 crushed cardamom pod)
2 tablespoons red miso paste, plus a little more to taste
1.2 litres warm water
2 handfuls chopped pūhā

Method

Heat the coconut oil in a large soup pot. Add the onion and cook on a low heat until it turns glassy and clear. Add the ginger, cumin, cardamom and miso, and stir through the onions.

Slowly pour the water into the pot, stirring all the while. Bring to a simmer, and cook for 20 minutes.

When you're 5–10 minutes away from serving, throw in the chopped pūhā – just long enough for it to wilt and shrink down a bit. Taste the broth, and if you'd like it saltier add a little more miso.

Use tongs to put the pūhā in the bottom of soup bowls, then pour the broth over top. Serve with crusty bread.

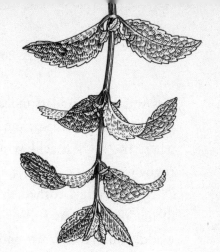

CHAPTER 3

Wild things growing by the water

Mint

I was on my long walk to school through town, across the river and up Manukorihi Hill. Nearing the school gates, I felt something hard hit my back. A slimy goo seeped into the back of my school jersey, cold against my skin. I reached around to feel where I'd been hit. I'd been egged again. I whirled around to see who had thrown it but the perpetrators were hiding.

Egging – throwing an egg at someone – was a common practice at our high school. Kids would scope out a good hiding place on the school route, chuck eggs from there and then duck down so the victim couldn't see them to retaliate. As a form of bullying, it wasn't taken especially seriously by the school staff, maybe because of its slightly slapstick nature.

Once I hit high school, I became a target for bullying for two crimes: I was intelligent and I was weird. My high school was small and underfunded, with several tired staff coasting their way to retirement, and had an upside-down values system, where the highest achievement was getting into the First XV rugby team.

By the time I turned thirteen, my brain was bursting out of my skull. I was full of questions and curiosity about the world, hungry to learn and to think. In class, I would burn through the day's lesson in about fifteen minutes and then ask for extra work. This quickly made me a liability to teachers who didn't want to do more than the bare minimum, so after a few months of asking I gave up. Sometimes I would sit and write angsty poetry in the back of my exercise book. Other times I would tell the teacher I had a headache and ask to go to the sick room. Then I'd bypass the sick room and head to the library.

The school librarian was a chain-smoker. We had an unspoken agreement that she wouldn't ask to see my hall pass so long as I wouldn't tell anyone about her sitting on the step of the open fire door and smoking in between class visits.

I'd drag a chair to a corner of the library and hide behind the rows of books, trying to make myself invisible, then spend the rest of the lesson reading before it was time to start the hourly cycle all over again. It was the beginning of a lifetime habit of hiding when life got overwhelming.

Luckily for my survival, me and my two best friends, Kylie and Dani, discovered punk just before we hit high school. We cut each other's hair into wonky spikes with shaved sides. This seemed to blow the minds of the pony-tailed girls at our school. The only punks they'd glimpsed around Taranaki were a pair that appeared for a few seconds in the music video for 'Poi E' by the Pātea Māori Club. Even though it was hard being outsiders

sometimes, punk gave us the bravado to be defiant in the face
of any negativity that came our way. We used vitriol as fuel.

When the bell went, I'd put my head down, grip a folder
to my chest like a shield and walk as fast as I could to my next
class.

'Hey, freak!' one of the guys from the First XV yelled out.
'Let me test how spiky your hair is!' He was holding something
and raised his hand. I started to run but he caught me and,
laughing, smashed half a mince pie into my hair.

I shook my head violently, shaking off the pie scraps.
'Thanks, asshole, I needed more hair gel.'

He and his mates hooted with laughter.

I ran into the bathroom and rinsed the mess out of my hair
under the cold tap. When I arrived late to my next class, the
science teacher shrugged and gestured for me to sit down. He
sat all the girls at the back of the room because, as he put it,
'You lot won't need much science to go off and have babies.'
With that level of encouragement, I dropped science at the end
of fourth form.

I had discovered punk in a chance interaction on the way
home from school in my second year at intermediate. I was
standing outside the Waitara post office, bored and wondering
whether to go straight home or to the town's small library,
where the two librarians were always welcoming and happy to
talk with me about books.

A sash window opened on the post office's second floor and a
head popped out. It was Gareth, a guy I vaguely knew through our
parents. He was a little older than me. My mother had mentioned
that he'd dropped out of high school – a disappointment to his
folks, who'd had high hopes for his intelligence. Since I'd seen
him last, he had morphed from an awkward, skinny farm kid in

a swannie into a picture of urban cool. He'd dyed his curly hair blue-black and it hung across his face. He had to lift his chin up to look at me through his long fringe.

'Oi! Lehndorf! What ya doing?' he called.

I played it cool. Lately I didn't really know who was friend and who was foe until the interaction had played out.

I shrugged. 'Nothing.'

'Come and do nothing up here for a minute. I got a record to play you.'

I had nothing better to do. I climbed the stairs and Gareth opened his door to a fug of sandalwood incense and instant coffee and a barrage of noise blaring from giant 1970s speakers. He was wearing black stovepipes and a Bauhaus T-shirt.

'I didn't even know there was a flat up here,' I said.

'Yeah, the only good thing about it is it's cheap. I want to move to New Plymouth but I can't afford it yet.'

I felt so unhip in my school uniform. As soon as I had a glimpse of Gareth's world, I wanted to throw out my whole wardrobe, all pastels and mesh influenced by 1980s pop, and begin again.

'Want a coffee?' he said.

'Okay. Milk and two sugars, please.'

He scoffed. 'Nah. Learn to have it black.'

I perched on the edge of a sagging brown velvet art-deco sofa and sipped nervously at the tar-like instant coffee.

He took off the record that was playing and slipped another one out of its sleeve. 'I *have* to play someone this. It's this group called Crass, from the UK. It's blowing my mind,' he said. 'Just got it today.'

He dropped the stylus on the record and a frantic-sounding woman screamed something I couldn't make out. I started to

ask Gareth what she'd said but he held up his finger. 'Wait …
wait … '

There was a minute of the sound of train wheels clattering
on a train track. It wasn't *music* … but then, up through the
clatter of the train, came an urgent beat and the women's
voice returned, yelping, 'Screaming babies! Screaming babies!
Screaming babies!'

Guitars crashed in and the song increased in urgency. With
every line of lyrics, she sounded more angry and more deranged.
Then she chanted a refrain: 'In all your decadence, people die!
In all your decadence, people DIE!'

I loved it. The disharmony and chaos, the bile. It sounded
like how I felt on the inside, brimming with frustration and
anger. I felt like the ground beneath me had fallen away, like
I'd slipped through a portal into my future. We sat listening
intently. As the song drew to a close with more clattering
train wheels, I looked at Gareth incredulously. 'What. Was.
THAT?'

He laughed. 'I don't really know, but isn't it awesome?'

*

After that, Gareth kept feeding me music. He was a few steps
ahead but I soon caught up. He lent me his copies of air-
freighted *NME* and *Melody Maker* and I pored over every word.
He told me about *Radio with Pictures*, an alternative-music
TV show that aired late on Sunday nights. I saw New Zealand
alternative music for the first time in the raw, low-budget music
videos on the show. It blew my mind that there was music
being made here in New Zealand, without big budgets or slick
looks. The video for The Verlaines' 'Death and the Maiden' was

just a bunch of homely looking students in hand-knitted jerseys skipping around a run-down Dunedin flat.

Gareth mostly got his albums from Ima Hitt Records in New Plymouth, so next time I was in the city I went to find it. It had wall-to-wall racks of records and outsized music posters; band T-shirts hung from the ceiling. I was all eyes and ears, trying to look calm and unaffected but full of excitement. Among the customers, I saw my first local punks, wearing hand-painted leather jackets with scraggly mohawks held upright with PVA glue.

There was a wooden rack beside the door full of photocopied handmade leaflets. A sign said *Zines*. Unlike most things in the shop, outside of my meagre budget, these were cheap, and some were even free. I grabbed all the free stuff and spent the five dollars I had on a selection of zines.

The bearded sales assistant took my money and said, 'Into the zines, are ya? If you make any, I'm happy to sell on behalf.'

If I make any? I could *make* something? And sell it … in a record shop?

With this exchange, my world rotated again. I was being invited to participate in this new world I was so taken with. Someone thought I might have something interesting to say.

I took the zines home and studied them like textbooks. There were articles about anarchism, vegetarianism, herbalism, vegetable gardening, the peace movement, feminism, Māori sovereignty, how to screen-print band shirts, how to tap a phone to make toll calls for free, how to rub a postage stamp with soap so that the recipient could wipe off the franking ink and reuse the stamp. It was a compelling mix of punk culture and practical life skills. I learned more from those zines than anything that was on offer at school.

At the back of each zine was the address of the author. They came from cities and small towns all over New Zealand, offering issues of their publications in return for letters, stamps or coins. I sat at my desk writing earnest letters to these kindred strangers. I frequently walked between my house and the post office to send mail to young punks around the country, knocking on Gareth's door as I passed by in the hope he'd be home to play me another record.

I'd found the key to getting involved in the local punk scene. Kylie, Dani and I started our own zine. We called it *Vox Populi*, voice of the people. Poetry, band interviews and articles spilled out of us. Zines were the perfect subculture for nerds. We all dreamed of being published writers one day. So why wait? We were through the doorway. We were in.

*

Taranaki in the 1980s had lots of local punk bands, and gigs were often held in the community halls of the countryside. They were ideal for these feral, shoestring gatherings – they were cheap and there were no noise restrictions because they were out in the middle of nowhere. So long as someone took responsibility for the Sunday-morning clean-up, the older people in the community didn't seem to mind too much.

We were the embodiment of 'make your own fun'; we had no choice. There was nothing else on offer for the region's freaks and weirdos. Dani's older sister would drive groups of us out to the gigs on the back of the family flatbed truck – not safe or legal, but we never got pulled over. We'd hold on to the dog chains as the truck bumped along, shrieking all the way.

The gigs were BYO everything. We'd open the kitchen hatches of the old halls and put drinks on the buffet to share. As well as cans of beer, there were flagons of home-brew and bilious fruity hooches – dodgy sly grog brewed in people's laundries and garages.

Sometimes we'd make a giant bowl of rocket fuel, tipping whatever alcohol we'd managed to find into the hall kitchen's biggest bowl. My friends nicked dusty half-full bottles of sickly liqueur from the backs of their parent's liquor cupboards to pour into the punch. If there was mint growing around the hall's back door, I'd rip some leaves off to decorate the rocket fuel, bringing jeers from the boys: 'Ooo, aren't we *fancy*?'

Every so often the three of us would put our money together to buy a bottle of a cheap, lethal brew called Purple Death. I liked the goth sensibility of its name. It tasted like synthetic strawberry mixed with cough medicine. The label boasted of the drink's 'distinctive bouquet of horse-shit and old tram tickets' and advised it was 'best drunk with the teeth clenched to prevent the ingestion of any foreign bodies'. The bright purple stained our clothes and teeth, and occasionally made for burgundy 'pavement pizzas' at the end of the night.

At the gigs, we'd stride to the front of the stage, close enough to smell the reek of unwashed armpits and rancid jeans. The older punks called us 'baby punks', but we didn't want to be anybody's mascots so we did our best to bring some big energy to the moshpit.

The hardcore punk music was an aural assault. The drums were hard, fast, relentless – not so much a rhythm as a roar. Guitarists thrashed their instruments around in the air as if trying to ward off an attack. When the music started, the crowd would surge forward until everyone was squashed against the front of the stage. We'd grab each other around the neck or shoulder until the moshpit's tide drew back. We'd pogo and thrash around, crashing against each other in a graceless ritual of leaping and falling. Some punk women stood towards the back and the edges, unwilling to risk damage to their carefully applied make-up and elaborate hair. But we three needed the scene credibility of going full tilt. We'd head straight into the centre of the chaos, jumping into the collective rage. In the pit, we'd jostle and thrash, our arms around each other's waists, crashing into the boys. It was our own kind of contact sport.

The moshpit had rules:

1. to mosh is voluntary; no one is to be pulled into the pit against their will
2. no punching or head-butting
3. no one is to be left on the ground; if someone falls over, lift them up right away.

I revelled in being hauled back up off the floor, slippery with spilled drinks, by massive punks twice my age and four times my size. At school I was mocked and belittled, but in this space I was included and uplifted. Keeping everyone on their feet was a collective effort, honour among vagabonds.

If the gigs got too intense I'd go outside in the field to catch my breath and have a moment. So far out in the country, the stars above were low and bright. Sheep stood in the nearby paddocks, as nervy as me, and I'd lean on the fence and call companionably to them in the long wet grass, our breaths steaming into the night air. The sheep gazed perplexed at the bacchanalian chaos disturbing their usually quiet existence. It was a strange mix of the urbane and the bucolic.

As country punks, we were a million miles from London and New York. Rather than city streets, the hills, rivers and beaches were where we found freedom from the eyes of adults. The politics and community cocreation of punk culture seemed to echo the energy of the natural world I'd grown up with; both were anarchic, unpredictable, self-organising and free. Both buzzed with unstoppable wildness. And, to me, they became forever enmeshed.

A good moshpit session is embodied catharsis. At the end of the night, I'd be filthy and covered in blossoming bruises – badges of pride. I felt like I was rehearsing for a life which would feel more real later, when I'd be old enough to leave and find a city to live in. I burned for a life without sheep, cows and paddocks, freezing works and rugby heads, possums and bush shirts, sexist dickheads and boring, boring, boring people.

*

The women in the punk scene were a beguiling mixture of punk toughness and goth witchy mystery. Some of them wouldn't give us baby punks the time of day but others were kind and took us under their wings. They schooled us in feminism and what they called the 'lost matriarchal arts': seasonal pagan rites and honouring the menstrual cycle. They dabbled in herbalism, handing around little bottles of handmade concoctions for emotional upset, for period pain, for hangovers. They carried large bags from which they produced all manner of compelling things: silver hip flasks, boxes of incense, clove cigarettes, black lipstick and Victorian lace hankies.

My family only drank black tea and instant coffee, so I'd never heard of herbal tea before encountering these women. A punk called Ruth made Dani and I a cup of peppermint tea in her flat one day. She ripped a sprig off a potted plant on her windowsill, threw it into a gold-rimmed vintage cup and poured hot water over it. That floating leaf seemed like the height of sophistication to me.

I learned about animism from these goth witches, the idea that everything in the cosmos is alive and has its own animating force. They made 'flying ointments' from illicitly foraged plants, like gold-top magic mushrooms and datura flowers, which transferred hallucinogens through the skin. They foraged the datura from Pukekura Park, New Plymouth's botanical gardens. The datura flowers were so dramatic and sinister, long white night-glowing blooms with petals like claws. I was too scared to take hallucinogens – I found the world psychedelic enough as it was – but was thrilled to be in proximity to people who weren't.

Kylie, Dani and I began to spend more time in the botanical gardens. There was so little to do that we often took to hanging out at parks, beaches, rivers and the bush. Empty schoolyards, abandoned rural houses, cemeteries, hay sheds and under bridges – we lurked anywhere the adults couldn't get in the way of our fun.

In the park, you could hire old wooden rowboats at the lake, painted bright red to match the lake's distinctive wooden bridges. These boats set the scene for our photoshoots, and we'd pose for each other in our punk and goth gear. We'd climb ashore the lake's small islands for photo opportunities and flower-pillaging. Standing in the long weeds, we'd stare dreamily out across the lake towards a fantasy of the future. Or we'd grasp bouquets of wild things growing by the water – white onion weed, yellow marsh cress and mint – to our chests, lie down in the boat and pretend to be dead. Op-shop Ophelias.

*

I started to bang heads with my parents. They'd seemed so capable and wise when I was small but now that I was questioning everything, they began to irritate me. They didn't appreciate my new-found radical politics. They believed in bootstrap ideology: all people needed to do to climb out of poverty was to work harder. Dad had only ever lived in our small town; he would joke that the only way he'd ever leave would be 'feet first'. Where once that had made him king of our world to me, I started to see it more as a kind of stagnation and entrapment.

Suddenly we occupied opposite poles: politically, aesthetically, ethically. I had no one in my family to talk to about all the ideas I was discovering through punk. Roy played rugby and seemed to fit in at school okay. I'd wind up Mum and Dad into heated debates that would end with me calling them hypocrites. They told me I was naive and would understand when I was older that life wasn't so black and white. When we were out in public together, I'd refuse to be seen with them, making them walk half a block ahead of me.

Dad couldn't stand the music I brought into the house. I'd blast hardcore punk from my bedroom stereo and he'd bang on my door. 'Turn that down! It sounds like the bloody bandsaw at work!'

They were busy with their own problems. Dad had been promoted to manager in the Borthwicks butcher shop, which brought with it a lot more stress than just being one of the boys. Mum had started a polytechnic course so she could find better work than her job at the supermarket.

My mother and I fought over the clothes I wanted to wear. Mum was a fine seamstress and an elegant dresser, and she loved to sew clothes for both of us. She wanted me to look nice. I wanted to look anything but nice. I was aiming for staunch and unapproachable – edgy. I wanted to wear ripped and ragged clothes covered in band patches and rows of safety pins, to tear down any expectation I would fit in when every day I had less and less respect for anything considered *normal*.

I didn't want to end up like my peers who got local jobs and married other local kids and never went anywhere. I wanted to find a place that valued creativity. I wanted long, intense conversations about ideas. I was seen and understood in the punk scene, but I knew I needed to leave Taranaki to keep on learning and growing.

No one in my family had ever been to university. I wasn't really sure what university involved, but I knew I was probably smart enough for it and that it could be my escape route.

By my senior year, both Dani and Kylie had dropped out. Dani had got pregnant at the end of fifth form and Kylie went on a 'work for dole' scheme so she could get the unemployment benefit for doing art – a smart move.

Without my friends, that final year seemed to drag on forever. Every day on my route to school, I walked across the long bridge over the river that bisected the town. I'd stop in the middle of the bridge, pick up a stone and whisper into it my intention to escape. Then I'd throw the stone as far as I could into the river. Those hurled pebbles were my daily offering to the gods of exit velocity.

My hometown had become a shoe that was too tight. I was blistering.

Mint headache balm

Makes approximately 200 ml

On the islands of Pukekura Park's lake, I picked water mint and apple mint at the water's edge. While mint is mainly known for its digestive properties (a mug of mint tea is a great help to the stomach if you've eaten too much), it is also a great way to treat a headache.

When you feel a headache coming on, drink a large glass of water and then gently rub this mint balm into your temples. Take your time doing it – the slow massage is part of the cure.

Ingredients
- 4 tablespoons recently dried peppermint (*Mentha* × *piperita*) leaves
- ⅔ cup olive oil or sweet almond oil
- 1 tablespoon argan oil
- 15 g finely grated beeswax (about 1½ tablespoons)
- 4 drops peppermint essential oil

Method
Add the dried mint leaves to a wide-mouthed glass jar with a plastic lid, and stir in the olive oil or sweet almond oil. Screw on the lid and allow to infuse for at least a week, up to 10 days. Keep in a cupboard out of direct sunlight.

Strain the plant matter out of the oil. The oil should be visibly greener.

Sterilise a small glass jar with a screw-top lid.

Put the infused oil, argan oil and beeswax into a small metal bowl. Take a small saucepan (small enough to rest the bowl on top) and half fill with water. On a stovetop over a low heat, rest the bowl on top of the water in the saucepan and gently stir until the beeswax has melted.

Take the saucepan off the heat and slowly stir in the peppermint essential oil. While the mixture is still warm, pour into the sterilised jar. Label and date the jar. The balm will last up to nine months if kept at a cool temperature. (A cupboard or drawer out of sunlight should be fine.)

CHAPTER 4

Thrift before dignity

Backyard rhubarb

Mum cried when she dropped me off at Massey University in Palmerston North. It was the end of an era for her, but I was too excited to dwell much on what I was leaving behind.

On my first morning away from home, I borrowed a bicycle and rode across the Manawatū River into the city centre. There were four sets of traffic lights to negotiate along the way. I'd never cycled through traffic lights before. Everything felt new and full of potential.

I wasn't sure how exactly university worked or what I wanted to do with my life except find creative, brilliant people and then follow their lead. No one knew me in Palmerston North; I was free of the bullies and the small-town small minds. Without the eyes of all the aunties, uncles and nannies watching me, I could recreate myself.

I set about working out how I could live as thriftily as possible. I was determined to be independent and the student allowance didn't go far. The more stuff I could find for nothing, the freer I would be. It was a creative challenge. What could I find? What could I make? Where were all the untapped resources of this new city? All my reading over the past five years about punk culture and anarchism had mixed together with my dad's approach to life to form a scrappy, survival ethos. I hadn't just moved to my first city; I had a huge playground to explore to test out my resourcefulness.

I looked out for anything with a *Free* sign on it. The range of items was broad: clothing outside op shops, boxes of excess produce on street verges, wood offcuts at a hardware store, dilapidated furniture dumped outside student flats. One person's cast-off was my new bookshelf or firewood or lunch. I was inspired by utopian visions of community, and I was on a mission to gather proof of people's generosity against all suggestions of the opposite.

I signed up for anything that would help me meet like-minded people: working as a DJ on student radio, writing for the student newspaper, collective art projects, volunteering at the local community-run music venue, The Stomach. It was the right tactic, and I soon made friends with other weirdos. I was trying to shake off my upbringing, which I found embarrassing, something to transcend rather than celebrate. But threads of it had come with me.

*

As well as clothes, books and records, I arrived at university with several boxes of straw-coloured kiwifruit wine. Mum's experiments with homemade wine were usually pretty successful. Once she even made a batch of emerald-green silver-beet wine for a St Patrick's Day party. It was pretty but tasted about as good as you might imagine a silver-beet wine would taste. She'd been unhappy with the kiwifruit batch, made from the seconds from the kiwifruit-processing shed where I worked during the school holidays. She'd declared it substandard but couldn't bear to throw it away, so it was relegated to the shed until she thought of some use for it. I retrieved it from there as I left for university.

When I moved into my room, I carefully stacked the dozens of bottles on their sides on a low bookshelf, as if they were a prized vintage wine. It was sour, cloudy and fairly unpleasant, but very high in alcohol content and, when diluted with lemonade, almost palatable. I shared it with my new friends, who called it 'Taranaki skull splitter' because of its effects the morning after.

*

One habit I couldn't shake from home was a preoccupation with finding food and sharing it with my friends. We were all so broke. Food was medicine to Mum, and she'd taught me how to make wholesome food from humble ingredients. It was ingrained in me, so I kept doing it.

When I was growing up, if Roy or I fussed about food, Dad would tell us about how he'd sometimes gone hungry as a kid. Money had been tight and there'd been times when my grandmother had struggled to feed her family. Dad had slept under old woollen army coats because there hadn't been enough blankets to go around. From a young age, he'd supplemented his diet with scrumped fruit, picked pipis out of the sand with a stick, cooked mussels on an iron sheet over a beach fire, and fished off Waitara's wharf. He learned the beach's terrain based on what food he could find; one reef had pāua, another mussels, a third crayfish. He'd sneak into the freezing works with his friends and take wool pieces with flesh still on them out of the waste bin. They'd lay these on the rocks at low tide and, on a lucky day, there would be crayfish stuck in the wool's weave the following low tide.

I used the skills Mum had taught me to feed my friends and flatmates on simple dishes made from sad supermarket-bargain-bin vegetables and foraged bits and pieces. Our flat fruit bowls were full of lumpen apples, tiny red plums and hard, rough-skinned pears that I'd found somewhere in my roaming. The cooking I'd learned was not fancy but rich in skills of preserving, stretching or reviving ingredients – the life skills of the thrifty. It was always easier to cook a big batch than just for one, so I loved to share what I was making.

These tendencies were not always welcomed. One day, when I offered porridge and stewed apple to my hungover flatmates who were sitting around blearily drinking black coffee and smoking cigarettes, one of them snapped, 'Christ, you're not the mother of us all, Helen.'

The comment stung. I knew my instinct to feed and share could be a bit intense – we'd all just escaped our parents and no one wanted more heavy-handed fussing – but I couldn't help it. If there was a big pot of soup or stew on the stove, I felt safe, secure in the knowledge there was enough food for anyone who might need some for the next few days.

Most of the student flats were run-down villas and bungalows. These old houses were utterly freezing; in winter, it was often warmer outside the house than in. We survived by piling on jerseys until we looked comical, like wool-swaddled snowmen. In one flat I lived in, the backs of the kitchen cupboards had wide cracks open to the air. A jasmine plant grew through them from the garden outside. Questing shoots threatened to ensnare our cans of baked beans.

'It's kind of romantic, don't you think?' I said to my flatmate.

'Romantic? No! It's just bloody freezing.' She laughed.

I loved the backyards of these old houses. Microcosms of abandoned wildness with overgrown bones of once-loved gardens. There was food to be found, if you were willing to creep through the knee-high grass of neglected lawns, which I was. I'd step gingerly through the long grass in my Dr. Martens in case there was broken glass or rusted scraps from tossed appliances, long since swallowed by the creeping green. Among the detritus there was treasure: old citrus trees, glossy rosehips on ancient rose bushes and scrappy perennial herbs that had continued to regenerate long after the people who planted them had moved on. I saw these garden remnants as assets.

'What are you doing back there?' my flatmate yelled from the security of the back door.

'Treasure hunting!' I replied, piling lemons into my arms, sprigs of mint sticking out of my jacket pocket.

'You weirdo!' She laughed, turning to go back inside. 'Let me know if you find money or booze.'

*

My parents sent love in the form of food parcels. *Eat. Eat.* Sometimes Mum sent me a packet of bacon by FastPost in a brown manila envelope. It'd arrive in our letterbox the morning after she mailed it. My flatmates were horrified, but I'd grown up with a butcher and I knew that bacon and salami were meant to last a while unrefrigerated. It was the whole point of their preserving process.

My flatmates' obsession with keeping everything – preserves, butter, eggs – in the fridge was neurotic to me; how did they imagine our ancestors had kept their food in the times before fridges? After I'd eaten the FastPost bacon a few times without dying, they began to accept my offers of bacon and egg sandwiches.

*

My friends and I treated op shops like our personal dress-up boxes for every gig and party. One day while I was op-shop sifting, a book drew me. Its cover had an attractive illustration of a cornucopia spilling out of a woven Māori kete. *Simply Living: A Gatherers' Guide to New Zealand's Fields, Forests and Shores* by Gwen Skinner featured beautiful watercolour plates of wild plants and herbs. I'd seen similar books from the northern hemisphere. On my shelf I had *The Countryside Cookbook: Recipes and Remedies* by Gail Duff, which, contrary to the bland title, was an exciting tome full of descriptions of wild plants by season, with both culinary and medicinal recipes. It, too, was illustrated with beautiful coloured plates of burgeoning wild plants in bucolic rural settings. But, because it was English, the seasons were all upside down and the folklore of the plants and places seemed very far away from New Zealand.

By contrast, *Simply Living* featured the New Zealand seasons and New Zealand native plants. The first chapter of the book had the romantic title 'Come gather wild plants'. I wanted to heed this invitation, so I bought the book and carried it along on my edgeland mooches, using it to extend my vocabulary of edible plants. I was *foraging*, a new word for an old habit.

Soon some of my friends were drawn into my Womble-like ways. We were cash poor but time rich. We'd go for bike rides scoping out the edges of parks and school grounds for overhanging fruit trees. Where a playing field backed on to suburban housing, there were often good yields of fallen fruit and walnuts. We hopped off our bikes and stuffed as much as we could carry into our backpacks.

My flatmates regarded walnuts as horrible, rancid things to be picked off the top of Afghan biscuits, so when I arrived home with a backpack filled with walnuts, they looked on sceptically as I shelled the nuts with a brick I'd found in the yard. But, once they tasted the fresh, just-toasted walnuts, they changed their minds. I toasted the nuts in a cast-iron pan on the stovetop then served them on top of buttered spaghetti with chopped parsley and grated Tasty cheese: a dish that seemed luxurious but cost us very little.

I made friends with a skate punk named Wilder. He told me about how he lived off dumpster diving. He hardly ever needed to pay for alcohol because he often found bottles of beer with ripped labels or dented cans in the supermarket dumpster. I volunteered to tag along with him one night so between us we could carry more stuff. We packed torches and put on backpacks, heading out after dark for a night-time rummage.

We found piles of bagged breads, fancy cheeses, food in dented tins, fruit and vegetables just a little past perfect. If anyone cruised by and started looking at us, we'd slam the lid of the dumpster and take off in different directions, me on my bicycle and him on his skateboard, baguettes sticking out of his backpack like ninja fighting sticks. We'd meet up again back at my flat and unpack, showing off our spoils to my flatmates.

I lost my childhood magnifying-glass necklace during one of these dumpster-diving sessions. I felt a bit sad but remembered Dad's philosophy of always needing to pay the piper, as he put it, in some way. When I realised it was missing from around my neck, a flatmate, who didn't approve of our dumpster-diving habit, said, 'Karma's a bitch.' I rolled my eyes at him.

I was philosophical. Maybe it was time to move forward from childhood things anyway. Another necklace would come and find me, I was sure.

Wilder and I liked to take food that we'd dumpster-dived along to class potluck gatherings. There was something very funny to us about watching our lecturers eat cheese and crackers that we'd fished out of a bin the night before.

*

English wild-food writer Richard Mabey, Britain's most famous forager, writes of the 'bramble-scrabbling, mud-larking [and] tree-climbing' involved in foraging for food. It's true that foraging quests sometimes compromise personal dignity. I've jumped fences to harvest field mushrooms, climbed trees for fruit and then struggled to get down with any grace, crawled around on my hands and knees in park grounds to gather walnuts, always taking risks, taking tumbles, wandering off the map. But, for committed foragers, a short-term loss of dignity is a price worth paying for the bounty – and for the sense of rumpty fun.

My friends were sometimes a little embarrassed by my audacity. Once my friend Sarah stood by, mortified, while I hung on to a sturdy fencepost with one hand, hanging over a deep, steep crevasse to reach a wilding Black Doris plum tree. I tossed the plums over my shoulder to where she stood, trying to catch them in an open bag before they hit the ground. A couple of times I slipped, rallied and thought, *Oh my god, I'm going to die for a plum.* She yelled out to me, 'Helen, I think your personal motto could be "thrift before dignity".'

At first I was embarrassed by this comment. I'd noticed that the way I'd been raised seemed totally different compared to the city kids I was befriending. I knew my thrifty ways could be a little eccentric, a little out of kilter, but I couldn't argue with her. It summed me up pretty well. Rather than staying bruised, I decided to claim it for myself. My interest in gathering *was* born out of dual impulses: the desire to connect to nature's wild abundance, and a deeply embedded dedication to thrift.

I translated it into Latin and called it out before meals when I was about to feed my friends from things I'd gleaned or found, my personal toast, in place of 'cheers': *Parsimonia ante dignitatem!*

*

It wasn't all mischief and fun; I was floundering a bit. Navigating university study was a challenge. I'd never learned how to write essays properly. Some of my new friends were talking about their planned trajectories for postgrad and careers; I didn't really understand what postgrad study was, or even why you might aspire to it. I behaved with a lot of bravado but the intensity of everything being so different from home took a toll.

One day in a history class, the lecturer was talking about 'the working class'. Her language was exclusive, distanced, as though to be working class was 'other', a subject for analysis and certainly not part of the university environment.

I raised my hand. 'I'm from a working-class background,' I said, my heart thumping from daring to speak up to a professor.

She raised her eyebrows. 'Well, perhaps you *were*, but you're not working class anymore. You're at university now. You've transcended.'

Someone else asked her to clarify what she meant. 'Well, look, if you've entered tertiary study, you're no longer working class. You become part of a systemic elite. You become … lower middle class, at least. People who have been to university can no longer claim to be working class.'

I burned with indignation. Why did *she* get to tell me what I was and wasn't? I felt like she'd erased my whole life with one dismissive comment. But I couldn't think of how to articulately push back, so I didn't say anything more.

My new friends didn't like it when I brought up class either.

'New Zealand's such an egalitarian society. I'm not sure we really *have* a class structure, do we? I certainly don't think about people in those terms when I meet them. It's not like in the UK,' said Sarah. But it was always the middle-class kids who wanted to downplay the idea.

As I got to know more people – new friends, flatmates, classmates – it felt like the middle-class kids were the thoroughbreds, trained all their lives in a sprint of high performance, long schooled in the subtle social codes of academia. Those of us who'd made it to university from working-class backgrounds were the workhorses, plodding behind, a bit blinkered. The need to suss it all out for ourselves meant our progress was slower, and peppered with awkward blunders and constant small social humiliations.

I took my fears and worries to the river, just as I had back home, when I'd sit under the Waitara bridge to hide from the bullies, egging and taunts of 'Freak!' or 'LehnDORK!'. The Manawatū River was wide, slow and dirty brown, just like the Waitara River. Because of this, it felt familiar. I took long walks along its edges, watching the swifts and swallows dance around at dusk. I'd pick fennel seeds for our flat kitchen and look for heart-shaped rocks to display on my bookcase beside my grandmother's tea-leaf-reading cup. The river has the Māori word for heart in its name, manawa, and it did feel like the city's heart.

I'd learned from punk how to put on a front of being plucky and fun so that I could attract friends, but inside I felt out of my depth. I would nod calmly through a lecturer's instructions as if I understood and then run straight to the library to see if I could find a patient librarian to explain the assignment to me.

My new friends were exciting, but I wasn't like them and I struggled to articulate why. I hadn't grown up with a family bach in a scenic locale, with childhood trips to Europe to be exposed to museums and culture, with intellectuals and academics among our family friends. My friends bought each other tight bouquets of flowers from florists for their birthdays, which seemed like burning money to me. Why spend good money on something that would die within days? Something you could find for free if you looked hard enough? Some of them had grown up vegetarian. How could I express what it was like to grow up around the freezing works and hunting without horrifying them?

*

I'd enrolled in an ambitious eight papers for first year, naively thinking that with my good performance at high school, I'd be able to sail through so long as I tried hard enough. It turned out that eight exams was two too many for me. I got through the first six, nervous and scared but determined, studying every hour I could. I mainlined coffee and popped NoDoz caffeine tablets so I could keep going into the small hours of the morning. If I didn't pass, I'd have trampled on the tender shoots of my new life before they got to unfurl.

By the seventh exam, Pacific history, I was exhausted and hollow. I opened the answer booklet, read the essay questions and felt a grey fog descend. Nothing. There was nothing coming. In my brain, the door to the information I needed had slammed shut. My heart was thudding and I was nauseous. I stared at the blue lines of the answer booklet until they started to swim. I wrote a sentence rephrasing the essay question as a statement. Nothing else followed. After half an hour, I packed up my things and ran out.

'Are you okay?' an examiner called after me, but I didn't turn back.

I spent the night in a state of emotional paralysis, horrified at the waste of money from going to the paper all year and then falling at the last hurdle. I hid from my friends, not joining them for dinner. I said I needed to study and climbed into bed with my art history notes. My final exam was the next day. I couldn't fuck it up.

The next morning, I dressed, packed my things and hopped on my bike. I cycled along towards the bridge that crossed the river, the university on the far side. But, just as I approached the bridge, I found myself swerving off down a steep dip to the river path. *What the hell are you doing?* I thought, but my legs kept peddling as if possessed.

I cycled along, dodging the dog walkers and passing the slower cyclists, until I got to a steep, grassy path. It was a spot I liked because it was out of view, a sort of green nest. I pulled off the path, threw my bike into a dense patch of lupins and mallow and ran down the grassy bank. I lay there, wrapped in the grasses, the river slowly slipping by.

While my classmates were sitting in the art history exam with their plastic bags full of pens, scribbling away on the booklets of lined paper, I was curled up in a ball trying to disappear. I felt around for the logical part of my brain, looking for the inner strength to propel me to get back on my bike, go to the exam. They'd probably let me in if I pleaded I'd had a flat tyre. But there was nothing. I sank into the ground.

I hid there for the three hours of the exam, my body in a frozen state of hypervigilance. After the year of bravado, I wondered if I was bright enough, strong enough to make it through university. In my last year at home, I'd felt like an outsider, the wrong shape to settle down, but I felt out of place in this new world, too. I hadn't managed to fully slot in. The solidity of the earth underneath me and the expansiveness of the sky above offered some comfort.

Far away from my flatmates, my tiny, claustrophobic bedroom, books, lecture halls and exams, impassive professors and the weight of everyone's expectations, I was cradled by my one constant supporter, the earth.

Rhubarb hooch

Makes about 4 litres

So much of my student life was about drinking that it seems appropriate to share an alcohol recipe for this chapter. The punks I grew up with brewed fruit alcohols, making cloudy hooches from whatever fruit they could find. Mum's fruit wines were a little more refined, clear and clean in flavour. She brewed hers in elegant glass carboys rather than large plastic buckets.

In the scraggly backyards of student flats there were often large and vigorous rhubarb patches in sunny corners. Rhubarb (*Rheum rhabarbarum*) makes stunning drinks because of its attractive pink colour. This recipe is for a fizzy rhubarb hooch, but rhubarb cordial is lovely, too. Rhubarb is wonderful paired with strawberries, so if you're drinking this hooch in summer, cut a strawberry in half, put it at the bottom of the glass and pour the hooch over top for a seasonal pink drink.

For a forager's alternative to domestic rhubarb, this hooch can also be made from the pest Japanese knotweed (*Reynoutria japonica*). The young shoots taste just like rhubarb. (Use only the younger shoots – nothing thicker than a finger.)

Ingredients
900 g chopped rhubarb (or young Japanese knotweed stems)
¾ cup apple cider vinegar
2 lemons, sliced thinly
680 g white sugar

Method
Sterilise a large bucket or fermenting crock. Combine all the ingredients in the bucket or crock, then cover with a muslin cloth and leave to macerate for 3 days.

On the fourth day, strain the liquid out and compost the fruit. Bottle into brown glass brewing bottles with swing-top lids.

Allow the hooch to sit for 3 to 4 weeks before drinking – it will get better the longer it sits. It will have some fizz, so take care when opening.

CHAPTER 5

Desire lines

Rose

I didn't like Maria much when I first met her. She seemed very loud and confident, and she approached every new person with a litany of questions: 'Where are you from?' 'What are your politics?' 'What are you passionate about?'

What are you passionate about? I imagined asking people back home that question and getting laughed at. Who even thought about life in that way?

She eventually turned the intense gaze of her bright blue eyes on me and the grilling began. I was a bit sarky and standoffish at first but she wasn't deterred. Her eyes didn't cloud over when I said where I was from; she leaned towards me. Each of my answers led to another question until I was telling her all kinds of things.

'A freezing works? Wow. I've never been inside one.' 'You've shot a gun? Oh my god, that's so hardcore. What was it like?' 'There's a punk scene in Taranaki? I thought it was all just dairy farms.' She seemed genuinely interested and, no matter what I said, non-judgemental. I softened towards her and a lifelong conversation began.

She told me that her father was a political journalist for the Christchurch *Press*. 'That must be where you get it from,' I said. 'All the questions.'

She laughed. 'Maybe. But don't you just find people so *fascinating*? Sociologically, I mean, or maybe anthropologically.'

Anthropologically? I didn't let on that I'd never heard the word and looked it up later: the study of human societies and cultures and their development. I'd never thought about my background as being a kind of culture of its own; it was just the water I'd swum in, and then through my teens a tether I was hungry to escape.

In first year I'd only enrolled in subjects I'd been good at in high school: English, history and art history. I thought that's just what you did. When I'd gone to our school's guidance counsellor to get advice, he'd told me that a BA was also known as a 'Bachelor of Anything' or a 'Bugger All' degree, and I'd be better spending my time doing a hairdressing apprenticeship. But then I learned from my new friends that you could take electives, interest papers in subjects outside your chosen major. I could study just about anything!

So in second year I signed up for an introductory anthropology paper. Maybe learning a bit about how cultures worked would help me feel less bisected? Besides, I liked the five-syllable word. It had gravitas and sounded important.

My anthropology professor was an American woman who didn't suffer fools. In the first session she asked us to introduce ourselves, to say our name and where we were from. When I said I was from Waitara, she said, 'Oh, that's funny. I actually know that town. I did field research there on the green-dollar economy.'

I didn't know what she was talking about. I felt the familiar combination of vulnerability, defiance and shame that university often elicited in me. But I was curious, too, so I asked what she meant.

'Well, you grew up there so you're no doubt familiar with it, but maybe you haven't heard it described this way. The culture of green dollars there, by which I mean the non-monetary economy, cashless exchange. Like, goods swapped for skills and vice versa, a self-managed economy but at the grassroots level.'

I was perplexed. Wasn't this how everyone lived? Wasn't she just describing life in every small town?

Green dollars. I turned the phrase over. It was true. Back home, babysitting was exchanged for vegetables. Car repairs swapped for the butchering of a body of beef on a farm. The laying of a concrete driveway paid for with a big feed and some beers afterwards. The small-town way.

But I didn't really relate to her name for it. To call it 'dollars' seemed to diminish the spirit of the exchange somehow. It diluted the ongoing and uneven dance of reciprocity as I knew it. The academic world was once again trying to nail down something that was by nature immeasurable. The name 'green dollars' didn't capture the subtleties woven through the relationships in the community. It felt like another case of a middle-class lens diminishing the lived working-class experience.

But the idea sank in and stayed with me. It was the first time someone from the university had reflected something of my hometown back to me. I told Mum and Dad about it and they thought that it was funny that you'd spend time studying it.

Dad adopted the name, though, and started calling everything he was gifted from a friend 'green dollars'.

'Didn't cost me anything. Got it through those green dollars,' he'd say with a grin when I asked where something had come from.

I started to feel a bit more pride about where I'd come from. People like Maria thought I was fascinating. The reciprocity in the community I grew up in had a *name*, was an *ideology*, an unusual thing studied by academics.

*

Maria was an anarchist, too, although she'd come to anarchism through student politics rather than punk. We became good friends and spent hours talking about how we planned to fix the world's ills. She talked a lot about her Scottish ancestry, telling me that as Pākehā we needed to learn about our own ancestry and our ancestors' roles in New Zealand history if we wanted to be informed citizens and useful allies to Māori. 'Disenfranchised Pākehā are no good to anyone,' she said.

I was impressed by her sharp intelligence. She was learning old Scottish words for things in the natural world. She practised pronouncing them aloud so she could include them in the poems she was writing.

I had Scottish ancestry, too, although I didn't know much about it. My dad's mother's family came from Clan Macrae, the moss clan. Nana told me that Clan Macrae had never had a chief; we couldn't be tamed. She also told me that we had witches in our family line and she was a witch who would put curses on anyone who crossed her.

'You just have to look at them like *this*,' she said, doing a ferocious, squint-eyed stare. 'Then when they walk away you point your finger at their back and you *hissssss!*'

My maternal grandmother had some witchy predilections, too. She had died long before I was born. She liked to read her friends' fortunes. My treasured possessions included her tea-leaf-reading cup and her fortune-telling book. 'Consult the Oracle!' it said on the cover. I took the book from flat to flat with me as though it held some essence of my grandmother. I asked it questions I couldn't ask her.

These small scraps of family story were enough to make me interested in all things esoteric. I taught myself to read tarot cards and carried forward various superstitions I'd inherited from my grandmothers, like not stirring pots with a knife because Nana said, 'Stir with a knife, stir up strife!' Both of my grandmothers were named Margaret and I carry their name as my middle name.

Dad had Nana's superstitious inclinations, too. As a teenager he'd discovered a human skull in the sand on Waitara Beach. 'I'm sure that old skull came with a mākutu on it,' he'd say any time his fortunes took a dip. Once he'd seen a huge albino eel in a creek. It had stopped swimming, broken through the surface of the creek and seemed to look right at him. He'd jumped on his bike and ridden home as fast as he could, unnerved. 'I don't know if it was good luck or bad luck, but I don't think I was meant to see it,' he said cryptically.

When I told Maria all of this she showed her usual enthusiasm for my stories. 'Amazing! My family are all total rationalists.' She was patient with my mystical leanings but I could never persuade her to let me read her tarot cards.

*

The longer I stayed at university, the more the total cultural fracture I'd felt in first year began to heal. I met a few other kids from similar backgrounds and we bonded over our small-town stories. I had some brief romantic encounters but mainly I didn't want to get too involved with anyone. There was too much I wanted to do.

Not long after first-year exams, I was cycling along the road when someone caught up alongside me. It was a guy I'd seen in some of my lectures. 'Hey,' he said. 'I didn't see you at the art history exam.'

'Uh, yeah. Didn't quite make it to that one. Had somewhere better to be.'

He laughed. 'Fair enough.'

His name was Fraser. We talked about what a dick the art history lecturer had been, and he asked me if I was going to be in town for the summer.

'Nah, I'm going fruit-picking down the South Island with a mate.' Unlike lots of my friends, I didn't have the luxury of taking the summer off. I needed to make money for the year ahead.

'Oh, that's a shame,' he said. 'Might catch you around next year, then?'

The traffic light's left arrow flashed and, before I could reply, he took off around the corner. Standing astride my bike, I stared after him until the car behind me blared its horn.

I hadn't noticed the light go green.

*

A neat concrete pavement winds around a bend in the river. Cutting across the corner of the pavement, a renegade dirt path has been worn into the grass by the treads of many feet: a desire line.

A desire line is where people have, over time, made a visible path; it's a triumph of collective human will over measured municipal planning. If I spot a desire line, I always want to walk it because locals know where the best shortcuts and hidden gems are. You never quite know where you will end up. Desire lines mark terrains in human scale. They tell a story about the people who walk the commons and where *they* want to go.

Desire lines often lead to good foraging spots, particularly wilding fruit trees like plums, pears and apples. The edgelands are full of desire lines.

At twenty, I swerved off course and made my own desire line.

Fraser was in most of my English classes. He'd tease me when I turned up to our 9 am tutorials bleary-eyed and wearing pyjama bottoms with my Dr. Martens because I'd had to scramble out of bed to get to class on time. Our friendship was a slow burn. I found him funny and sweet but sometimes he'd hold my gaze a second too long and I'd break off the conversation, running off to a meeting or to the library or to anywhere else but that searching look. I had a sense that, if we attached, our connection would be something I might have to take seriously, so, like an eel, I'd slip quickly around him and keep on swimming.

In our final year, he asked me if I wanted to be 'study buddies' for exams. He was still living at home. His mother was an artist and their family home was a warm, ramshackle bungalow with terracotta-orange walls and unusual contemporary paintings covering every available space. His parents had paintings by some of the New Zealand artists my high school art teacher had talked about, like Nigel Brown and Michael Smither. It blew my mind that it was possible to *own* paintings by artists who'd been in textbooks; I'd thought you could only find them in museums and art galleries. It was the bohemian house of my dreams. I'd never been anywhere quite like it.

The garden was romantic and sensual, all sprawling lilies and oxeye daisies, trailing with roaming, redolent old-fashioned roses. We got to know each other in long study sessions on a blanket under a large plum tree. Fraser was funny and made me laugh more than any boy had before. He seemed to know just how to nudge me out of my tendency towards melancholy. On those warm spring afternoons, the smell of the roses and lilies was intoxicating, often lulling us from our notes into a distracted haze. As the days passed, we studied each other as much as our literature texts.

I was torn. The timing was terrible. I was planning to leave as soon as I could. I wanted to travel, to go to the UK and take myself on pilgrimages to the homes and gardens of the writers I'd just spent three years studying. I wanted to go and find the haunted fragments of old Albion – the Green Man, the chalk horses, the sunken burial sites of Viking ships. I wanted to see the plants described in the poems I'd been writing essays about: the poppies and the hedgerows, Tennyson's 'long fields of barley and of rye'.

Just before our final exam, Fraser asked me to read his tarot cards. He was a rationalist like Maria but still a little intrigued. I didn't really like reading for sceptics. It felt like a waste of my time and theirs. But I figured it didn't matter. I'd be gone soon and, besides, a tarot reading in the garden was a fun way to procrastinate reading notes about 'The Lady of Shalott'.

For extra theatricality, I tore a fat rose bloom off his mother's overhanging plants and strew the petals in a loose circle on the blanket to frame the cards as I lay them. He laughed his way through the usually solemn shuffling and deck-splitting that precedes a reading, then I lay the cards in a Celtic cross spread. The final arc of cards corresponded to the future, and they were a heady mix: the sun, the ten of cups and, finally, the lovers. That final card in that particular spot – the immediate future – knocked us both into silence. Then Fraser looked at me, gooey-eyed, his scepticism temporarily washed away by romance.

Oh, damn it, I thought. *No! I need to leave! The timing is off!* But there the cards lay.

A few weeks later, when I was moving out of my flat, Fraser offered to help. It was a tatty old art deco place. After a hectic day of lugging boxes and vacuuming dusty corners, I returned from dropping a load of stuff to the op shop to find him on his hands and knees, sleeves rolled up, scrubbing away at the filthy oven. It was full of the cooking debris of many previous tenants. I didn't dare tell him we'd never bothered to clean it ourselves after gingerly peering inside and declaring it a lost cause. Here was a man willing to clean what was possibly the city's grottiest oven, just so I would be guaranteed to get my tenancy bond back. Now *that* was true love.

*

A year on from the oven-cleaning incident on a stormy spring day, we were married at All Saints Church in Palmerston North. We chose it for its beautiful architraves and stone carvings. In place of biblical scripture, our reading was Matthew Arnold's 'Dover Beach', a poem we'd studied in our Victorian literature paper. The poem's message can be described as 'the world is utterly terrible but at least we have each other'. It was not the most romantic of poems, but it matched Fraser's pragmatic sensibility.

As we left the church, our parents showered us in rose petals that Fraser's mother had collected from her garden that morning. We chose rose-gold wedding bands, a nod to the roses surrounding our first kisses, engraved with the words 'where the sea meets the land' – a fragment of a line from 'Dover Beach'. It summed us up: opposites in harmony.

My friends – alternative types, punks, lefties, musicians and artists – saw marriage as an obsolete institution, a controlling tool of the toxic patriarchy. They didn't understand why we were bothering and some of them turned up to our wedding ceremony stoned. Even Maria, usually unreservedly supportive, said, 'Love, I just don't get it. I'm going to have to trust that it makes sense to you.'

I didn't see what the big deal was. Where I was from, people often married young. Many of them had a pair of kids before they turned twenty-five. I was stubborn, forging my own desire line; the more horrified responses I got, the more it strengthened my resolve to do it.

Fraser loved nature, too, although rather than foraging and food-growing, he liked to take off into the wilds. He was happiest tramping solo with just a hammock to sleep on, strung up between a pair of trees. A storm chaser, he sought out terrible weather and loved the ice-blasting winds and storms of winter hiking. From him, I learned the exhilaration of stomping down a wind-blasted winter beach. We took photos of each other almost horizontal as we leaned into gales on wild beaches.

Foraging was new to him, but he was gracious about my magpie tendencies. He was happy to help fill a cardboard box with windfall fruit or harvest wild herbs, but he was always an absolute stickler for rules. If there was any question about legitimacy of access, he'd walk away saying, 'You're on your own for this one, sorry.' If I suggested he do something even slightly boundary-pushing, he'd shake his head. 'Nope, sorry, I'm not a Lehndorf.' I tolerated this jibe because it was based in truth; my family did have a rascally edge.

He loved books as much as me. The literature degree we'd done was old-fashioned, the curriculum largely English literature with just one paper covering all of New Zealand literature. By the end, we'd spent three years steeping in writing from the past 500 years in the United Kingdom – good training for an OE skewed towards literary and mystical sight-seeing with a side serving of my romantic interest in England's flora and fauna.

Fraser's ancestry is the usual New Zealand Pākehā mongrel brew of Scottish and English, and also German, Scandinavian and Russian. His name, Fraser, is Scottish for 'curly-headed one'. He has tight curly hair, in the manner of Janet Frame. He was keen to climb a Scottish mountain or two, to walk the land of his forebears.

I'd never been out of the country before. We started making plans to head off to England's 'green and pleasant land'. We bought tramping gear, stacked up some savings and pored over copies of Lonely Planet's *Great Britain*. I packed northern-hemisphere plant guides so I could seek out some of the witchy-sounding plants that I'd never been able to find growing at home, like vervain, mandrake, mistletoe and mugwort.

I was hungry to see if anything I encountered in the northern hemisphere would resonate with me, make me feel more like the box I had to tick on official forms: European. I resolved not to return to New Zealand until the land in the United Kingdom gave me a gift, something that would feel like a sign of ancestral acknowledgement.

I knew just what form of gift I would ask for: a mystical notion seeded in me by my grandmother.

Sweetbriar rose elixir

Makes approximately 500 ml

The roses that were the backdrop to my early romance with
Fraser were cultivated old-fashioned David Austin roses, which
his parents collected. For foragers, there are several roses to
be found in New Zealand's wilds, including multifloras, French
roses and ramblers. My favourite is the sweetbriar rose (*Rosa
rubiginosa*), the blooms of which have a lovely apple-rose aroma.

As with many good foraging plants, sweetbriar rose features
on many pest-plant lists. Like the blackberry, sweetbriar rose is
a rambler – hard to contain and, if left unattended, capable of
choking waterways and dominating landscapes, climbing up to
3 metres high. It usually has small white-and-pink blooms, flatter
and more open than the grandiose tight balls of standard roses
or the blousy loose heads of an old-fashioned rose. Both the
petals and the hips can be eaten or used medicinally. The seeds
have a hairy fibre around them that will irritate the throat and so
needs to be removed. Forage the petals and hips in late summer
to mid-autumn.

Rosehips are very high in vitamin C, much higher than citrus
fruit. They are also very high in pectin, making them a good
addition to jellies and jams. During World War Two, when
imported fruits were in short supply, the rosehip came to the
rescue. An array of glowing red rosehips drying in a basket is
also a cheerful sight. As the hips wrinkle and the colder months
advance, they are a reassurance that we have the medicine and
the resilience to get through another long winter.

This simple elixir is made from sweetbriar rose petals. Rose
is said to have a heart-opening quality, and a tablespoon of this
elixir can give you a little bit of warmth and steadiness to the
heart if you've been feeling vulnerable or wounded. It can help
restore your trust in life and help you relax enough to find your
enthusiasm again. And, as well as being medicinal, it's delicious.

Tinctures and elixirs often fetch very high prices in health
food stores and herbal dispensaries, but they are easy to make:
a few simple ingredients combined in a jar and then time does

the rest of the work. No cooking required and no preserving skills or complicated equipment needed. Once you've made one, you'll soon get addicted to the possibilities.

Ingredients
2 handfuls sweetbriar rose petals
300 ml vodka or brandy
250 ml honey (or glycerine for a vegan alternative)

Method
Put the sweetbriar rose petals into a 600 ml jar, filling to halfway.

Pour over the vodka or brandy, filling to halfway.

Fill the rest of the jar by slowly pouring in the honey. Stop pouring when the liquid level is a couple of centimetres from the top, so there is room in the jar to shake and turn the elixir.

Put the jar in a cupboard where you will notice it often (near your tea or coffee pot is a good spot). Let it brew for 4 weeks, giving the jar a good shake every day.

After brewing, strain out the rose petals. Bottle the elixir into dropper bottles or small dark glass bottles. Take a few drops on the tongue in moments of emotional vulnerability.

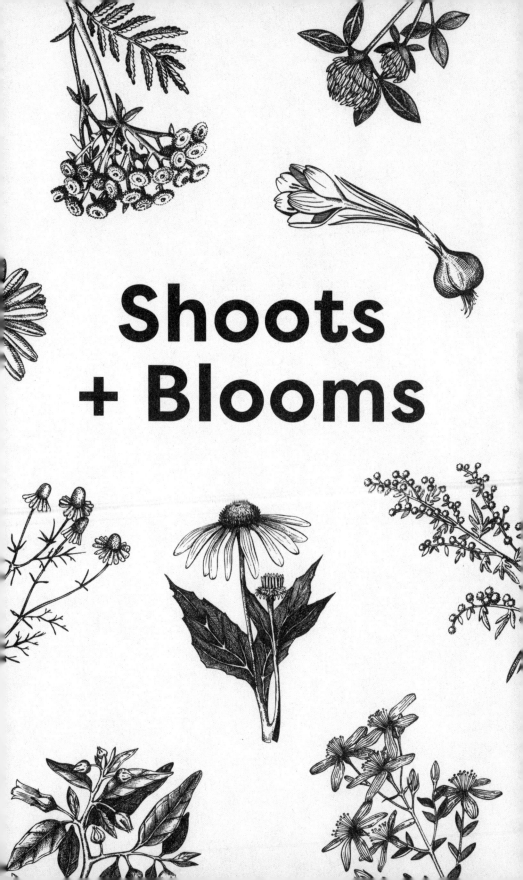

Shoots
+ Blooms

CHAPTER 6

Underwater days

Dandelion

When I was small, as a prop for her storytelling about curses and evil eyes, my grandmother would pull out her hag stone and let me look through the hole. Hers was local, from Hāwera's Ohawe Beach.

'It's an eye of nature, eye of stone. I can see the future through the hole,' Nana said. 'What do you see?'

I peered through the hole but all I could see was her face staring back at me. 'Nothing. Just you.'

'That's because it's mine,' she said. 'You need your own. But you'll have to find it yourself.'

Hag stones, also known as witch stones, snake eggs, hex stones, fairy stones, holy stones or eye stones, are stones with a natural hole clean through the centre. They get their name from a folkloric belief that the hole is a portal; it's said that peering through will enable you to scry or see otherwise unseen worlds. The hole in the centre means the stone is also a circle, a kind of naturally formed ouroboros, the ancient symbol for infinity. As talismans, they are said to protect. Because the holes are formed by water, it is believed that the energy of the moving waters that created the hole remains in the stone.

Witches call stones the earth's bones. In my reading of English literature and folklore, I had become drawn to the idea of the hedgewitch. Hedgewitches are the ultimate foragers, people of the edgelands and the margins, taking their wisdom from places others don't look at or even notice. They were the first bioregionalists; boundary-walking and boundary-tending is their practice. The word 'hedgewitch' comes from the Saxon *haegtessa*, meaning hedge-rider, and the words 'hedge' and 'hag' have the same root.

With the various mystical stories I'd heard growing up, I felt like I'd inherited a slant way of seeing the world. I looked at life sideways, my head on a lean like a magpie's. My one constant question was *Why? Why* was it like that? Was that the only way it could be? In the style of Groucho Marx, I yearned to belong but also mistrusted anything that accepted me too readily.

I didn't view witches as gnarled old crones boiling newts in a cauldron, only appearing at Halloween. Witches were once respected healers, teachers and valued members of the community. They knew plant medicines and understood the interconnectedness of all life. They were the healers for their family lines, up and down the ancestral chain.

I had hedgewitch longings. I was drawn towards a deep relationship with plants but I knew I had so much to learn. I needed to open myself up to a lifelong conversation with the natural world, and to the world of signs and synchronicity.

*

As the plane left New Zealand, I spent the hours in the sky wondering if I would find my own hag stone in the UK, a new circle to gaze through, a graduation from my childhood magnifying glass. I thought about the infinite potential of a hag stone hole, a portal to the complicated mysteries of the cosmos.

*

Fraser and I landed in England on a brutally cold winter day. From the airport we took our first ride on the underground and emerged into the watery daylight of Brixton tube station, heavy with fumes from a resident incense seller.

My friend Maria was also on her OE and had already been in London a while. She'd found a flat for the three of us, and Fraser and I were grateful to have something already organised. As we trudged from the tube to our new home, bleary from the long flight, we saw the fountain in the centre of Brixton's shops had frozen solid. The streets were filthy with litter and grime. We stopped and stared at the large pool of dirty grey ice, our skin still sun-kissed from the New Zealand summer day we'd just left. I felt like I'd slipped into an underworld.

The flat had low rent but what we didn't pay for in money we paid in suffering. It was a hovel above a takeaway shop whose poor ventilation meant that our clothes always smelled like burnt cooking oil. The toilet was leaky, the boiler broke down with tedious regularity, leaving us freezing, and the floor was so crooked we would roll marbles down it to amuse ourselves. The flat was advertised as 'furnished', which meant our bedroom featured a mattress directly on the floor and, inexplicably, a ladder, which we used to hang our clothes. The small living area had a row of seats ripped from a theatre in lieu of a sofa.

Across the road was the Hobgoblin, a cosy pub that we came to use as our detached living room.

Fraser and Maria immediately got sick with a terrible, feverish cold. Our flat was too small and grim for me to hang out in all day so I went exploring South London with little money but a large capacity for walking.

I spent a lot of time in the Brixton library, leaning on the radiator and researching potential trips: the South Downs Way and Scotland's West Highland Way. I read about the sacred sites of Cornwall and Devon, and dreamed of finding the plants of wayside and hedgerow that I'd read so much about in my foraging books. The green life in the books seemed a million miles away from the Brixton winter outside.

Wandering around Brixton market, I found a stall selling Hoodoo tools. I looked carefully at all the apothecary jars of dried herbs and potions; I wanted to try everything but I'd have to wait until I earned some money. My eye was caught by a white candle, pocked with dried sprigs of catnip and sage. The writing on the side had instructions on how to burn it for 'fast luck'. This distinction amused me – not just good luck but fast luck. Fast luck was just the kind of luck I needed in this vast new city so I bought the candle, figuring the five-quid price tag would be a bargain if the candle delivered on its promise.

I'd read that the margins of London's cemeteries were a good place to find wild plants, so I skulked off to Camberwell Old Cemetery. In winter, it was a gothic place that matched the mood of the weather, full of mossy stone angels and marble sheets cracking and crumbling with the sinking of the dead. I saw ravens for the first time, flapping across the sky like lost patches of night. I spotted daylilies, hostas, hyacinths and oxeye daisies. It was a good place for my first try at plant-scouting, but it didn't feel right to take plants from a cemetery so I made do with taking photos. Then, walking towards the cemetery's exit, I saw a twenty-pound note lying on the ground.

The candle's price plus fifteen quid? Fast luck indeed.

*

The right to forage requires access to the commons, land which belongs to everyone. The United Kingdom has a long history of the commons being central to the wellbeing and happiness of its common people – the landless, the peasants and the poor – who, historically, depended on food grown in and foraged from common land to supplement their diets and incomes.

Most of the UK's commons have been lost or encroached upon over the last few hundred years, and now only 3 per cent of its land remains in commons. A conservation body called the Open Spaces Society (of which the artist William Morris was an early member) was established in 1865 to defend the UK's remaining commons; its victories include Hampstead Heath, Epping Forest and Wimbledon Common, all large tracts of wild land that have been preserved for everyone to enjoy.

The Countryside Act allows for foraging of the 'four Fs': fruit, foliage, flora and fungus. It also allows for something poetically called 'the right to roam', meaning anyone can explore and harvest from these common lands.

Fraser and I had landed in England at a tumultuous time in the history of the commons. The Criminal Justice and Public Order Act of 1994 had recently been brought into law. A fight was raging about the freedom of people to gather on common lands, to travel them and to organise activities like the outdoor dance parties that were such a feature of the emerging electronic dance music scene. These dance parties, coupled with the

New Age traveller movement, had led to a harsh government response.

New Age travellers were groups of people, usually working class, who opted to live freely in mobile homes like caravans, vardos and house trucks rather than be broke and disenfranchised in the city. They would meet up on common lands and create pop-up villages for the duration of their stay, forming the communities they struggled to find in urban centres.

The Criminal Justice Act forbade any gathering in a public place of more than twenty people – a huge assault to freedom of movement and self-organisation, and another blow to England's long history of the commons. However, the government's attempt to squash the New Age travellers and the rave scene seemed to only fuel resistance. It felt like the latest conflict in an archetypal battle as old as civilisation.

Maria, Fraser and I had heard a little about the acts of resistance against the Criminal Justice Act from political groups we were involved in back in New Zealand. As soon as we could, we found our local Reclaim the Streets group in South London. Groups were sprouting up all over the country, and Reclaim the Streets events saw a whole village's worth of people appear out of nowhere and stop traffic to create pop-up dance parties, causing the whole city to have to push pause for the rest of the day.

If there was a battle going on to try to suppress personal freedoms, we were going to be on the side of the rights of the commons. We started going to Reclaim the Streets meetings and helping to distribute leaflets. It was a great way to make some English friends. We also took care to go to as many locally organised fundraising raves as we could, dancing for the cause.

*

My first months in London had a dreary quality. It was dark on the way to work and then dusk encroached just after 4 pm. Fraser and I had forgotten to make time for having fun before we hunkered down to the winter slog of earning money for our summer travels. With hours spent literally underground, travelling on the tube to our unenjoyable jobs – Fraser was temping in a bank in the city, I was teaching high school English in Woolwich Arsenal – London felt like heavy layers of grey on grey. It was like living underwater.

My enthusiastic personality seemed culturally at odds with the South Londoners I taught alongside. I couldn't stand their dour outlook and hardwired cynicism. Fraser's colleagues were amused by his Monday-morning stories of exploring wider London's green spaces. Many long-time Londoners didn't seem to go far from their home boroughs.

With no friends to be found at work, I started going for walks in my lunch hours, looking for any small green patch or plant to admire. In front gardens near the school, I found stark branches of wintersweet and bushes of winter honeysuckle, both plain-looking blooms with seductive, citrusy scents – true winter treats. My plant guide said that winter honeysuckle was also called kiss-me-at-the-gate, so I pocketed a bloom to take home and hold above Fraser's head like mistletoe.

In a Peckham Rye charity shop, I found a book called *Street Flowers* by Richard Mabey, my favourite famous forager, full of beautiful drawings of plucky city weeds growing through the cracks, bricks and edgelands of London. Mabey admired the city's weeds, observing how tenacious and resourceful they were against all the odds. He seemed to embody the voice of the weeds. The book espoused such a radical reframing of urban wildness that it forever changed the way I looked at edgelands.

There were still traces of England's close connection to field, hedge and haw to be found on the supermarket shelves, in products I hadn't seen in shops back home: elderflower cordial, rosehip syrup, damson jam, teas made from wildflower blends. There was even a popular dandelion and burdock fizzy drink, which the company had been making since Victorian times, the label said. The main ingredient was sugar so it probably didn't hold many of the health properties of these two wild plants, but I took it as evidence that eating the weeds still held a place in the collective memory of the UK.

On weekends, Fraser and I sought out the city's parks, reserves and cemeteries, hungry for any restorative dip into the green world. Hampstead, an ancient woodland heath on one of the highest points in London, became a balm to me when I was struggling with the city's constant grey. On Saturday mornings, we'd head north across the river for long walks in the heath that culminated in a bit of foraging: lemony sorrel and dandelion leaves to add to our picnic sandwiches. I'd fill my pockets with yarrow flowers to take home for cups of tea.

But, however much I enjoyed the heath, I quickly grew more loyal to our local parks: Dulwich Park, Battersea Park, Clapham Common and Streatham Green. With fewer people around and wilder edges, they made for good foraging wanders.

Whenever I found a wild edible in London, it gave me a small sense of resiliency beyond what humble handfuls of chickweed or cups of fennel tea might suggest. It was also transgressive fun. In the parks, it was soothing to find some familiar friends, like dandelion, chickweed, fennel, red and white clover. People could be challenging, but plants are always friendly and these small moments of recognition had the effect of making anywhere feel like home, at least in the moment of discovery.

The storybook Englishness of the parks, with their yews and wildflowers, squirrels and foxes, ravens and wrens, made me second-guess how I experienced them. Was my delight at seeing these creatures and plants only because of my formative soaking in the children's books of Cicely Mary Barker, Kenneth Grahame and Brian Wildsmith? Or could it be that there was something deeper happening? Was it possible that there were dormant memories of place in my bones and DNA, waiting to awaken when my feet stood on ancestral soils? Or were these flares of recognition and excitement merely imagination coupled with my romantic tendencies? Every spark of recognition and connection I felt was immediately rained on with doubts.

It was complicated to reach backwards and look for clues of belonging, like trying to catch hold of a ghost. I had to let myself be content with small glimpses of the ghosts I was never going to be able to grasp.

*

Once Maria and I had connected into the mycelial networks of London's anarchist community, opportunities opened up, we made more friends and the city started to seem more accessible. Through urban squats, community gardens, protests and street festivals, we were welcomed into the wilds of London's grassroots.

I noticed that at the end of the day at Brixton market, the stallholders would stack piles of boxes at the road edge, ready for Lambeth Council rubbish trucks to collect the next morning.

The fresh fruits, vegetables and herbs looked fine but wouldn't survive another day's haulage and storage so the stallholders chucked them out.

One day, after the market had closed, I picked up a box off the ground and began to fill it with some of the better-looking rejected produce: spotty bananas, bruised apples, bags of spinach beginning to wilt. I braced for someone to come up and challenge me but people streamed on past, unfazed. I relaxed and began to take my time. I saw a mound of mangoes on top of one rubbish pile; a few had bruises but otherwise they looked fine. Mangoes! In the middle of winter! I took them home, gave them a good wash and we three sat around scraping the aromatic flesh off the long pits with our teeth, like we were trying to devour the sun itself.

*

Wherever you find yourself living, you have to find a way to give back. Fraser, Maria and I had received a lot of support and resources from the city, so it was time to contribute too. One spring Saturday, before the 1997 general election, we joined a protest event called 'Never Mind the Ballots: Reclaim the Streets'. Marches were organised along several of the city's main arteries, coming in from the four directions and converging in Trafalgar Square at the city's heart. We joined the South London march.

People were dressed in theatrical costumes and musicians played instruments as they strolled. As the crowd began to move slowly north, the three of us slipped in behind a drumming troupe, their supporters carrying a huge banner of a sun, sewn from a patchwork of upcycled fabrics. The frenetic beats kept our spirits up on the long walk from Brixton, across the Lambeth Bridge, to Trafalgar Square.

I looked out across the Thames, euphoric to be part of this crazy carnival, shoulder to shoulder with hundreds of colourful strangers. We were marching for creative freedom and for the commons. It was unlike the earnest, angry protests I'd attended back home. The Brits knew how to bring a joyful mischief to their acts of resistance. The spring sunshine was beating down and the drummers in front of us dripped with sweat. We sacrificed our water supplies, emptying our water bottles over their heads to cool them down.

After several hours of walking, we finally made it – thirsty, sunburned and sweaty – to Trafalgar Square, where thousands of people from marches from the north, south, east and west of the city had converged in a huge gathering of an impromptu, wayward tribe. A huge sound system on a trailer was towed by a bicycle fleet into the centre of the square, near the iconic lion statues. Loud techno music started to pulse out of the massive bass bins.

Fraser and I lost Maria for a while but then she reappeared carrying several bottles of water. We drank until our thirsts were quenched and then poured the rest over our heads. We weren't used to hot weather in London. It felt like the sun had come out especially to show support.

Nearby a young couple were bobbing to the beat. Both were dressed head to toe in bright green and the woman had a large yellow dandelion on her hat. The man was wearing a green tweed suit with a handmade headpiece like a dandelion seedhead; it had wires sticking out with delicate tufts on the ends. He held up a sign: *We Are The Weeds They Cannot Kill: Reclaim The Streets.*

I couldn't take my eyes off the pair. They were so beautiful. I turned to Maria. 'Look! We're the weeds! We ARE the weeds!'

She couldn't really hear me over the music. She tugged my backpack off my shoulders and yelled in my ear, 'Shut up and dance!'

*

I'd survived the London winter and saved enough money to buy my freedom for the summer. Fraser and I planned to start off walking the south coast, gradually working our way along the mystic sites of the country, before heading north to walk Scotland's 100-mile-long West Highland Way at the summer's end. I was desperate to finally travel. Fraser wasn't enjoying the grind of London. 'We didn't travel all this way to struggle,' he said. I'd done my best to find the city's pockets and patches of green but, after a few months of the cramped boundaries of urban nature, I was hungry for an immersion in England's wilds.

I wasn't going to find a hag stone on the streets of London.

Dandelion hot chocolate

Makes 1 large mug

Dandelion (*Taraxacum officinale*) is one of my favourite weeds – beauty of the commons, disruptor of monocultures. A symbol of resistance around the world, it's able to grow in the smallest cracks in the concrete and thrive in the most challenging of settings. Its distinctive jagged leaves, scruffy blazing flowers and trouble-making seedheads are often used in logos for resistance movements and campaigns, such is its reputation for defiance and tenacity. When I see a dandelion growing vigorously out of some unlikely crack in the concrete, I hold up a closed fist in respect.

Dandelion is a universal plant, richly represented in folklore and herbal histories. It appears on almost every continent and yet, despite being a powerful nutritional and medicinal plant, it's rarely cultivated. The inulin in dandelion roots helps gut flora, and its bitter leaves are cleansing for the liver – we'd all benefit from munching a few wild dandelion leaves every day.

Dandelion's life cycle echoes the elemental forces: the blazing yellow flower head like a little sun; the ethereal round white seedhead, beloved of artists and romantics everywhere, a glowing moon; then the seeds with their downy, fairy-like pappus, floating out far and wide like the stars above us.

Much money, poison and effort is used to try to eradicate dandelion, but it's unstoppable. I can almost hear it laughing at human attempts to keep it down. It's at the front of the 'protest march' of pioneer weeds who move in to repopulate disturbed soil; with their deep, fat roots they are soil healers.

Almost every part (apart from the seedheads) can be eaten or used in medicine. The blooms can be made into a cheerful yellow wine that has a floral and slightly bitter flavour (like the bitterness of almond or green tea).

The toasted and ground roots of dandelion make an earthy and highly nourishing drink, often called a 'coffee' and suggested as a coffee substitute. However, I think to call the dandelion-root beverage 'coffee' does a disservice to both.

It's unlike coffee's energising blast. Dandelion-root drink has almost the opposite effect; it is very grounding and calming. Mixed with chocolate and spices, it's one of my favourite drinks for that mid-afternoon slump when I don't want to frazzle my adrenals with more coffee, but some kind of gentle boost would be welcome. It has a pleasant toasty, earthy flavour, offering coffee's bitterness without the subsequent acidic stomach and adrenal jitters. It's great if you feel like your mind has been whirling all day – it will help put your disparate pieces back together.

If you don't have dandelion in your own garden, you shouldn't have to walk too far to find some. It grows everywhere. It's a great plant to forage because it's so common. Be sure to harvest from friendly places that are unlikely to have been sprayed.

Dandelion root is available at most health food shops if you don't have the time or energy to make your own.

Ingredients
- 1 tablespoon freshly ground toasted dandelion root
- 1 teaspoon organic cacao powder
- ½ teaspoon ground ginger
- ½ teaspoon ground cinnamon

Method
To prepare the dandelion root, take a trowel and carefully dig around the plant's taproot. This requires some patience – it won't yield easily. Give the harvested root a good scrub and chop off any hairy or spindly bits that will burn in the oven. Chop the root into pieces a few centimetres long. Spread the pieces out across a large shallow dish (a pizza pan works well) and roast at a low heat, around 100 degrees Celsius, for a few hours until they are dried. To check if they are well toasted, break a piece. It should be brown on the inside, not white. Allow to cool and then store in an airtight jar. Grind just before use.

To make the dandy hot chocolate, put the ingredients into a large (300 ml) mug or cup. Slowly pour just-boiled water over top, stirring vigorously all the while. Both the dandelion and cacao can be silty so need a good deal of mixing. I tend to leave the spoon in and give it a stir between sips.

If you prefer a sweet drink, add honey or brown sugar to taste. You can also add milk or nut mylk if you like, but I like the intensity of it without.

CHAPTER 7

Chalk cliffs call

Wild greens

In London, I'd signed us up as WWOOFers – willing workers on organic farms. The scheme gives volunteer workers food, board and land education on organic farms in return for a few hours' work each day. They're basically working holidays, with some education in the mix. It seemed a good way to meet locals, learn land-tending skills and travel to places we wouldn't see if we stuck to the tourist routes. Fraser was a little sceptical. While I tend to bound up to people enthusiastically like a daft puppy, his attitude to strangers is more 'assume the worst to avoid disappointment'.

Fraser was a master of packing light. My backpack was heavy with pocket wildflower field guides and my journal, which I planned to use to take notes on what I foraged and to scrawl the drafts of poems. I liked to hike in vintage dresses paired with bicycle shorts, never willing to compromise sartorial considerations for my physical endeavours. Waving us goodbye at Paddington Station, Maria's boyfriend laughed at my sagging backpack, calling out as I walked off to the train, 'Oh my god, Helen, you look like a dog dragging its arse!'

My teaching colleagues had thought the idea of WWOOFing was bizarre. 'What, you're gonna go dig fields for random strangers? And get paid *nothing*?' But I refused to be deterred.

Our first WWOOFing destination, Blacklands Farm, was an intimidating sight as we walked up the driveway. Surrounded by a looming yew hedge, the house had a black thatched roof and stony entranceway. Near the East Sussex town of Battle, it was a sheep and vegetable smallholding. The house was listed with the National Trust. It had been built in 1679, during the reign of Charles II.

'This house is twice as old as Pākehā New Zealand,' I said to Fraser.

'Let's hope they've updated the plumbing a few times then,' he replied in his usual dry fashion.

Stuart and Diane, our hosts, were an austere pair undergoing a midlife sea change. They'd recently moved to the farm from London after leaving jobs in academia. Fraser and I found ourselves sharing a tiny attic room (we could only fully stand up in the room's centre) with a pair of young Japanese travellers. Dressed in matching pastel shell suits and bright white trainers, they were sweet and confused, didn't speak English, and seemed very unwilling to go near the farm's muck. We did our best to help them across the language barrier.

Diane had a good knowledge of plants, and when I came down holding my plant guide she took me for a walk around the farm's edge. We found plants I hadn't seen before: agrimony, bittersweet, toadflax, navelwort and jack-by-the-hedge. I picked small pieces to press in the pages of my journal. She picked some horehound to make a cough medicine.

Stuart soon put us to work in a field he planned to turn into arable land for crops. He gave us mallets to break up an old concrete pad.

'That should keep you busy for the morning,' he said cheerfully. He didn't join us, instead headed back inside for a second coffee.

After twenty minutes of bashing at the concrete in a fairly futile way, Fraser stopped to catch his breath and glared at me. '"Willing" workers, eh?'

I shrugged apologetically and started singing, 'Breakin' rocks in the hot sun … '

Fraser snorted, not amused.

After a couple of hours, I went inside to find Stuart. 'I don't mean to be rude, but do you reckon we could do something less like demolition and more farming-related for a while?'

He walked us to the field's boundary and put us to work chopping and grubbing out waist-high nettles and tangled nests of blackberry. With inadequate gloves and blunt tools, we were soon covered in bramble scratches, our arms flaming with nettle burn. The change of task didn't improve Fraser's mood.

When we showed up at the large kitchen's wood-fired Aga stove for dinner, Stuart served us nettle soup with cheese and nettle-flocked bread, followed by blackberry crumble – the incidental fruits of our day's labours. He chuckled as he filled our plates. Although both dishes were delicious, we were too weary to laugh.

From the point of view of our Kiwi pragmatism, the couple seemed a bit tentative and ineffectual. I noted in my travel journal, *They are not really farmers, but intellectuals ... faffing around on the land.*

Fraser and I liked to learn new things and we had been taught by our families the value of working hard. With this chronic earnestness, we had a bad habit of somehow managing to turn leisure time into more work. After a week of days spent wrestling with concrete and nettles in return for weedy dinners, and nights spent in the baking attic on a lumpy wire-based bed, we realised we'd done it again. We had got the balance of 'working' and 'holiday' wrong. Blacklands had been a good shift in gears from the pace of London life, but we needed some freedom and fun. We left the farm for the south coast.

*

We began the South Downs Way at the eastern end, leaving from Eastbourne. A 100-mile coast path between Eastbourne and Winchester, the way features dramatic sea views, winding through idyllic farmland and historical sites. The beauty of the South Downs Way is that most days begin with a steep grunt uphill, then once you're up on the tops the rest of the day is rolling grasses, high above the beach, and sparkling sea vistas.

Sussex is also home to sites of the Bloomsbury Group literary movement. I was a little obsessed with members Virginia Woolf and Vanessa Bell, and we planned to wander off the way to visit their houses.

The less money we spent, the longer we'd have freedom before we had to settle down and find work again. So, when the South Downs guidebook suggested walkers book accommodation at pubs and bed and breakfasts in villages near the track, we were scornful. The very idea of it: finishing each tramping day in a cosy bed and breakfast, coddled by hot showers, hot pub dinners and soft beds. What was intrepid about that? We were used to DOC (Department of Conservation) huts and hunters' digs, which were free or cost a small amount for a hut pass.

Ignoring local guidance, arrogant, cash-strapped and stupid, we set off with our tent and camping stove. We weren't going to let the lack of information about campsites or friendly tent pitches get in the way of our intention to do the walk for free. We grunted our way up Beachy Head to Birling Gap with no accommodation booked, no farmers contacted, no worries about our fate, no clue.

We were also used to the deep immersion of the New Zealand bush, where it is possible to be hundreds of miles from other people and to really get away from it all. As we walked, we began to realise we weren't going to be immersed in any deep forests. England's long history and dense population meant that civilisation was all around us, all the time. There seemed to always be a country pub or village shop within half a kilometre. Instead of being grateful for this proximity to food, beer and other comforts, we spent our first few days a little deflated.

If New Zealand's farms looked young, like they had recently been carved out of the land, then England's looked as if they were slowly being reabsorbed, with low, sinking buildings and crumbling stone walls. The countryside was denuded of forest, too. The wilds we'd been reading about at university existed more in cultural memory than in the present day.

But, while there were no dark Tolkien-esque forests to be found, there were other natural delights. Using my guidebook of English wildflowers, I found plants growing wild that I'd only ever seen domesticated in New Zealand gardens. In drifts along the track's edge, I saw mounds of pale yellow-green primroses, purple hyacinths, brilliant blue chicory flowers and field scabious. It wasn't the intense, dense dark green of the bush at home, but the other consolations of the English countryside were considerable. The narrow, winding roads were edged with tangles of sweetbriar roses, blackberry brambles, hawthorn and native honeysuckle, Shakespeare's 'luscious woodbine'. I'd found my first hedgerows. The field edges were coming to life with dots of small, bright flowers: buttercups, blue speedwell, cowslips, red poppies, cornflowers, wheat, rattle and red and white clover. We spotted sunbathing newts on stone walls. There were Mediterranean herbs, thyme and wild marjoram, growing happily around the boulders of the chalk hills. They cheered up our humble camp-stove pasta. One day while we were picnicking in a meadow, a bright green grass snake slithered slowly across my hand, like something from a Greek myth.

We passed lots of English walkers on the route. Calling themselves 'ramblers', they had a quirky uniform of swishy wet-weather gaiters over their boots, pairs of walking sticks, tweedy hats of various shapes and styles, and, most amusingly to us, they wore maps tucked into A4 plastic sleeves on strings around their necks. It was endearingly dorky.

On the first day of walking, we made it to the crest of sister two of the Seven Sisters cliffs just as dusk was beginning to encroach. This was the moment when a sensible English person would have wandered off the way and down the lane to a nearby pub or bed and breakfast. Instead, we found a thicket of gorse and blackberry that looked like it could offer a bit of camouflage. There was no one else around. All the other walkers had left for their accommodation for the night.

We stomped on the bracken to make a flat square for our tent, then rolled a couple of large rocks over to be our camping seats and cooked up a hearty brew of what Fraser called 'camping slop': a one-pot wonder supplemented with foraged greens including dandelion leaves, plantain and bittercress. We watched the sun go down over the ocean and, in the dusk's dim light, put up our tent and spent a cosy freelance night sleeping in the nest of bracken.

The luck of that first night did not continue. It was often difficult to find discreet corners to hide our small tent. One night, after a day of beautiful views walking past fields edged with giant red poppies, dusk started to fall while we were in the middle of a farm path, exposed on every side.

We could have turned back to Alfriston, which we'd only just passed through. We didn't. We could have tried to find the farmer to ask permission to strike camp. We didn't. A combination of shyness and doggedness got in the way of good sense. We winged it and put up our tent near some scrubby trees, over the fence from the walkway's edge. It felt like we were sleeping right on the road – because we kind of were – and I took a long time to get to sleep.

A couple of hours later, a sound like a very loud fart just near my head woke me up. I elbowed Fraser. 'What was that? There's something outside!'

He woke up, blearily groped for the torch and stuck his head out of the tent.

'Oh dear.'

Fraser tends towards understatement in the face of adversity, so I was immediately alarmed.

'What?' I hissed.

I crawled out of my sleeping bag and looked out. We were surrounded on all sides by enormous red bulls, steam unfurling from their ringed nostrils. There were about twenty of them in a circle around our tent. If we startled them, they could have easily stampeded, crushing us. We froze. They gazed back impassively; it was hard to tell if they were annoyed or just curious.

We pulled our clothes and boots on, and stuffed our gear away as quietly and calmly as we could. Fraser jerked his head at the next paddock over. It looked empty, but it was hard to be sure in the dark. I grabbed our packs and scuttled. Fraser lifted the whole tent, still standing but freed of its guy ropes, and tossed it over the fence. We secured the tent into the hard chalk of the path as best we could and crawled back inside. We wrapped our unzipped sleeping bags around ourselves, but this time we stayed dressed with our boots on in case we needed to bolt again. I tried to sleep but kept sitting up in wide-eyed panic at every small sound.

Then, around 1 am, I heard gunshots. I panicked, assuming we were being shot at by an angry farmer. We could see three men in the next paddock over.

'Oh bloody hell. What shall we do now?' I hissed. 'Shall I yell out to let them know we're here?'

'No! They might shoot at us!' said Fraser.

'They're rabbit hunters, not murderers,' I said, frantic to get out of a potential firing line.

But Fraser's distaste for talking to strangers stretched to this extreme situation. 'Look, they're not going to shoot towards the cattle. Just be quiet and lie still and we'll be okay.'

He was infuriating. He'd rather risk injury than come clean. I was grateful they didn't seem to have hunting dogs with them.

We lay still, scarcely daring to breathe, and clutching each other. About an hour later they finally left.

I got no more sleep that night. At the merest inkling of the morning's light, we packed up, hopped the two fences and took off back to the way. We trudged up to the clifftop, where, exhausted, we made coffee and porridge and spread our soaking gear out to dry in the dawning sun.

Even after this night of frights, we continued trying to force our New Zealand tramping style on to English territory. We were slow to let go of the idea that we wouldn't be doing it for real if the day's walking was bookended by chintzy bed and breakfasts with TV and full English breakfasts. After a final low point of sleeping in scrappy bushes beside a busy roundabout, where we had to kick aside a carpet of chip packets, beer cans and cigarette butts to make a space for our tent, we caved in. We did the rest of the South Downs Way like the locals, booking ahead and paying for comfortable accommodation.

Later, when we walked the West Highland Way from Milngavie to Fort William, we found that Scotland's hiking culture resembles New Zealand's a little more closely. Scotland has a system of bothies, simple sleeping huts or shelters that are free for anyone to use. The huts are maintained by the Mountain Bothies Association, who serve 'to maintain simple shelters in remote country for the use and benefit of all who love wild and lonely places'. Fraser used this discovery as further evidence of the superiority of Scottish culture.

*

I held a hope that if I visited enough sites where famous writers had created great works, some of the atmosphere might rub off on me, as though writing success was contagious. While walking the South Downs Way, we took a weekend off to visit some of 'Bloomsbury Sussex'. In Virginia Woolf's garden writing hut at Monk's House in Rodmell, her final home, I sat down for a precious minute at her writing desk, soaking up the atmosphere.

The next day, we woke up in a little white cottage facing out to sea and spent an absorbing morning visiting Charleston Farmhouse, the famous Bloomsbury Group enclave and pilgrimage site for wannabe Bohemians everywhere. Every surface, every lampshade, every bowl and even the radiators were hand-painted with fruit, flowers and other decorative motifs by once resident artists Vanessa Bell and Duncan Grant.

We left Charleston and walked three miles north on a path that cut through farmland to Berwick Church, a tiny rural church featuring a large mural of 'The Annunciation' by Vanessa Bell. We'd decided to walk there rather than get the tourist shuttle because we wanted to experience the journey as Vanessa and Duncan would have – on foot, across the fields near their home. We reached a rise on the path and stretched out ahead were golden fields as far as we could see. Bordering the golden wheat and barley were wide strips of wildflowers: red poppies, blue speedwell, purple clover, yellow cowslips. We stopped in our tracks, overwhelmed by the very English beauty of it.

I shrugged off my pack and climbed the wooden fence separating the walking lane from the field. I waded into the thick poppies.

'What are you doing now?' Fraser shook his head, reluctant to trespass.

'C'mon, look at this! I think we died in the night and went to heaven,' I said.

I walked through the wildflowers, running my hand along their tops until I found an especially thick patch of cornflowers and poppies. Slowly, I lay back into the thick bed of flowers. Fraser looked both ways, then hopped the fence and came to lie beside me. From our perspective on the ground, the sky was framed by the bright red and blue flowers.

I poked a cornflower behind Fraser's ear. We gazed up at the fluffy clouds. Skylarks darted overhead.

No church could top this.

'I think this is where we go next,' I said. 'Heaven is an English wildflower meadow in midsummer.'

My journal entry for that day read, *One of those rare perfect days.*

Foraged wild greens soup

Serves 2

One of the joys of foraging is learning how many of the green things in the grasses and margins can be eaten. In foraging guides, there are descriptions of dozens of green leafy things that can add a substantial nutritional boost to a humble soup or 'camping slop'. It's empowering to discover that you don't need to go without fresh greens while camping. It also eases the load of things you need to carry with you.

You might find some of these humble greens around a tramping or camping site in New Zealand: garlic mustard (*Alliaria petiolate*), bittercress (*Cardamine hirsute*), chickweed (*Stellaria media*), dead-nettle (*Lamium purpureum*), chicory (*Cichorium intybus*), cleavers (*Galium aparine*), dandelion (*Taraxacum officinale*), young dock (*Rumex obtusifolius*) leaves, fat hen (*Chenopodium album*), mallow (*Malva* species), pūhā (*Sonchus oleraceus*), nasturtium (*Tropaeolum majus*), nettle (*Urtica dioica*), onion weed (*Nothoscordum borbonicum*), oxalis (*Oxalis incarnata*), purslane (*Portulaca oleracea*), plantain (*Plantago* species), sheep sorrel (*Rumex acetosella*), sweet violet (*Viola odorata*) leaves, wild lettuce (*Lactuca virosa*).

Take care while foraging *Urtica dioica* that you are confident in your identification. New Zealand's native nettle (*Urtica ferox*) is poisonous. Consult your foraging guides. Nasturtium is very peppery and spicy, so add in a little for flavour but don't make it the bulk of your greens. Dandelion greens are bitter, so only add a few. Aim for a mix of leaves.

This recipe makes one small potato stretch quite far, and uses the foraged greens to add flavour, visual interest and nutrition.

Ingredients
   2 tablespoons dried onion flakes (or 1 small chopped onion)
   a generous slosh of olive oil
   1 small potato, chopped into cubes
   1 teaspoon garlic powder
   500 ml water (or thereabouts)

2 generous handfuls foraged greens, chopped
a small grating of cheese (optional)
salt and pepper, to taste

Method

In a pot or billy that holds at least 600 ml, sauté the onion in the olive oil. When the onion is soft and glassy-looking, add the potato and garlic powder, stirring to coat well in oil. Add salt.

Cook, stirring occasionally, for 5 minutes.

Pour in the water and bring to the boil. When the potato has softened, drop your greens into the pot for the last 5 minutes of cooking. Stir well.

If you're lucky enough to have a bit of cheese with you, sprinkle some on top and enjoy the feeling of freedom that comes from eating a dinner sourced from your home for the night!

CHAPTER 8

Wandering the West Country

Thistle, gorse and lemon balm

The way I was wired, too much time around concrete, metal and a constant throng of people overwhelmed me. If I couldn't put my bare feet on the grass or find plants to sit with, I would end up frazzled, with a kind of white noise taking over my brain.

After the summer's long days turned to autumn, I made a case for moving somewhere new. Fraser thought we should stay in London because there were better work opportunities and we'd only just found our feet. But we seemed to spend most weekends escaping London anyway, hungry for our nature fix.

A friend from home, Fi, was living in Bristol. I knew we only needed one good friend to plug into a new place. I would miss Maria a lot, but London was in constant fast forward and I needed a place that moved at a more human pace.

Fraser agreed to move if I found a job to get us through the transition. That bit turned out to be easy – Fi said I could work at the café she was managing. We moved west.

Bristol was smaller and greener, with large gardens and reserves to forage and learn from. It was also a gateway to many of England's most potent mystical sites, and there was the matter of my ongoing hunt. When we'd walked the West Highland Way in late summer, I'd trailed a little behind Fraser, eyes to the ground, looking for a hag stone. No luck.

'I'll guess I'll find it in the West Country,' I said to Fraser.

'You said that about Scotland.'

I had hoped to find it in Scotland, land of Clan Macrae and Fraser's ancestral Clan Campbell. We'd bought every postcard and leaflet we could find in Scotland about our clans – their history, tartans and terrains – and mailed them back to our parents.

'I think it didn't find me in Scotland because it will be the end of searching when I find it. It will mean it's time to go home.'

Fraser was patient with my murmurings, but, ever the pragmatist, he threw a *Time Out Bristol* towards me. 'Speaking of searching, find us a flat.'

*

Fi was working for a New Zealander who owned a string of cafés; he'd single-handedly saved Bristol from bad coffee by introducing Kiwi-style flat whites to the West Country. The Monday after our weekend move to Bristol, I started work as a barista in one of his cafés, the Boston Tea Party. We found a tiny bedsit in Clifton, with a bed that folded down out of the wall, like something in a sitcom. It was partially underground, and our living-room window had a view of the feet of passers-by on the footpath outside.

The weekend we moved in, Fraser suggested we go furniture shopping but I encouraged him to be patient – the city would provide. Sure enough, the next week there was an inorganic-waste day. We rescued a wonky coffee table and two 1950s lounge chairs with wooden legs, upholstered in a mustard 1970s boucle, off the pavement for nothing.

My Bristolian workmates were friendly and gracious. They teased me about my flat vowels. My workmate Ben was particularly amused. 'Bin? BIN?! She's calling me rubbish again!' They were far less reserved and polite than the Londoners I'd met. They could be endearingly blunt and also melodramatic – every small inconvenience was dubbed 'a total nightmare'. I was moved by the way Bristolian friends called each other 'my lover' as a form of affection.

I volunteered to do the unpopular first shift, opening up the café at 6 am and working the high tide of people flooding in for their morning coffee. It was early and busy, but I liked both because the shift passed quickly and my workday was all done by 2 pm, leaving me with plenty of time to explore.

Foraging was much more exciting in Bristol. In the Downs, Bristol's largest reserve, I found wild hops growing around the edges of the park. I'd never seen hops growing wild like that before. I picked the pretty pale green flowers, dried them until they became a pale straw colour, then drank them with catmint for a sleep-inducing tea. In the plant-essence world, hops help you relinquish tight control and allow you to relax and to dream. This echoed how I felt since making the move from London. I could let go of the cockroach-like carapace I needed to get by in the big city and be a little soft again.

The council used bay trees for municipal landscaping so I dried bay branches on our radiator. I supplemented gifts with small jars of bay leaves I'd foraged from the park. I found lush patches of wild garlic in the Downs and, in the wood's edge where the sun dappled through, waves of wild strawberries. Also known as alpine strawberries, they look like their cultivated cousins except they're much smaller, almost fairy-sized.

Foraging wild strawberries requires both agility and patience. To find these tiny treasures I had to get on my knees and crawl around the forest's edge. The little red jewels liked to hide under the jagged trefoil leaves, requiring a measure of tenacity to find them. Half an hour of picking resulted in dirty leggings and a small handful of bright red, heavily seeded fruits that I tried to eat singly, mindfully, savouring each one, but it was hard not to just throw them into my mouth in one greedy toss.

The forests of the West Country were airy and light green, with drifts of wildflowers beneath the trees. I found my eyes habitually searching for the dark, distinctive outlines of ponga, kareao vines and cabbage trees, and not finding them. Bristol's bright copses were such a different experience.

Yellow was a colour common in the understory: the pale lemon of cowslips, wild honeysuckle and primroses, and the rich butter yellows of lesser celandine and yellow corydalis. Back home, a patch of bright yellow on the horizon either meant a kōwhai tree or, more often, gorse, the scourge of farmers everywhere.

*

Fraser suggested we walk from Bristol to Bath along the River Avon. He'd found an admin job working for the local council so, while I was out wandering on weekday afternoons, he was cooped up in an office, itching to explore. In New Zealand, he liked to travel from town to town by bike or even on foot, just to prove to himself he could make the trip without a car. The Bristol to Bath walk went along the river and canals, taking five hours one way.

Along the path we found blackberries and more wild garlic. We added these to our picnic lunch. I picked hawthorn berries to take home and make into a savoury sauce, a little like HP sauce. (Later, I would label it 'BB sauce' for 'Bristol to Bath'.)

Fraser could have done the walk much faster without me; my foraging forays made us slower. But there was so much to look at. I loved seeing the narrowboats on the canals with their distinctive Roses and Castles folk-art decorations of stylised flowers in bright colours. We passed a narrow arched wooden bridge, much too narrow for humans, with a sign beside it saying *Take Care: Chickens Crossing*. We also saw a man walking a large pig on a leash.

After a pint of beer at a canal-side pub in Bath, we jumped on a bus and were back in Bristol in less than an hour.

*

Fraser and I wanted to visit Land's End in Cornwall, a craggy rock hunkered precariously on the Atlantic Coast, and England's most westerly point. At university, our Romantic literature textbook had the painting 'Wanderer above the Sea of Fog' by Caspar David Friedrich on the cover, and I wanted to go to Land's End so I could recreate this image, using the long-suffering Fraser as my model. Lover of the old stories and myths, he too was attracted to the poetry of being able to say we'd stood at Land's End.

The first time we tried to visit, a flash rainstorm flooded all the roads near the site, forcing us to turn back. On our second attempt we got closer to the bluff by driving along narrow lanes cramped between businesses and small dwellings, but again the weather was refusing to cooperate and we soon hit roiling clouds of mist and car-rattling winds.

We stopped and climbed out of the car to try to glimpse the coast, but we were bead-blasted by hail. The sea was a surging swell that boomed and spumed over the shrieking of the winds. Drenched, we clambered back into the car.

'This is crazy, Helen,' said Fraser. 'Even if we can get there, we won't be able to walk near the edge. It's too dangerous.'

I wasn't going to get my Romantic painting re-enactment, but we were so close.

'One more try,' I pleaded.

Fraser sighed and turned the key in the ignition.

We tried a different thin country lane, a little further inland and away from the roar of the sea. Suddenly a blast of wind clashed the power lines together overhead, and a power pole fell across the lane in front of us with a dramatic shower of blue sparks, narrowly missing our car.

'Okay, I think that's a definite no,' said Fraser as he hastily reversed.

We wanted to see Land's End, but apparently it didn't want to see us. It was time to accept the land's refusal.

That night, safely back in Bristol in our rickety wall-bed, Fraser said, 'I think we couldn't get to Land's End because we haven't made the same pilgrimage at home. We haven't been to Cape Reinga yet.'

It sounded like the sort of thing I would say. Sometimes the diehard rationalist could surprise me.

*

Wanting to carry on the activism I'd started in London, I went along to a local Reclaim the Streets meeting in a community centre in Bristol. The organiser asked four people to walk to the four corners of the room and said to the gathering, 'They'll hold up a sign showing the type of action they're doing, if you could get up and go over to whichever one you're most interested in.'

In one corner a woman with dyed black hair wearing a mirrored kurta held up a sign saying *Green Activism*. A guy in the opposite corner held a sign saying *Art Activism*. I dithered for a moment, but I was intrigued to find out what green activism might involve so I walked over to the woman. Her name was Jude and she needed more guerrilla gardeners for her group. I didn't know what guerrilla gardening was but I was intrigued.

'I'm so burnt out from being *against* all the time,' said Jude. She did look tired. 'I need to do something that's a big YES for a while, something *positive*.' Jude had spent the previous year living in the forest at the Newbury bypass protests, an ongoing forest occupation by protestors to try to stop England's ancient forests being cleared to build a motorway. Maria had spent some time at the protest, too, while Fraser and I had been on our walking trips.

As Jude explained it, guerrilla gardening was another attempt to reclaim the commons. People planted fruit trees, herbs and medicinal plants in waste and common urban lands to beautify them and for the benefit of all. Free planting to reignite people's interest in access to shared land made sense to me. I was seduced.

I joined the phone list for the group. We met up at the community centre soon after to make seed bombs, burying wildflower seeds in balls of clay to hurl from a distance on to wastelands so the wildflowers would grow. We took walks along scrappy industrial parts of the river and poked willow sticks into the ground as we walked along. We hoped the trees would grow and restore the depleted ecosystems, inviting life back to the polluted shallows.

Jude inspired me with her passionate rhetoric. 'I work for the earth first. Whatever supports life informs my actions.'

She was a poet, too. As we got to know each other, I gave her some of my poems to read. She was kind when she gave me feedback. 'I think you're a bit too much in your ideas. Readers don't want to sit in your *brain*; they want to sit in your *world*. Where's the *stuff* of your world? The weather, people, places … the plants?'

Some of the other guerrilla gardeners were foragers, too. They made practical use of the spiky plants of the edgelands, plants I'd been raised to consider the very worst weeds, with nettle beers, gorse flower cordials, pickled burdock roots. I sampled everything I was offered, keen to expand my palette. I couldn't wait to tell Mum and Dad that I'd been eating nettles, thistles and gorse, like some feral human goat.

*

The café planned to take a coffee stall to the annual Glastonbury Festival. Fi and I volunteered to join the 'Glasto Gang' and we got Fraser a place on board the trip, too.

We drove the work van to the site to set up the stall a couple of days before the festival began. It was a glowing summer day as we entered Worthy Farm, the rolling green fields emptied of cows for the festival's duration. After that first golden day, the sun abandoned us and the heavy rains began. It was going to be a muddy Glasto.

I worked short four-hour shifts off and on all through the day and night. With the intense bursts of work followed by inadequate snatches of sleep and quick dashes out to explore, the festival took on a bizarre, dreamy quality. Behind the coffee stall, we lived in a revelrous encampment of small tents sinking into mud, separated by a slippery wooden-pallet walkway. Fraser and I slept with our gumboots on, our muddy feet sticking out of the tent door, and a mound of damp sleeping bags over our fully clothed bodies. We learned to sleep on our backs like a pair of bog vampires.

I could tell what kind of drugs customers were on by how or what they ordered. The stoners bought a lot of cakes and crisps. Those on ecstasy were bug-eyed, chewing gum intensely as they bought bottles of water. The trippers stood in front of the counter for long periods, wide-eyed and swaying slightly, struggling to form words.

At the top of the site was a large section called the Greenfields, ring-fenced off from the rest of the festival and intended as a safe haven. Here were the children's spaces, soothing art activities, chill-out yurts, environmental groups and healing tents. I gravitated there in my time off, although the green of the fields was soon a sea of whipped mud.

A stall with medicines and upcycled pixie dresses caught my eye. Its sign read *Green Witch*. I wandered over and bought a herbal tincture for period pain off the stallholder, a woman called Megwyn. She was open and friendly and pulled up a round of wood so I could sit down. She asked me about New Zealand's native-plant medicines and I felt some shame that I couldn't tell her much. I thought I knew the word for Māori plant medicine, rongoā, but none of the wisdom within.

When I asked her what her favourite wild plant was, she said, 'Lemon balm, because it follows me everywhere. It's like a little sister.'

Being sisterless, I loved that idea. I told her about the guerrilla gardening I'd been doing back in Bristol and she made a huffing sound. 'Travellers've been doing that forever. Sow it along the wayside, and then we come back when the season's right to harvest.'

She went into her tent and came back with a glass bottle of pale yellow liquid and two cups. 'Carmelite water. You had it before?'

I hadn't. It was refreshing and delicious. She said it was an ancient drink, made from lemon balm and angelica – an antidote to the crazy atmosphere of the festival. The lemon balm was good for calming the nerves, and the angelica for soothing the indigestion from all the dodgy camping food.

I had to get back to my next shift. I thanked her for the drink and the tincture, and for giving me some new plants to look up.

'You're welcome, my lover. And don't go back to New Zealand without finding yourself some meadowsweet. It's the Druid's plant – always brings you luck.'

I found Fraser back at our camp. He was buzzing from having just seen the Chemical Brothers play in the dance tent.

'Oh cool! I just had an ancient drink with a real Traveller witch!' I said.

He rolled his eyes. 'Of course you did.'

*

After the festival wound up and the crowds left, we had two more days stuck in the quagmire to slowly pack up the stall. As Fi and I took a squelchy walk to the general store to replenish our stash of crisps and cans of Coke, we passed a cool vintage clothing stall, with racks of bright shirts and dresses from the 1960s and 1970s, a rainbow of florals and paisleys. But the double racks had sunk; the clothes on the bottom were melting into the mud.

A small, wiry woman with a blue mohawk was throwing the top rows of clothing, still somewhat clean, into the back of a large yellow van. Fi found us a pallet to stand on so we wouldn't sink, and we stopped to talk to her.

'Oh, *mate*!' I said, waving at all the sunken muddy clothes. 'That sucks! What are you going to do?'

'Ha! Nothing. Have to get back to Germany for work. I just leave it all here.' She laughed at our shocked faces. 'It's okay. I made my money.' She waved her arm towards the sunken, bog-soaked clothes. 'Can be all yours! If you want to deal with the mud.'

I looked at Fi.

'Oh, I dunno ... ' she said. We were both sleep-deprived, filthy and physically exhausted.

I grabbed her arm. 'C'mon! Look at all these amazing vintage fabrics! We can do it!'

We bought five large black rubbish bags at the general store, then squelched back to the stall. At first we tried to be discerning about what we took but it soon became clear this was pointless, time-consuming and messy, so we threw clothes in the bags haphazardly until we ran out of room. It took a few trips to lug all our loot back to the coffee stall.

Our boss, Al, groaned when he saw the pile of muddy bags. 'You have got to be kidding me.' But he was a good sort and let us fling them in the back of the van on top of a tarp.

As we drove out, the farm was all churned mud, rubbish and abandoned belongings – a dystopian ocean of filth as far as the eye could see.

*

Back in Bristol, the clean surfaces and straight angles of the flat felt jarring after a week in the Glastonbury trenches. It took Fi and I days of soaking clothes in large buckets and continuously running the washing machine at Fi's flat to clean up our muddy bounty.

First we chose some things for ourselves. Then we draped everything else around the furniture of Fi's living room and invited our friends over for a giveaway party. The living room turned into a mad communal dressing room as people tried on clothes in front of mirrors we'd propped against the sofas. Clothes flew around the room, tried on by person after person in a flurry of mad, sweaty fun. Our friends couldn't believe we'd got it all for free.

'Yeah, and in the middle of a paddock,' I said.

It quickly became my favourite UK 'foraging' story.

*

In the Greenfield stalls at Glastonbury, I'd seen some hag stone necklaces on waxed linen cords. They weren't expensive, some ten quid, some twenty, but I wanted to find one in the wild. A hag stone needs to come with an origin story, and I wanted a better one than 'I bought it at Glastonbury'. A hag stone should be gifted from a special friend, or found swimming in wild waters or out on a walk. Not purchased.

Wearing a hag stone was a signifier that you were literate to the liminal, open to the world's signs and synchronicities. For me it was also an homage to my grandmothers. I'd been searching these ancestral lands for almost two years now. When would my hag stone find me?

Carmelite water

Makes approximately 750 ml

The first recorded version of Carmelite water dates back to 1379. So-called because of its association with the Carmelite nuns and monks of France, it is an old tonic recipe that the nuns and monks referred to as 'the elixir of life'. That may be something of an exaggeration, but, as Megwyn had told me at Glastonbury, it does serve as a nervine tonic and digestive aid. It also tastes very good – fragrant and unusual.

In New Zealand, both lemon balm (*Melissa officinalis*) and angelica (*Angelica archangelica*) can sometimes be found in edgelands. They are usually garden escapees, but I've found lemon balm at bush edges in some surprisingly remote places, miles from the nearest human dwellings. The seed must have been carried by birds.

Sip a small glass of Carmelite water after dinner to aid digestion and calm the nerves.

Ingredients
   1 cup chopped fresh lemon balm
   ½ cup chopped fresh angelica
   zest of 1 medium-sized lemon
   a generous pinch of freshly grated nutmeg
   1 bottle inexpensive white wine

Method
Put the fresh ingredients at the bottom of a large jar. Pour the wine over top. (Keep the wine bottle.)

Stir well and leave to macerate for 24 hours.

After the mixture has macerated, strain out the plant material and rebottle into the wine bottle. Label and date.

Gorse-flower cordial

Makes approximately 500 ml

Gorse (*Ulex europaeus*) is one of New Zealand's most noxious invasive weeds. But when I saw gorse growing in the hills of its native Scotland alongside its sister plant, purple heather, it made sense in its land of origin. Both plants have a similar scrubby density. They interweave, their blooms creating vivid yellow and purple patchworks across the rolling Highlands. In Scotland, gorse is also known as 'whin' or 'furze', the latter sounding particularly delightful in a Scottish accent.

In the medieval Celtic ogham alphabet, the letters correspond to different sacred plants and their spiritual qualities. Most relate to trees, like oak, willow and yew, but there are a few related to plants. Both heather and gorse have their own letters, which shows the significance they once held in early Celtic culture – not pests but sacred plants.

Gorse flowers have a pungent coconut smell and a mild coconut-almond flavour in the nectar at the plant end of the bud. This cordial carries that lovely smell and is a pretty straw-yellow colour, too. For me, it's consistently pleasing to make something delicious out of such a maligned plant.

Getting up close and personal with a gorse bush takes a measure of determination – the spiny prickles are treacherous. To harvest gorse flowers, wear strong gardening gloves. Take a large paper or fabric bag and a pair of scissors with a fine blade. Hold the bag beneath the blooms and snip the blooms off at the base, letting them drop into the bag. To make a 500 ml bottle of cordial, you'll need about four generous handfuls of blossoms, so settle in!

Ingredients

600 ml cold water
150 g white sugar
juice of 1 small lemon
zest of 1 orange
4 generous handfuls gorse blossoms

Method

Make the sugar syrup first. Bring the water to the boil in a medium-sized saucepan, then add the sugar and stir until it is completely dissolved. The liquid will reduce down a bit.

Remove the sugar syrup from the heat, then add the lemon juice, orange zest and gorse blossoms. Stir gently to combine, then cover with a muslin cloth or clean tea towel and leave to infuse overnight.

Sterilise a 500 ml bottle or jar. Strain the plant and fruit matter and bottle the cordial in the sterilised bottle or jar.

The cordial is shelf stable until opened, then keep in the fridge.

Dilute according to your taste – one part cordial to three parts water works well as a rough guide.

How to eat a thistle

Jude the guerrilla gardener taught me that it is possible to eat the stalk of a young thistle (*Onopordum acanthium*). Thistle is best harvested in spring, when the plant is still young, as it grows very fibrous through the summer. Bees, birds and butterflies all adore the vivid purple thistle flower; it ought to be celebrated for its contribution to biodiversity rather than seen as a prickly pest.

In Europe, some farmers' markets still sell bunches of thistle stalks. Like many foraged foods, it takes some measure of tenacity to harvest, and then time to prepare, but you'll be rewarded with a sense of pride in your efforts. If you can make a thistle palatable, you'll know you're unlikely to ever starve.

Plus, thistle-eating is an essential life skill for any aspiring poet.

Harvest a young thistle carefully, with gloved hands, and then strip back the sinewy, rougher outer greens. Inside, there should be around 30 centimetres of tender and crisp midrib. It has a similar consistency to the inside of a broccoli stalk and a mild artichoke flavour. Grate raw into a salad or chop and steam as a side vegetable.

CHAPTER 9

Hag stone hunting

Meadowsweet

Fraser and I had a list of sacred sites in the south of England we wanted to explore, looking for any feelings of ancestral connection. On weekends, we ticked them off: the Uffington chalk horse; the Cerne Abbas Giant, a chalk man with a large erect penis carved into a hillside in Dorset; Stonehenge; the standing stones of Avebury; Glastonbury Tor, which we climbed before drinking sanctified water from its sacred spring.

Some sites were fenced off and charged an admission fee to see a fancy educational display curated by a conservationist body. These places made for an odd experience – the mystic made municipal. Any hope of a direct experience was diluted by the security cameras and long sets of rules. I preferred the freer, wild places, where it was still possible to walk right up to the structures and touch them, where sometimes, if you were lucky, you were the only person there.

We also went on country walks, passing through small villages. We'd try the door of any church we passed. Many were left unlocked during the day. Inside there might be medieval stonework or Victorian stained glass to admire. The gardens of these small churches were good places for a scenic rest stop, and there were sometimes communal orchards that invited fruit-picking – dregs of the commons.

Every time I had a visceral reaction to a sight, felt a stirring in my core, something like deep recognition, I immediately started to second-guess myself. *It's because you've seen it in a film,* my doubting voice would say. *You read about it in a book.*

And yet there were experiences that felt like they sank all the way in, unfurling some coiled epigenetic memory. Steep Scottish mountains covered in purple heather with a gleaming black loch below. My first glimpse of the white cliffs of the South Downs. The moody moors and fens of England's north, land of my coal-mining ancestors. I had never seen anything like them back home, and yet my first feeling was one of deep recognition.

An electrical charge would travel straight to my core, briefly winning over my analytical mind, and I would be able to surrender to the moment. It was always the land, the plants, the hills and the weather that brought on these moments, rather than cultural phenomena like galleries, museums or historic buildings.

Fraser and I had studied a Wordsworth poem about Tintern Abbey in the Wye Valley. We were keen to see it for ourselves as a reward for the essays we'd had to write. One weekend we crossed the long bridge to the west, into Wales.

The Tintern Abbey ruins were shrouded in an early mist the morning we walked there from our campsite. It added to the ghostly atmosphere that the place has even on the brightest day. The ruins were every bit as impressive and affecting as Wordsworth had described over a hundred years before; there was no hyperbole in his poem.

After walking around the ruins for a long while, soaking in the feeling of time out of time, we wandered off the track near the abbey. We wanted to take a walk and explore the forest, and scope for any potential dinner ingredients.

In a gloomy forest copse, we walked around a large ash tree just as the spring sunshine burned the morning's mists away. We stood before a large dell of bluebells. The flowers were dense and luminous. We'd caught the blooms in their moment of perfect expression. The sun was shining in luminous ropes through the trees and the bluebells appeared to be glowing.

We sat down and leaned our backs against the ash tree in silence, absorbing the magic of the vibrant blue, the sunlight and the scent, until the damp ground began to chill our bones. I didn't want to leave but, just as soon as it had flared, the magical light faded.

*

Our working visas were close to running out. I was still working at the café. I'd only meant to take the barista job as a stepping stone, but I'd got attached to my colleagues and to the freedom of the 2 pm finish time.

When I wasn't working or on nature walks, I was writing poems. Maria was writing madly, too. We exchanged letters full of draft poems between our two cities. I went to London for writing weekends and stayed in her Hackney squat. We'd go to poetry gigs or to read at open-mic nights. At a poetry café in central London, a mystery guest at open-mic night turned out to be the famous punk poet John Cooper Clarke. We got a lot of mileage out of saying we'd 'read with John Cooper Clarke' – technically true, but a bit of an exaggeration.

Fraser was bored in his council admin job. My only ambition was to create a simple life of nature, beauty and good friends, and hopefully to one day write a book. My career ambitions looked a bit like the Bloomsbury Group sitting in deckchairs in the garden at Charleston, drinking tea and talking about Very Important Ideas while deadheading the dahlias.

We started to turn our gazes towards home. I enrolled in a year-long creative writing programme for the following year. Fraser, ever the practical one, applied for journalism school. If he was going to write, it would be in a way that had some hope of earning us a living. We had plans in place and flights home booked.

Our remaining weekends were quickly filled up with visiting friends and chores. But I was determined not to leave the country without seeing Tintagel Castle, the famous site of Arthurian legend, and nearby Merlin's Cave. We booked a campsite and took off.

Legend has it that Merlin carried a baby Arthur Pendragon through Merlin's Cave to Tintagel Castle. The cave is a giant hag stone formed by sea erosion. Around 100 metres long, it can be entered at Tintagel Haven at one end and exited at West Cove.

Fraser and I visited on a bright summer's day. We'd timed our walk down the steep and precarious cliff path to the cave for when the tide was out. When we arrived, we were the only people on the beach, a beautiful wild sand and shingle cove with a dramatic tall waterfall just before the cave's entrance.

The attractive, wave-worn slate of the beach was just asking to be picked up and stroked for the pleasure of its smoothness.

Then, inside the cave, I saw it: a large, dark grey stone. At first I doubted my eyes, but I stooped over and picked it up. Smooth and oval, it fit perfectly in the palm of my hand. Near the top of the stone was a hole, a small perfect circle. My heart beating fast, I peered through it to the oval of light at the tunnel's far end. Hag stone within hag stone.

'I found my hag stone!' I called to Fraser.

'Of course you'd find it *here*.' He laughed, shaking his head incredulously. Fraser indulges my esoteric leanings at just the right moments, allowing small cracks of magical thinking in his pragmatism.

'I should probably leave it here. It's Merlin's Cave! What if taking it carries some kind of curse?'

But Fraser had reached his limit. 'Nah, I don't think Merlin would mind.'

I pocketed the stone while we explored, turning it over in my hand while I turned over in my mind whether or not to take it. The cave ceiling was dripping salt water, and we perched on a crag to look out to sea, imagining the tunnel full of clanking Arthurian knights. I'd imagined the cave as a dwelling place, somewhere Merlin had lived, but it was a passage – jagged, wet and inhospitable.

I wanted to take the hag stone with every fibre of my being; it was the culmination of months of looking. That I'd found it in this sacred site was eerie, almost a cosmic joke. Maybe the story was gift enough? I'd imagined the hag stone I would find would be craggy, brownish, imperfect, like Nana's one from Ohawe beach. This was a smooth-surfaced stone, the precise deep grey of the black iron sand of my Taranaki childhood.

The sea-worn hole was so perfect it looked intentional, as if a person had carved it rather than time.

I decided I couldn't have it both ways. I couldn't ask for signs and then reject them when they arrived. A friend from home had once told me, 'If you want more miracles in your life, you have to leave the door open a little to let them in.'

We ate our picnic and explored the nearby rock pools.

That night in the tent, as I undressed, I pulled the stone out of my pocket. I held it out to Fraser. 'I guess I did decide to take it.'

'It climbed aboard,' he replied, enabler of my magpie tendencies, 'right at the eleventh hour.'

I laughed. 'Well, eleven *is* my favourite number.'

*

Our campsite was by a stream, surrounded by a copse of trees. The next day, strolling the edges where the plants grew thickly, I saw a large patch of glowing white flowers. The plants had airy clusters of fuzzy flowers on top of elegant, tall, burgundy stems. As I approached the fence to look more closely, I saw a tall woman with long grey plaits and bright pink gumboots picking a large bunch of the blooms and putting them in a bucket.

'Excuse me for bothering you, but what is this plant?' I asked. 'I don't know it.'

She smiled. 'It's meadowsweet, or queen of the meadow. You must smell it.' She held out her bouquet and I put my face into the frothy flowers. Hundreds of tiny stamens tickled my nose. The smell was sublime, the clean floral of elderflower but with notes of almond.

'That's divine! What are you going to do with it?' I asked her.

'I'm going to make cordial.'

She said her name was Lucy. She lived in the nearby village, and the campsite owner had given her foraging privileges in return for bottles or jars of whatever she made from her finds.

I remembered Megwyn at Glastonbury telling me that meadowsweet was the Druid's plant. Druids are shamanic pagan priests. I asked Lucy if she knew anything about that.

'Yes, that's right. They flavour their mead with it and make medicines, but I like making cordial because of how it holds the smell.'

Her use of the present tense made me curious. Did she know some living, practising Druids? I loved bumping into other foragers; they were so generous with their knowledge. I was yet to meet an unfriendly forager.

I picked a few blooms to sniff and to sketch in my journal. I was on a high. My hag stone had found me. England's goodbye gift. What was ahead through the stone's portal for me?

*

For our goodbye get-together in Bristol, we had a big picnic lunch on the Downs. We crossed the Avon over the huge suspension bridge to meet up with Fi, my café workmates and our other friends. I wore one of the dresses Fi and I had rescued from Glastonbury's mud and my hag stone.

I'd lugged along bags of books, dishes and clothes to give away to my friends.

'Don't you want to take this back home?' they asked.

'No, you take it. It came easily so it goes easily.' I trusted in the flow of stuff, of life.

As the sun and beer worked their magic, we went from sitting in a circle in the open field to crawling into the shade of a large oak. One by one, our friends wandered off home. I stood up to give each person a long hug goodbye. Eventually, it was just Fraser and me left. We lay back among the tree's roots in the dappled light.

The beers had me feeling philosophical. Who was I at the end of this two-year pilgrimage? I felt a little more tempered than I had when I'd left New Zealand. At university I'd been a question mark in the shape of a person, a fledgling fresh from the nest that didn't know which direction to fly.

I'd learned that solace and medicine would always be elemental for me: earth, sky, water, plants. The bones of my ancestors might be buried in the UK and Europe, but I loved my birthplace the best, with all the complexities of what it meant for me to seek to *belong* there. I needed to live in a place where I could enmesh myself in a lifelong quest to know the land. I didn't want to make that commitment to Europe. It wasn't home.

I held my hag stone up against Bristol's blue sky and looked through the hole. What could I see? Wellington ... wrangling with words ... a snug harbour ... steep hills ... another new city to explore. I hoped there'd be a book in my future. I really wanted to achieve it for my parents, to give them the gift of our family name printed on a book's cover.

A pair of magpies flew across the frame of the hole. English magpies have elegant white bellies, unlike the ones from home, which are sturdier with white backs. I lowered the stone. *Two for joy*, I thought, remembering the words from the childhood nursery rhyme. *One for sorrow, two for joy.* But then I saw two more following behind. It was a little family. *Four for a boy.*

'Hey, corvid alert!' I nudged Fraser. He liked corvids and was always delighted by England's crows and ravens.

There was no response, except for the sound of soft, hops-induced snoring.

Meadowsweet granita

Makes approximately 600 ml

The drug aspirin was originally made from the salacin compound found in meadowsweet (*Filipendula ulmaria*). Meadowsweet has a long history of being a sacred plant. It has been found in Bronze Age burial sites in Scotland and Wales, the flowers left on bodies as tributes to the dead.

Meadowsweet is also known as 'mead wort' because it was once used to sweeten mead, and 'brideswort' because the flowers were thrown at new brides, a sweetly scented natural confetti. It's a plant of romance: queen of the meadow, queen of the ditch. And, as the Druid's plant, the blooms help us to be our genuine selves, courageous in our own beliefs.

Meadowsweet doesn't grow prolifically in New Zealand but it can be spotted in the Auckland and Waikato regions. The seeds and plants can be purchased for growing in the home garden, where it makes a lovely addition to any mixed herb or flower bed.

It's a bloom of the high summer, and its unique scent is good infused in dairy-based desserts, like panna cotta or ice cream. I like it in lighter dishes, cordials, teas and granita, as it seems to holds its aroma a little more this way.

If you can't find meadowsweet for this recipe, elderflower is a good substitute.

Ingredients
200 g caster sugar
600 ml water
zest of 1 lemon
juice of 3 lemons
4 cups meadowsweet flowers

Method
Make a sugar syrup first. Bring the water to the boil in a medium-sized saucepan, then add the sugar and stir until it is completely dissolved. The liquid will reduce down a bit.

Remove the pan from the heat. While stirring, add in the lemon zest and juice.

Add the flowers. Stir them through the liquid a little, and then allow to steep until the syrup cools to room temperature. (You can steep it for longer if you have time.)

Strain out the flowers and the zest. Put the mixture into a plastic container and freeze overnight.

The next day, blend the frozen syrup to aerate it, until the texture is light and flurry-like. If you like an airier granita, repeat the process one more time (freeze, then blend).

CHAPTER 10

Where the sea meets the land

Kōkihi and St John's wort

We didn't tell our families we were coming home. We travelled down the North Island, surprising them along the way. Four sets of surprised reactions made the trip a lot of fun. First my brother, Roy, in Auckland, then my folks in Waitara, where Mum poured coffee down herself when she spotted me through the window. Next were Fraser's folks in Palmerston North, and finally we popped up unannounced at Fraser's sister's work, in Wellington, where in true sibling fashion Bronya greeted him with a tearful, affectionate 'You *bastard*!'.

We had nothing. We'd spent every cent on travel. At first we'd kept a bit aside but then, just before leaving Bristol, I saw a poster advertising seven-quid plane tickets to Paris. We blew our tiny nest egg on a final whirlwind weekend of Monet paintings, Montmartre flea-market wanders and flan pâtissier.

I asked my parents for a small loan so we could pay a tenancy bond for a flat in Wellington. It pained me to ask them, but Fraser and I couldn't start making money until we had somewhere to live. They were not impressed we'd let ourselves get so close to bare bones.

'But I'll always have Paris,' I said to Mum, quoting *Casablanca*. She clicked her tongue and raised her eyes skyward. I promised to pay it back as soon as I could.

We got a tiny, damp flat in Newtown, built hard against a concrete wall that seemed to constantly trickle with water. It was the best we could afford. Wellington greeted us with weeks of endless rain, and a month or so after moving in, our kitchen ceiling collapsed, covering everything in ancient plaster dust.

But it was wonderful to live on a coast again. I hadn't lived on the coast since leaving Waitara.

'Let's make a pact to visit the sea every day,' I said to Fraser. He'd never lived on a coast before and agreed we should make the most of it.

We tried to honour our pact, sometimes going late at night, when, alone on the beach, we'd strip off our shoes, socks and jeans and run through the dark, into the icy ocean up to our thighs, gasping at the cold.

There were no hag stones on Wellington's south coast, but I did find another kind of eye: the sea-snail shell, cat's eye. There were dozens of them in one particular bay. I was taken by the grey spirals whirling in to the white centre. As we walked, I picked up any good specimens and over the months slowly filled a jar with them.

I put the jar on our front windowsill because cat's eyes were said to have protective powers, similar to the blue-glass evil eyes I'd seen on my visits to Greece and Turkey. The spiral was a potent symbol of infinity – the evolution of an ever-expanding circle, helping to ease transitions and welcome new seasons of life.

I had one large white cat's eye made into a chunky silver ring. If someone was venting at me in a vampiric fashion, I would put my right hand, where I wore the ring, softly on to my chest over my heart and envisage the ring's eye protecting me and any bad vibes going back to sender, like Wonder Woman's bracelets of deflection.

On beach wanders, I gathered kōkihi, also known as beach spinach or New Zealand spinach. In Pākehā history, it's known for being used by Captain Cook to combat scurvy in his crew; he made a kind of ferment from it. In Australia, it's known as warrigal greens.

I recognised kōkihi from the beaches in Taranaki, where it was often thrown into pots of boil-up if there was no pūhā to be found. I liked its salty tang from the sea spray. It was an easy one to harvest if I'd left my pocketknife at home because the succulent stems easily yielded to a pinch of the fingers. When I found kōkihi, I knew that dinner was sorted. I would blend it into a bright green sauce and serve it with potatoes and boiled eggs.

*

The writing course was inspiring and pushed me to improve. I loved talking about writing with people who took it seriously. After absorbing Jude's advice about populating my writing with the tangible *things* of the world, I'd swung too far in the other direction. I received critiques that said my poems sometimes read like unadorned lists of the world's wonders. I understood what my teachers meant, but I also thought, *Have you looked out the window lately? Everything is so alive!*

Did a vibrant yellow honeysuckle vine *need* my measly adjectives? Was the brilliance of a blazing red maple in autumn sanctified or diminished by an attempt to capture it in words? I knew at their zenith these questions undermined the need for writing altogether, and I didn't want to do myself out of a job before I'd even really begun. Everything I wrote felt like fumbling through the dark towards an expression of life's ultimate ineffability.

On National Poetry Day in 1999, my classmates and I went into the centre of the city and installed a pop-up poetry booth, where we wrote poems on demand. I scrawled mine in vivid marker on dried autumn leaves I'd collected from Central Park. We took turns to read, climbing on to the base of Cuba Street's bucket fountain and shouting our poems to bemused passers-by. We chalked poems on the footpaths. We were determined to hold a presence for poetry there all day. It felt important, like the people of Wellington needed to have their day disrupted by poetry – acts of public poetry for the collective good. We handed out photocopied poems by famous New Zealand poets. One man pushed his hands into his pockets and refused to take the James K. Baxter poem I was proffering.

'I don't take street propaganda,' he said testily, swerving past me.

'But it's not propaganda! It's poetry!' I called after him.

'Even *worse*!' he yelled over his shoulder.

*

We were broke again, but this time not so much in a fun way. Wellington was expensive. We scraped by on our student loans. Fraser got a job at a petrol station. A friend got me some night shifts in a bank call centre. I was terrible at that job; I never hit sales targets and couldn't find it in myself to *care* about making profits for the bank. The only good thing about it was that the office was on the tenth floor of a skyscraper on the Terrace with a view of Wellington Harbour. I daydreamed through my shifts, swivelling in my chair to gaze out to sea and scrawling scraps of poems on my desk planner. Artists and punks didn't work in banks.

We always made rent and bills, but sometimes food was in short supply. I didn't want to ask our families for help again. I was the one who'd decided to study *creative writing*, something my parents thought of as a nice hobby but not anything you could make a living from.

I clung on to my belief that the city could provide. We just had to find where to look. But it felt harder than before, less like a game. We turned up at every art opening and book launch, trying to eat enough to form a dinner from the wide platters of catered canapés without being too obvious. On Sundays we went to the five-dollar vegetarian feasts offered by the city's Hare Krishnas. When the local chapter of Food Not Bombs set up impromptu soup stalls at community events, we queued up, holding our mugs out for the long-cooked lentils. We made a twenty-kilogram sack of potatoes last a whole month by combining them with what I gathered from Wellington's coast and green belt: chickweed, onion weed, wild mustard. And we ate a lot of meals of 'fancy ramen': two-minute noodles made slightly more nutritious by the addition of a handful of greens and a tablespoon of peanut butter.

It was just for a year. We could handle it. Once we had our qualifications, we'd get decent jobs and turn it all around. Fraser would become a journalist and I'd get some nice government job to fund my stupid poetry habit.

Sometimes a box would show up, a care package from Mum and Dad full of Mum's preserves and a few tins of whatever she'd found on special at the supermarket that week. They always seemed to arrive at the right moment, just when I was having a despairing day.

*

One day, walking to my course, I went past a bakery and felt a wave of nausea wash over me as the bready aroma wafted past my nose. I rushed to the edge of the path and doubled over, throwing up my breakfast into a Te Aro gutter. *What the hell?* I put it down to eating something dodgy and tried to lose myself in the day's work.

But when the bouts of nausea had followed me around for a week, I had to submit to reality. Numb with fear, I bought a pregnancy test from the Newtown New World.

Fraser said, 'Well, you can't be pregnant, because the timing is awful. But also, if you are pregnant, it'll be fine.'

Both things were true – as much for us as for all who've had a baby arrive in this world unplanned.

I did the test. Fraser and I sat and watched as two blue lines slowly emerged across the small white window.

I sat on the toilet and cried. It wasn't meant to happen this way. We had nothing. We lived in a hovel. I hadn't published a book yet. We were too young. But I was twenty-eight. I knew plenty of people back home who had multiple kids by my age.

While I cried, Fraser laughed for ten minutes straight. I stared at him.

When he finally stopped, he apologised. 'I'm sorry. That was odd. I think it was just, you know, inappropriate male pride. I'm fertile! And also, I dunno, at least now we know what we're doing next.'

The future had announced itself. So much for my hag stone. I hadn't seen this one coming.

Later that week, I wrote in my journal, *The pregnancy book I got out of the library says the baby is just quarter of an inch long.*

A mere smidge. So small.

So huge.

*

Maria had returned from the UK, too. She'd decided to live in Dunedin. On leave from work and study, I scraped together a plane fare and went down to visit her. I figured it would be my last holiday for a long while.

She'd already made friends in Dunedin, a characterful bunch of environmentalists, hippies and artists. She took me to visit a group who were living on Mount Cargill. They were squatting rent-free in a clearing in the bush, living in a caravan on blocks, a large canvas tent and a kind of roofed tree house that'd been knocked together, called Whare Mānuka. The toilet was a long drop and they got their water from a natural spring. They were broke and a bit feral, but they also seemed totally free. I didn't mention my night shifts at the bank or my writerly ambitions. In that environment, my Wellington life seemed unhip and uptight.

We stayed the night. Away from the lights of the city, the sky was inky dark with low, bright stars. I lay awake listening to the haunting cry of a resident ruru. I felt like we'd driven right off the map. I wanted to live like these free tree people.

Truth was though, even in summer it was freezing at night. The bed we slept in was damp and I couldn't get warm, even though I was sleeping in my jersey and woolly hat. It was miles from anywhere. I wondered what Mum and Dad would think about me living like a hobbit among the trees. Besides, it was no place for a baby. But it fed my fantasies of what life could be like all the way off the grid. On rough days, my mind would wander back to the Mount Cargill squat, seesawing between the beauty of a free life in the trees and the less romantic practical constraints.

After a couple of days in Dunedin, Maria and I threw sleeping bags and food into her car and took off on a roadie. We op-shopped and camped our way around Southland, sharing clothes and spending the evenings writing and talking about poetry. We walked the Kepler Track.

Maria lost her watch on one of our lakeside walks. I suggested we retrace our steps to try to find it but she shrugged. 'Nah, it's a sign for me to step out of clock time for a while.'

It was true. Time had taken on a malleable quality, and it was wonderful to spend some stretchy, expansive time with her. The trip had a melancholic tinge to it. It was the end of a season for me. *Maiden, mother, crone.* I could feel that I was stealing time from responsibility, from planning, from all that was ahead.

Around the pebbly shores of the southern lakes, I saw thickets of St John's wort, a modest, scruffy-looking plant, but one with many medicinal properties. Its yellow flowers mirror the sun, blooming at summer's apex. Up close, they have multiple fine stamens, like rays of sunshine. When I held the leaves up to the sun, I could see they were covered in tiny holes, the *perforatum* of the plant's Latin name. St John's wort is considered a pest plant in New Zealand, but medicinally it's an asset.

I felt lucky to stumble across St John's wort right at the moment of its brightest blooming. I'd read in one of my plant guides that making a medicinal herb oil from its flowers harnessed the summer's heat and vitality, bottling and banking it for a boost on winter's darkest days. I was keen to try it. Wellington winters were long, dreary and grey, and I needed all the help I could get to make it through another one. The baby was due right at winter's heart.

With my pocketknife, I harvested a paper bag of the flowers and tender tops, and when we got back to Dunedin I bought a bottle of sweet almond oil from a pharmacy. I tipped out a third of the oil, chopped up the St John's wort with scissors, and stuffed it into the bottle so it could slowly leach its red goodness into the oil. It was a better souvenir of my Southland summer than anything I could have found in a tourist shop.

Too soon, it was time to go home. At the airport, Maria hugged me hard. She pulled off the blue handknitted jersey she was wearing and handed it to me to take on the plane. She'd found it at an op shop in Invercargill and we'd been sharing it on our travels. It was the perfect amount of lived-in, the bottom band stretched and loose.

When I got my photographs from the trip developed, Fraser asked why we were wearing the same jersey in all the pictures we'd taken of one another. 'It looks like you're wearing some kind of uniform.' He laughed.

I loved the jersey, but she'd found it first.

'I can't take it,' I said. 'Finders keepers.'

'Don't be silly,' she said. 'I'll get it back off you when I come north. It'll come back to me eventually.'

Over the autumn and winter months, the St John's wort oil slowly turned a brilliant red. And I grew a baby under the warmth of that Invercargill op-shop jersey.

Wellington green sauce

Makes approximately 500 ml

This sauce is a version of a dish I ate in Europe that I made often using foraged greens when Fraser and I were first living in Wellington. The original German green sauce features parsley, cress, chives, salad burnet, sorrel, chervil and borage leaves. This version features a mixture of easily foraged greens.

Ingredients
    2 cloves garlic, crushed
    2 tablespoons olive oil
    1 large handful kōkihi (*Tetragonia tetragonioides*) leaves
    8 borage (*Borago officinalis*) leaves
    1 small bunch onion weed (*Nothoscordum* × *borbonicum*) stems
    1 handful chickweed (*Stellaria media*)
    1 cup sour cream
    1 cup plain yoghurt
    1 teaspoon mustard
    1 teaspoon sugar
    juice of ½ a lemon
    salt and pepper, to taste

Method
In a medium-sized saucepan, sauté the garlic in the olive oil over a medium heat.

Turn the heat to low and add the kōkihi, borage, onion weed and chickweed, stirring until they are wilted and cooked through. (You want to end up with around 1 packed cup of cooked-down greens.) Take off the heat.

Mix the sour cream, yoghurt, mustard, sugar and lemon juice in a large bowl. When the greens have cooled a little, drop them in the bowl and blend everything together with a stick blender. Add salt and pepper to taste.

To serve, pour ½–¾ of a cup of the sauce into a shallow bowl. Add room-temperature boiled potatoes on one side of the dish, and a boiled egg or two chopped in half on the other. Garnish with chopped flat-leaf parsley.

St John's wort healing body oil

Makes approximately 600 ml

St John's wort (*Hypericum perforatum*) is known for its wound-healing properties. It's also taken orally as an antidepressant. It's a healer of nerves, both in the body and in the psyche. St John's wort harnesses healing solar power from summer's peak to help restore balance through the ups and downs of the seasons, and to assist with the endurance of pain.

If you crush a St John's wort flower between your fingers, you'll see it leaks a dark red substance. This is what will slowly turn your oil from a pale straw colour to orange or red (depending on how long you leave it to infuse).

Don't wash fresh St John's wort. Just give it a good shake to dislodge any small insects or debris, then leave in a sunny spot for a few hours so any excess moisture evaporates off the plant material.

I use this oil all over my body through the winter to keep my spirits up. It has a warming effect, too.

Ingredients
1 cup fresh St John's wort
600 ml almond oil or extra virgin olive oil

Method
Chop up the blooms, stems and leaves of the St John's wort for faster extraction of the plant oils.

Put the oil and chopped St John's wort into a wide-mouthed 1 litre jar. Put on a plastic lid and shake vigorously to mix.

Cover and let sit for up to 4 weeks. Shake the jar occasionally to mix and ensure the plant matter stays under the surface of the oil. The oil will slowly change colour to a vibrant red as the St John's wort releases the goodness of midsummer sun into the oil.

After a month, strain out the plant material using a fine sieve or muslin cloth.

Bottle in a sterilised dark glass bottle or jar. Label and use within a year.

CHAPTER 11

Birthing the sun

Nasturtium and pine

Pregnancy brings with it a biological urge to nest.

After years of tiny gardenless flats, we moved into half of a Newtown villa with just enough room for a baby and a small, sloping backyard – bare lawn with a cherry tree and a small lemon tree. It wasn't much of a garden but I felt happy to have one at all. The city's green belt was a short walk from our door. Within ten minutes I could be high up in the pine forest with a grand view across the city. I loved sitting up in the trees listening to the screeching monkeys and roaring lions at nearby Wellington Zoo.

Fraser and I enlisted a pair of wise and staunch hippie feminist midwives. I wanted to try for a home birth. The midwives read my very wholesome birth plan impassively, with no ironic eye twinkles, no hint of scepticism. Fraser was supportive of the idea. If we needed a Plan B, Wellington Hospital was literally just around the corner.

I went into labour on the last day of June 2000. While I was on my hands and knees groaning through contractions, midwife Liz raised her hands towards the ceiling and rotated her hips as though she were slow-motion hula-hooping. She stared into my face. 'Wo-MANNNNN!' she roared in an empathetic battle cry. 'You can do this, Wo-MANNNNNN!'

Fraser was too taken aback by her ferocious intensity to even raise an eyebrow.

At my antenatal classes, I had been coached to come up with images of opening and expansion, so that when the pain got bad I could go within myself and bring these visualisations to my mind's eye. The instructor had said this might help keep me soft and malleable, prevent me from tightening my body against the pain.

As the tides of pain passed through my body during labour, I closed my eyes and imagined a rose unfurling in slow motion, from tight bud to open bloom. I imagined circles rippling outwards across water, as from a pebble dropped into a pond. In my mind, I stared through the hag stone's portal, imagining my baby coming towards me.

I laboured in a birthing pool, but the baby was born on the floor. Liz put him on my chest. He smelt ancient, primeval, of blood, musk and sweetness. He was long, with huge feet. He mewled like a kitten. He was beautiful. A baby! *My* baby?

Afterwards I gingerly took a shower with a towel gripped between my legs, then I got into pyjamas. I ate two big bowls of chickpea curry and drank an entire pot of tea in one sitting. I'd never known thirst or hunger like it.

We named him Willoughby, an old English word meaning 'farm by the willow tree', inspired by Fraser's love of archaic languages and the willow-tree hut my brother and I had played in as kids.

Through that first winter of his life, I'd rub the ruby-red St John's wort oil I'd made on my South Island trip into his hands and feet, and into my own.

'Bottled sun for my little son,' I said to him.

The oil's soothing properties calmed my frayed nerves and helped him off to sleep.

*

What you birth, births you back. I'd taken on a new form but it took a while for me to fully inhabit it. The ghost of my old self hung around while the new version stared into mirrors in deep disorientation. Willoughby was no more trouble than the average baby, but that was still quite a lot of trouble. For the first time in my life, I was doing something where reading books on the topic didn't seem to help much. This one was all on me and my better instincts.

I dug up a small patch of the backyard lawn against a sunny fence and began to grow food. I wanted to be sure of the provenance of my baby's first vegetable mashes. I built the garden while Willoughby lay on a blanket on the grass. The backyard was tiny but at least we could be outside in the elements, out of the dark ground-floor flat. In Willoughby's first spring, I planted a row of sunflowers so he could watch them grow, bright and strong, and hopefully follow their example.

Exhausted from night feeds, I lost hold of my sense of clock time and the days passed by, slippery and indistinct. It was hard to write poems. Writing from a watery, vulnerable place resulted in a lot of watery, terrible poetry.

I wrote in my journal, *Little bean, little turtle. So small but you fill the house. Fill the hours like once you filled me. I am both softer, more raw, more open to the world's pain, and also stone-like, impatient with bullshit, strong in my dedication.*

I used to put wild jasmine in the jar on the windowsill and then one day it was lavender instead. Mum put it there when she came to visit the baby.

Medicinal, comforting. The smell of mothers.

*

We were the first of our friends to have a baby; they were all busy at work or study. The baby didn't fit in with the cool, urban vibe of the performance poetry scene. I felt like I'd failed in some way, diluting our edge. My writing group would hold meetings in busy bars and then say, 'Just bring the baby!' like he was a fashion accessory, not a mini human. One wrote a sarcastic poem that began, 'So now it's breeding time.' I tried to keep on participating for a while, but soon dropped away.

With long, lonely days to fill, I'd pack Willoughby into his sling and we'd start our day in the misty pine forest at the top of Coromandel Street. We'd wander the green belt's endless meandering paths. It was somewhere to go and something to do, a sanctuary. It was good to get away from the domestic disarray for a while – the table cluttered with food-glugged bibs, *Where the Wild Things Are* and piles of bills.

The forest nearest our house was full of pines and spruces, with a thick and buoyant carpet of orange pine needles to lie Willoughby down on for nappy-changing or resting. I sat with him and stared out at the roofs of all the houses. When I was feeling disoriented and displaced, a higher vantage point was soothing.

The bright green spruce tips on the pines called out to me, so I harvested some and made menthol-favoured tea. I poured the dregs of the pot over a cloth to wash the baby's face with.

I picked green pine cones for making pine syrup. The first step was to tuck the pine cones into a jar of sugar. The slowly seeping pine resin eventually dissolved the sugar, fermenting and turning into a dark syrup. I'd spoon it over pancakes or add it to hot water to make a sweet, cleansing drink.

*

The top branches of our backyard cherry tree were just outside our kitchen window. I hung a ceramic bowl in the branches and put a concoction of lard and seeds in it for the birds so Willoughby and I could watch them feed while we were at the dining table.

One morning as I sat feeding Willo, gazing into the treetop, a hefty brown rat with a pink, worm-like tail raced along a branch to feast from my bird buffet. I leaped up and banged on the window and the rat scuttled away. A wave of revulsion passed through my body. Willoughby startled and began to cry.

I went straight outside and cut the bowl down. It felt like a manifestation of the shadows I had been sitting in – something to do with plans, expectations, destiny – and it heightened my awareness of the malevolent forces that had seemed to arrive when I became a mother. I washed my hands with soap and hot water over and over, as though if I scrubbed them hard enough I could wash away my brooding thoughts.

Instead of forging a path into writing, I'd stumbled into motherhood. The baby filled all my time, took all my energy;

how would I ever have any capacity to write again? But many women before me had managed to do both. Becoming a writer and becoming a mother were entwined, ever-evolving life-long passages, not destinations. I felt stretched, tugged, flattened and enriched by both, and never very graceful at either.

*

Across our back fence was a creche. I was soothed by the sounds of small children playing, guided and chided by the calm adult voices of the teachers. It was a kind of company.

I was hanging out laundry one day when one of the teachers, a beautiful woman wearing a brown homespun jersey and long bone earrings, called out to me. 'Don't spose you'd mind sharing a few of your lemons?'

Our small tree was laden with bright yellow fruit.

I smiled in recognition. Here was someone just as cheeky as me, a kindred spirit. 'For sure! Let me just go grab a bag.'

'Oh, no, just a couple, eh? I don't want to be a pain.'

'It's cool. I like sharing.'

While I filled a plastic bag with lemons, she told me her name was Hana. She'd moved down from a small town in Hawke's Bay because her partner was at jazz school. She was warm and laidback in a way that felt familiar from my own hometown.

We got talking about how expensive the city was, how we were doing everything we could to save money. After that, we'd sometimes chat over the fence and if I had something to spare out of my tiny vegetable garden, I'd pass it to her over the fence.

'I haven't got anything to give you back,' she said a few times.

'All good,' I'd reply.

I'd hold Willoughby up to look over the fence at the children playing, and Hana would sometimes lift up a random child to say hello back.

*

One day in spring, the nasturtium plant growing over the hedge between our garden and the creche was returning to life. While I was talking to Hana, I picked some of the bright orange flowers to put in a vase for a bit of colour on the next damp Wellington morning.

'You know you can eat that stuff, eh?' Hana said to me.

'I think I've read that, but I haven't tried it yet.'

'Oh, you have to. It's really good. You can eat all of it: leaves, flowers, even the seed pods. Smell your fingers.'

I sniffed. 'Ha! They smell kind of like mustard?'

'Yeah, that's it. Peppery. A bit weird at first but good once you know what to expect. You can put it in salad. Eat a bit every day and you won't need vitamin C pills anymore.'

I'd never thought about getting vitamin C from anything except pills and citrus fruits. I tentatively nibbled at a leaf. The flavour was intense, a clean, hot explosion in my mouth.

'Woah! That's actually really good.'

I looked at the plant, winding its way up and over the hedge, bright green and vigorous. There was so much of it and it was growing rampantly in our backyard. And, unlike my vegetables, no coddling was necessary.

She picked one of the trumpet-shaped flowers and said, 'Suck on the end. Nectar.'

I was familiar with doing this with the honeysuckle flowers of my childhood.

'I learned it growing up,' she said. 'My nan taught me about what's around that you can eat.'

That night I made a salad with nasturtium leaves and flowers in it. I was delighted that the flower has such a pungent, intense flavour – not the floral sweetness you might expect.

The next day, Hana gave me a recipe for poor man's capers – pickled nasturtium pods – handwritten on the back of a child's crayon drawing.

I became a nasturtium bore. Every dish I took to potluck dinners was covered in nasturtium flowers as edible decoration. I made mayonnaise with chopped nasturtium. I experimented with mashing nasturtium into butter instead of garlic. I stuffed the leaves with rice, making foraged dolmades.

I noticed that the leaves grew more pungent and peppery with the warmth of the day, like the sun's heat was cooking the flavour deeper. The pungency of the plant seemed to have a unifying effect on me, pulling my brain back into my body, interrupting my racing thoughts to anchor me in the present.

This peppery crawler grew more beautiful to me the more time I spent with it. I learned the bright flaring trumpets were frost tender and would slump into a dead dark mass in the cold. The flowers were the shape of gnome hats, and the lily-pad-shaped leaves seemed to float above the plants, like little umbrellas. In the early morning, the round leaves cradled dew drops that shone like gems. The flowers ranged through all the hot tones, from orange to red to yellow. I read the name came from the Latin *nasus torquere*, meaning nose twister, because of its pungent smell. I was smitten. I began to see it everywhere.

*

Another day when I was chatting to Hana, she held up a cup with leaves floating in it.

'I'm not sposed to bring my cuppa into the playground, but the boss is away today,' she said.

'What's that floating in it?' I asked, always nosy.

'It's kawakawa with a bit of ginger. It's good.' The tea was a bilious dark green against the white of the ceramic.

'The holey one?' I asked. My knowledge of native plants was not especially good. Dad had taught me and Roy a lot about native birds and fish, but not so much the names of the plants we walked through.

'Yeah, the holey one. It's good stuff. Keeps you healthy,' she said.

The next time I was carrying Willoughby around up in the green belt, I looked out for a kawakawa bush. I didn't have to look far. Soon I started to see it everywhere, too. Another plant I could forage to add to my growing list.

The tea had an iron quality and smelled just like the New Zealand bush. Researching the plant, I read that the ripe orange kawakawa fruit could have a mild psychedelic effect if a large quantity was eaten.

I was always so glad to see Hana for an over-the-fence chat. Her dry, pragmatic humour was just the same as that of folks back home. But I didn't quite know how to take our chats beyond these incidental situations into something more deliberate. I planned to find the courage to ask her to hang out after work one day.

One week, I didn't see her head over the fence at all. The next I asked one of her colleagues where she was. He told me that she'd left quite suddenly. Her partner had dropped out of jazz school and they'd returned to the East Coast. I was gutted. Another fleeting city connection was gone.

Nasturtium and kawakawa became forever connected to Hana in my mind, just as horehound was connected with Diane from Blacklands farm, and meadowsweet with Megwyn the green witch and Lucy the forager. Plants yoke us forever to the people who teach us about them.

I'd had enough of fleeting friendships and failing to find my feet. Being broke and canny wasn't so fun with a baby to fret about. My thirtieth birthday was looming with no book in sight, no sense of what I was doing with my life. I'd meandered and wandered my way through my twenties.

Maybe it was time to grow up. Whatever that meant.

Pine syrup

Makes approximately 570 mls

This traditional food of Russia and Scandinavia is a magical recipe. The resin from the green pine cones slowly macerates and ferments the sugar into a rich brown syrup. In countries where early spring was still snowy, this syrup was a prized source of vitamin C when it was otherwise scarce.

Cones from different trees have different flavour profiles. Pine is the strongest, whereas spruce and fir cones make for a milder and more complex flavour.

Pick very young pine cones in spring or early summer. Take care that you're picking cones from an edible tree. Yew trees are poisonous, for example, as are ponderosa pines and Norfolk pines. Consult your guidebooks. If you can cut the pine cone in half with a sharp knife, it's green enough to make syrup with. (You won't be able to do this with a mature, dry pine cone.)

Ingredients

approximately 20 baby pine cones
up to 3 cups white or brown sugar

Method

Wash your pine cones and pat dry with a tea towel.

Cover the bottom of a clean pint jar with white or brown sugar, then add a few green pine cones. Continue this process, adding layers of sugar then pine cones, until the mixture is a couple of inches from the top. Make sure sugar is the last layer. The syrup will ferment while it macerates, so leave a little bit of bubbling space.

Put the jar in a dark place, somewhere you won't forget it (near your tea or coffee pot is a good spot), and leave to macerate.

By day 6, the water and resin of the pine cones should have mostly rendered the granulated sugar into liquid.

Leave for 4 weeks, remembering to turn the jar every time you think of it. Give it an occasional shake and open the lid to 'burp' the jar when you see a bit of bubbling happening.

After 4 weeks, pour the mixture into a medium-sized saucepan over a low heat and slowly bring to the boil. Simmer until the mixture thickens to a syrupy consistency. The darkness of the syrup will depend on how long you simmer it for.

Strain out the pine cones by pouring the syrup through a fine sieve or muslin cloth. This will take a while.

Bottle in a sterilised jar, label and date.

Use as you would maple syrup, on pancakes and desserts or in hot or cold drinks. I like to add it to black tea.

Poor woman's capers (pickled nasturtium pods)

Makes approximately 400 grams

Pick green nasturtium (*Tropaeolum majus*) seed pods in spring or early summer. They must look pale green, not beige, as a beige colour means they are beginning to dry. Avoid the dried pods of late summer as they will be too tough.

Use a mild vinegar to pickle nasturtium pods, like apple cider vinegar or white wine vinegar. Make sure the vinegar has an acidity level of at least 5 per cent to ensure your capers will be shelf stable.

By the time you open your jar of poor woman's capers, the pods will have lost both their pale green colour and their intense peppery flavour. You'll find a yellow, mellow-tasting 'caper'. They are great sprinkled on a salad or a sandwich, or added to pasta, and they're also good with fish.

Ingredients

1 cup green nasturtium pods, freshly picked
300 ml cold water, plus more for soaking your nasturtium
    pods
1 cup salt
1 tablespoon sugar
300 ml mild vinegar
peppercorns (optional)
fennel (*Foeniculum vulgare*) sprigs (optional)

Method

Put the nasturtium pods into a large bowl and cover with cold water. Leave to sit for ten minutes, to allow any little insects or garden debris to float apart from the pods. Drain and return the clean pods to the bowl.

In a separate bowl, make a brine by mixing together the cold water and the salt.

Add the brine to the pods and soak overnight.

The next morning, drain and rinse the seed pods.

Find a jar with a plastic lid that will fit your pods. Sterilise the jar.

In a small saucepan, dissolve the sugar in the vinegar over a low heat.

Pour the seed pods into the jar, then pour the vinegar mix over the top. Add a few peppercorns or a sprig of fennel if you'd like to infuse the liquid with more flavour. Screw the lid on tightly and label.

Leave to sit for 3 weeks before eating.

CHAPTER 12

Back to the swamp

Urban olives

After graduating from journalism school, Fraser landed his dream job as a technology journalist for the *Dominion Post*. He loved it, especially getting to review tech products, which meant lots of free goodies. But, just a few months after he started, the technology section of the newspaper was axed and all the tech journalists were made redundant.

It was a shock. We found ourselves with a new baby, no car and suddenly no income. We were once again navigating leaner territory. Through a contact, I was offered a high school teaching job in our old stomping ground: Palmerston North. Fraser would take over caring for Willoughby while he job-hunted. We jumped at it. It was a bit of solid ground in a moment of free fall.

I'd failed at establishing a career in England and Wellington. If anything I'd gone backwards, going from teaching secondary school in London, to office admin, to working as a Bristol barista, to aimless odd-jobbing in Wellington. Then I'd wandered into the biggest yet poorest-paid job in human history: motherhood.

I hadn't gained much traction with my writing either. I felt like I was in my early university days all over again. There seemed to be invisible rules in the writing world that I wasn't privy to – another sphere of impenetrable middle-class codes. There weren't many voices like mine reflected back at me in the writing world. But I didn't want to give up on my notion of myself as an observer, a writer. My year of writing study had given me some essential tools: the tenacity to keep on trying, the skills to edit my own work, and some necessary grit.

Our Wellington friends were horrified we were moving back to Palmerston North, the butt of endless jokes about how boring it is, a city carved from a flax swamp. Palmerston North's residents had gone some way towards reclaiming the city's swamp origins: the annual alternative music festival was called SwampFest and locals referred to the city as 'Swampton'. It's hard to punch down on someone ahead of the joke.

I wasn't worried about moving back to Swampton. Unlike in Wellington, Fraser and I would have a chance at being able to afford a house there one day, and, after living in three bigger cities, I missed the slower pace of life there, the wide river and the big sky.

Our first flat was just two blocks from the river. It had an open fire. We walked along the river every day, going home through a pine glade where we would fill the bottom of the pram with pine cones and sticks for kindling. Willoughby's first acts of foraging were picking up pine cones for our fire. Just learning to talk, he'd call them 'kine pones'.

Foraging felt easier in Swampton too. There was a lot to be discovered on a neighbourhood wander, and I found daily contact with the river restorative. I loved the fennel that grew all along the river path. I enjoyed its grace at every stage of growth, from the first bright green feathery fronds in spring, to the bright yellow umbels in summer, to the towering black dried seed heads at winter's heart.

There were also swathes of yellow lupin. When Fraser was a child, he earned money by harvesting lupin seeds for a local conservation project that was using them for riparian planting. It seemed a romantic way to earn money to me. I liked to imagine Fraser as a young boy, shaking dried lupin pods into a paper bag for pocket money as he walked the very places we were now walking with our new son.

*

There's an old English poem about the encroachment of the commons.

> *They hang the man and flog the woman*
> *Who steals the goose from off the common*
> *Yet let the greater villain loose*
> *That steals the common from the goose.*
>
> *The fault is great in man or woman*
> *Who steals a goose from off a common*
> *But what can plead that man's excuse*
> *Who steals a common from a goose?*

The poem's message is that yes, occasionally people might take more than they should off the commons, from shared resources, but the far greater crime is that people have no access to land at all. Foraging requires a culture of commons, areas that belong to everyone – or no one and therefore everyone, such as abandoned lots, railway margins and scrappy industrial edges. Nature is endlessly generous. Many humans have lost their way in reciprocating this generosity, but a little 'commons sense' could help us return.

Some Indigenous Australians talk about the importance of 'walked-for food' – knowing the foods that can be found walking distance from where you live. A bush forage is always a treat, but in Palmerston North I became most interested in what I could find within walking distance of my own house, pushing Willoughby in the pram. Out foraging, I felt my smallness and enmeshment with where I was living. I came to care for the land and for the people around me. These slow walks were a good antidote to the pressures of my new job.

As I pushed the pram around the wide, flat streets of our neighbourhood, I'd watch the ground. If I saw fallen fruit I'd look up and try to find where it fell from. There were rich spoils: plums, feijoas and slightly path-bruised apples from overhanging urban fruit trees. Willoughby was a good fruit spotter, too. If I was lost in my thoughts, he would scout and call out, 'Mama, feijoa on the ground!' I carried rolled-up cotton bags in my jacket pockets, just in case.

I also looked for clues of what other people were up to, their signs and desire lines. I looked at all terrains with a magpie's eye, open to being surprised, looking to collect the shiny, the edible, the abandoned. Each day I asked the city what it had to offer, and what I could give back.

When I found something, it gave me a feeling of good luck for the whole day. Maps of fruit trees and herb patches began to form in my mind – personal, psycho-geographical maps from my wanderings and foraging. As the seasons flowed, Willoughby and I walked in all weathers and watched as the spring's blossoms turned into summer's blooming fruit.

So many of the urban gardens we passed were scrappy, neglected or full of mistakes – odd plant combinations, ambitious schemes gone wrong. A lexicon of thwarted plans, urban migration, human error. But I loved *all* the gardens. I loved where weeds came in and grew in tiny crevasses that didn't seem to have any soil. I loved the twee, tidy gardens around the brick units down the end of my street where the widows lived – all pansies and polyanthus and tight little roses. I loved the student-flat gardens, with their car-crushed comfrey and gnarled old lemon trees. There was a tender place in my heart for the kindergarten gardens: old tractor tyres full of scrappy marigolds and strawberry plants, matchbox cars and spilled glitter.

Every garden was a victory garden.

*

I was keen to make more friends with kids, so I made a handwritten sign: *Are you a mother of young children who believes in social justice and would like to meet other mothers for sharing ideas and maybe growing food together?* I put them up on noticeboards around the city. I got a few phone calls and invited everyone who replied around for a cup of tea: Madz, Caro, Cath, Rachael and Alice, all terrific women – funny, bold and practical. Between us we had nine kids, a small gaggle of unruly rascals that romped around my garden.

'Maybe we could call ourselves MAMA?' I said at the first gathering as I poured tea out of a large enamel pot, always keen to infuse the most incidental gatherings with a wider purpose. 'For Manawatū Activist Mothers' Association?'

'Or maybe we could just keep meeting up for cups of tea because it's fun?' said Madz wryly.

So we did. We shared a love of food gardening, op shopping, home herbalism and foraging, too. Our gatherings usually involved sharing in some form – passing around kids' clothes, our own clothes, spare food from our gardens.

I wondered if there were other locals out there interested in foraging. Madz and I started up a Facebook group: Manawatū Urban Foraging. We were startled when, after just a few days, the page attracted hundreds of followers. There was far more interest than we'd imagined. We used it to share photographs of our local harvests, ways to use what we'd foraged and tips about where to find things.

The swift velocity of the page captured the interest of the *Manawatū Standard*.

A journalist, Bronwyn Torrie, contacted us to ask if we would take her foraging. The idea of trying to wrangle all our kids while putting on a show of foraging was unattractive. Instead, Madz and I suggested we make a 'locavore lunch' from local and foraged ingredients. Bronwyn took us up on the offer.

We enlisted our friend Toni to help with the cooking. We made elderflower pancakes, nasturtium pesto on sourdough and a cake decorated with foraged flowers. Madz had olives she'd foraged from an urban street and preserved in a herb-flavoured brine. I'd made cordial from foraged lemons, which we poured into vintage teacups.

When the article came out, it was very strange to see a bit of our lives reflected back through a stranger's eyes: 'A small army of plucky foragers is on a mission to liberate food from rotting on the ground, and they're recruiting,' the article began.

Bronwyn had spent a couple of hours with us while we talked about all sorts of plants we'd found, their nutritional properties and where the good foraging places were. But, in the way of any savvy journalist, Bronwyn led the article with two of the more outrageous things I'd said in my nervous babbling. 'Lehndorf hates food going to waste. In fact, when she was a poor student, she would dive into rubbish bins and "liberate" food scraps,' it read. Then: 'She is preparing to feast on road kill which is sitting in her freezer, but she insists it isn't as feral as it sounds. "My dad is a hunter and recently when he came down to visit me he hit a pheasant with his truck, and it was such a beautiful bird and such a shame, so he stopped and picked it up. It wasn't like picking up a yucky, squishy possum."'

I was mortified. Somehow I'd managed to make foraging seem like a mad fringe activity.

When Madz said that she grew a lot of vegetables, Bronwyn had to be convinced and peered through the weeds for evidence, illustrating the difference between how foragers and non-foragers tend land and see gardens.

'Upon closer inspection, there *were* broccoli, cabbages, garlic, fledgling fruit trees and so on,' the article read. 'Unlike most gardeners, Madeline embraces oxalis and adds the weed to salads.'

We also said the thing that few people want to hear: learning to forage takes time. 'It has taken the women more than a decade to know which weeds are tasty and which can kill, and they would be lost without their foraging bibles.'

After this publicity, our Facebook page took off.

*

All the foraging, gardening and gleaning had given me peasant hands, which I was proud of. Hardworking hands, a bit rough-looking, covered in bruises, scratches and cuts. Fingers often stained with berry juice or turmeric or pollen. I kept my fingernails as short as possible but even so they often still hung on to a fair amount of soil, despite comprehensive scrubbing with a nailbrush.

Dad has hardworking hands. There's a crude, hand-poked tattoo of a cross that a friend did when he was a teenager on his third finger. The tip of one finger is missing from a run-in with the bandsaw. His left thumbnail is constantly serrated with small cuts where he tests the sharpness of his knives. I always look at people's hands when I first meet them – hands are more revealing than faces. I respect hardworking hands more than the soft palms and long, manicured nails of more refined folk. There is great dignity in the evidence of hands used in physical work.

The word 'peasant' is often used as a pejorative, a demeaning word to suggest someone uneducated, coarse or heathen. But many Pākehā come from Europe's peasant stock – the working-class servants, shop girls and farmhands who jumped on ships to the impossible-to-imagine down under in the hope of a better life. Among my own ancestors were Danish sailors, Novocastrian coal miners, German farmers. People who worked in the elements.

When I imagine back beyond the recently planted grove of my family tree – my parents, grandparents, great-grandparents – and feel further back into the dark forests of deeper history, there dwell land-literate ancestors who inspire me to try to learn the land, too.

The United Nations defines a peasant as 'any person who engages [...] in small-scale agricultural production for subsistence and/or for the market [...] who relies significantly [...] on family or household labour and other non-monetized ways of organizing labour, and who has a special dependency on and attachment to the land.' By this definition, I am proud to identify as a peasant ... though perhaps this comes across as an affectation.

In the *Manawatū Standard* foraging article, Madz had put forward the radical idea of getting to know your neighbours. 'When Madeline and her husband, Simon, moved into their Feilding home four years ago, they quickly made friends with neighbours and began to trade their feijoas for homegrown apples. "Actually, if you knock on someone's door and ask them for something, it's a magical, normal moment. Why not share the love?" Madz said.'

Those first years back in the Manawatū were all about learning the land and sharing the love. And very soon we had another member of the family to extend that love to.

Peasant pottage from field and forest

Serves 2

A pottage is an old English dish made from the shared gifts
of the commons. A kind of savoury porridge, it makes for a
warming midwinter lunch. In medieval times, for special feasts
and festivals, it was served in cob-shaped bread.

Throw in whatever wild greens you can forage to make your
pottage deeply nutritious as well as heartening. Every pottage
you make will taste a little different depending on the pungency
of the wild greens. Some possibilities are: fat hen (*Chenopodium
album*), sorrel (*Rumex acetosa*), bittercress (*Cardamine hirsute*),
dandelion (*Taraxacum officinale*) leaves, oxalis (*Oxalis incarnata*),
young nasturtium (*Tropaeolum majus*) leaves, young plantain
(*Plantago* species) leaves, clover (*Trifolium* species), young
borage (*Borago officinalis*) leaves, and nettles (*Urtica dioica*).
The main thing is that your pottage contains a good amount of
greens local to you.

Take care while foraging *Urtica dioica* that you are confident
in your identification. New Zealand's native nettle (*Urtica ferox*)
is very poisonous. Consult your foraging guides.

Some people make pottages with turnips or pearl barley.
I don't much like turnips and prefer oats to barley, but, like many
peasant dishes, pottage is forgiving, designed to be adjusted to
suit personal preferences and to use what's available.

On a winter's day, lean over a bowl of peasant pottage, warm
your hands on the steam, and see if you can imagine your way-
back people doing the same thing.

Ingredients
   a knob of butter
   1 white onion, chopped
   1 small carrot, chopped
   1 small parsnip, chopped
   500 ml water
   1 generous sprig fresh thyme
   salt and pepper, to taste

¾ **cup rolled oats**
2 handfuls foraged wild greens, chopped
grated cheese, to serve
crusty wholemeal or sourdough bread, to serve

Method

Melt the butter in a medium-sized saucepan over a low–medium heat. Add the onion and cook until glassy, then stir in the carrot and parsnip. Cook until the vegetables begin to soften.

Add the water, thyme, a pinch of salt and a good grind of black pepper. Bring to the boil, then simmer until the carrot and parsnip are cooked.

For the final 5 minutes of cooking, add in the oats and wild greens. Stir until the oats cook and thicken the brew.

Serve with a little grated cheese and crusty bread.

CHAPTER 13

Value the margins

Chamomile and lawn daisy

After a couple of years saving, Fraser and I were able to buy our first house. In our usual bumbling way, we got the formula for real-estate success upside down and bought the best house in the worst street. It was a tiny ex-state house in a rough neighbourhood, but it was *ours*, after years of renting. We were busting out of it from day one, but what it lacked for in inside space it made up for in garden – an old-school quarter acre.

Willoughby was growing up fast and I wanted him to have a sibling.

We'd better have another baby soon, before I lose my nerve, I wrote in my journal.

The second baby was born at home as well, this time in the birthing pool. When he emerged, I looked down and saw his face through the water. It seemed like he swam up to me, although this can't be what happened. Now I had two suns, two bright forces to orbit every day.

We called the new baby Magnus because he was strong and broad-chested, unlike his brother, the long and willowy Willoughby. Magnus is an Icelandic name and the saint of Scotland's Orkney Islands. Fraser chose it, both as a nod to his Scottish ancestry and in homage to Magnus Magnusson, the translator of the Icelandic sagas he loved to read.

It's a powerful name and Magnus was a powerful force right from the time he was born, so different from his careful, gentle brother. At first we called him Magnus the Mighty, until after a while that wasn't so funny.

I switched from high school English teaching to tutoring university creative writing courses so I could be at home more often to care for the children. I built another food garden, keen to feed the kids good, organic vegetables.

*

I began to read about permaculture, a design system for land tending that uses principles drawn from observations of the natural world. I was drawn to these principles, both in the garden and beyond. They made sense to me. I sat with each one, pondering the philosophy beyond its application to vegetables and compost heaps. The principle I was drawn to the most was 'value the margins'. It spoke to the potential of the commons – what could be possible if we looked at land through a lens of possibility and sharing. I also interpreted it as an appreciation of the biodiversity to be found at the edges of the land, an appreciation of the forageable.

To value the margins is to value the weeds. What makes something a weed is fairly arbitrary and dependent on cultural bias and human priorities anyway. A plant that is a pest to one person – a dominating bully, a threat to flowing waterways and diverse forests – might be an edible or medicinal resource to someone else.

I liked to wander through the principle's metaphoric possibilities. At the margins – in the garden, on the land and in society – was where all the unpredictable and interesting things happened.

A forager is a margins dweller, an edgewalker, always wandering off track, looking down for windfall or up for fruiting trees. Mooching to the sides of paths for edible greens and herbs. An ambulant muncher, distractedly chewing on 'weeds' picked while on the go. A conduit for chance, seeker of serendipity, explorer extraordinary. No one values the margins more than a forager.

When I would research plants I'd just discovered, the first hits would often be sites like Weedbusters and AgPest. Sites for how best to eliminate the plants. Sometimes the same plant would appear on both weed-buster sites and foraging or herbalist sites. The description on the foraging or herbalist sites was often reverential, poetic, romantic. On the weed-busting side, the same plant was described as invasive, a pernicious pest, the language pragmatic, derogatory and focused on 'control'.

I was resistant to the idea that nature needed to be controlled. I shared my garden with all manner of flora and fauna that had different needs from me. Together, we formed an ecosystem. Why should I be the only creature in the ecosystem who got a say?

But both sites were worth reading. The weed-buster sites often had excellent identification photographs and up-to-date details about where the plant might be found.

Sometimes the qualities listed on a weed-busting site might be prized in another context: 'Hawthorn produces many long-lived, well-dispersed seeds. It is extremely tough and versatile, long-lived, tolerates both hot and cold temperatures, damp to dry conditions, and can withstand salt, wind, shade and heavily damaged soils.'

In other words, it was utterly tenacious. A resilient survivor.

Foragers don't see weeds as pests. A weed is a plucky volunteer. Weeds are innovative, brave. They appear, seemingly out of nowhere, to heal the soil in marginal lands. They interlope, uninvited. Nature's squatters. Hybrid roses might falter and cosseted exotics turn yellow despite luxuriant tending, but weeds will thrive in the sourest of soils. Weeds are living examples of the saying 'nature finds a way'; they are the jazz hands of resilience.

Foragers are able to hold both possibilities at once. They understand that plants like blackberry or gorse are an absolute headache for land management, but they also appreciate what the plant has to offer.

*

Behind our new house was a stream flanked by stopbanks that were thick with green life. The real-estate agent who'd sold us the house had called the stream a storm drain, but I learned from an article in the local newspaper that it was actually an urban stream, the Little Kawau. It had once been a valued source of food to tangata whenua Rangitāne o Manawatū, full of eels, kōura, watercress and pūhā. Rangitāne were unhappy about the streams in the city being treated as 'drains', poorly tended and full of industrial runoff.

They were trying to educate local Pākehā about the streams in the hope that better knowledge of the history could turn the streams' fate around.

With the principle of 'value the margins' in mind, I lifted the boys over our back fence and we started to explore the edgelands behind our house. The banks were thick with comfrey, which I cut armfuls of for layering on to my compost heap. We also found useful garden escapees like mint, lemon balm and nasturtium, plus a lot of less desirable things, like tradescantia, convolvulus and ivy. The city council occasionally came by with ride-on mowers and did their best to cut a swathe through the rioting green along the streams, but in between their visits the plants sprang back in their unstoppable way. Soon the banks would be wild and weedy once again.

Willoughby and I trudged along through the knee-high grass and greens. I carried Magnus on my back in his baby sling. The boundaries and binaries of the gardening world – crops versus weeds, cultivated versus wild – were blurring and seemed to make less sense to me all the time. These urban edgelands, right on our doorstep, unloved and marginal to many, became our playground and natural medicine cabinet, full of helpful volunteers.

*

Sometimes I head out for a foraging walk with a loose mental list of things I hope to find, but it is rare that foraging sessions work that way. Either something unexpected pops out at me or I don't find anything tangible but come away restored in ways I couldn't have predicted. Foraging is slow. I trust that I will find just what I need, even if I can't always predict what that might be. What is meant for me will find me.

One late August day I was out for a bike ride along the Little Kawau. In some places it looked like little more than a big open drain. I was winter-weary, feeling flat and heavy with responsibilities. The sky loomed overhead and the world felt like a grey old pointless place.

I pedalled through an underpass beneath an arterial road and popped out to see a huge patch of German chamomile growing on the steep stopbank of the stream. Chamomile can sprawl and look sad and scrappy, but this patch was new-season perfection. The flowers were white and fresh, the green bright, the feathery leaves waving in the breeze. I hopped off my bicycle and scrambled down the bank into the thick of it.

A dense, straw-like smell rose up all around me as my footsteps released the volatile oils of the plant. Above, the clouds opened and sunshine flooded down. The chamomile was so dense, so beautiful.

Chamomile is a de-stresser, a herb of the young, a reliever of anxiety. It's often found in bedtime herbal tea mixes because of its ability to relax and restore. I have a hippie aunty who used to brew chamomile tea into a yellow rinse for brightening her white blonde hair. (She also used to go barefoot, and once, when told she couldn't go into a country pub with her bare feet, sat down in a nearby paddock and quickly made herself some macrame 'sandals' from the long grasses.)

I believe in synchronicity. I believe if I hold my head at the right angle, one ear towards the ground, the earth will speak to me through the plants and birds and waters. The chamomile patch said, 'You don't need to feel so heavy. You have a young heart. Enjoy our beauty, and remember your own.'

I sat with the chamomile, inhaling its medicine and absorbing the message. I picked enough to fill my bike basket. I would dry it for a buoying tea to keep me going through spring. The tangible harvest was a treat but the experience of happening on the patch right at that low moment was the greater gift.

*

My efforts to grow food for my family made me appreciate wild foods all the more. Edible weeds regenerated themselves and needed no tending. They were attuned to the subtleties of microclimates and seasons in ways that cultivated vegetables, at the mercy of my randomness and distracted guardianship, couldn't be. They often sprouted earlier, grew faster and had less trouble with pests than the food I was trying to grow.

It felt like to eat the wild plants I foraged was to eat this innate intelligence. They brimmed with vitality.

*

As Magnus grew and became more mobile, he, Willoughby and I explored further along the streams, the living veins of the city. Each stream had a different microclimate, range of plant life and level of care – or neglect, depending on the neighbourhood. In between weeds and trees, there was sometimes less attractive surprises: fly-tipping, abandoned supermarket trolleys, broken televisions, piles of rotting clothes. It was also where some of the city's best graffiti art could be found, on the backs of suburban fences and the walls of culverts, opportunist expressions on concrete canvases.

We found many delights from overhanging backyard trees: plums, pears and mandarins. I also found more unusual fruits, like medlars (an heirloom fruit that requires 'bletting', or semi-rotting, before it can be eaten), guavas and loquats. Seeing properties from the stream rather than the street was oddly intimate. We saw vegetable gardens, bicycles, trampolines, garden sheds, recycling bins, rabbits, cats, dogs, guinea pigs … lots of busy, happy mess.

*

Willoughby was delighted to have a little brother. The four-year gap between he and Magnus meant he was a great helper, old enough to fetch clean nappies and spoon vegetable mush into Magnus's ever-hungry mouth.

Motherhood had knocked the certainty out of me. Post-children, everything was nuance. Like most artist-mothers, I struggled to keep my creative practice going. Writing was scrawled down between family demands. My journal was always open on the table with a pen lying in its gutter, in case a poem fragment came to me while I cooked, fed and tended. Rather than emerging as an artist, I was beginning to feel less visible, backed into the shadows by the demands of care.

One day Willoughby picked up my digital camera and took a photograph of Magnus and me in our backyard. I looked at it later that night. In the picture, the garden was full of vegetables and calendula, outdoor toys were scattered all around the yard. Magnus was running away from the camera. I was sweeping the concrete with a yard broom, wearing a vintage dress over jeans, my jaw set in determination. It was not an attractive photo but I liked how it captured the Sisyphean quality of motherhood.

There she was, the archetypal tired mother, trying to maintain some kind of order while all around her children made chaos, undoing the effects of her labours at the very moment she was conducting them.

*

At first Magnus met all his developmental markers but around the age of two things began to change. He didn't seem to be learning language and he began to be destructive and violent. His behaviour became challenging. He would become distressed at the beach, terrified of the ocean. He would sit in the garden, throwing clods of soil at the fence and watching them smash. He could do that for an hour if I let him, before the repetitive fixation would unnerve me and I'd distract him on to another activity.

He was obsessed with swings. He would scream and tantrum if I tried to take him off the swings, attracting concerned looks from other parents at the playground. He suffered night terrors, and would wake in the night howling and distressed. We couldn't soothe him back to sleep. The whole family became sleep-deprived.

We were looking so hard for all the ways he was 'normal' that we became wilfully blind to the high level of his quirks. But after a while we couldn't deny it anymore. Our boy seemed out of kilter with the rest of the world.

Home was hell for a while. Broken crockery, broken light bulbs, food was thrown against walls and ground into the carpet, drawers and cupboards were emptied on to the floor as soon as they were tidied. On one gloomy spring day he smashed a living-room window. Magnus the Mighty had turned into Bamm-Bamm.

Imagine living with a gremlin. Not a Spielberg-style gremlin of the 1980s film, but a gremlin in the old-fashioned sense. A being bent on destruction. A chaotic sprite who seeks to undo everything you do, to get in the way of progress, to break the unbroken. This is what is was like living with Magnus. He liked to break plates. He enjoyed the sound of crockery smashing into the wall and would laugh a strange, hollow giggle. He seemed to have a strength, daring and agility beyond his years. He was fearless.

He would climb up Fraser and me as though we were mountains, standing on our shoulders, squashing our heads down into our necks. He would grind his chin into the top of my head. He would empty the cutlery drawer with a crash. He would hurl his toys over the back fence to hear them plop into the stream behind our house. He would ride his tricycle at full speed into the fence and laugh when he crashed, even though he'd hurt himself in the process.

One day Magnus ran up to a friend's small daughter and shoved her in the chest, sending her flying backwards. She landed heavily on her back and her head made a terrible sound as it hit the concrete. After some cuddles and care, she was okay, but I was horrified. That night I said to Fraser, 'We can't risk letting him be around our friends' kids anymore.' Although home was no fun, we stopped being able to go out anywhere either. I couldn't cope with the hypervigilance needed to keep everyone safe. Over time we became isolated.

Because of his speech delay, Magnus would repeat everything I said. We later learned this phenomena is called echolalia. Echolalia sounds like it ought to be some beautiful phrase of music, but living with it was less musical. Some days I felt like I lived with a giant, chaotic parrot.

'Oh no! Why did you break Mummy's pot plant?' I said to Magnus.

'Oh no! Break Mummy's pot plant! Break Mummy's pot plant!' he replied.

I constantly looked for some reassurance that he was happy inside himself, that he was okay. It was so hard to tell. I used his echolalia to hear what I needed to.

'Magnus is happy?' I would say.

'Magnus is happy, Magnus is happy,' he would chant back blankly.

One day, when I was talking to Mum on the phone, I said, 'I just don't know what I'm doing wrong. Nothing seems to work. No amount of positive reinforcement affects his behaviour. And I can't tell if he's happy or not.'

'Do you think you're getting depressed?' she asked me.

'No,' I said. 'I'm not depressed, just having a normal reaction to a difficult situation.' But when I got off the phone I thought to myself, *If this was a job, I would definitely quit.*

I lay in bed at night dreaming of escape. I thought of the tree houses on Mount Cargill. The feeling of being in a tent on top of the chalk hills in England, looking out to miles of ocean. I wrote a long poem called 'The Stay-at-Home Mother Contemplates Flight'. It all felt too hard, too raw, not what I'd signed up for. I'd only ever had a vague sense of what direction I was heading in, and now I'd lost all control. I started to feel like my life was totally off the leash.

At home, I was failing, flailing, slipping, but when I took the boys out – to the stream, to the playground, to the river track – there was a bit of space for us all to just *be*. Nature's green hum, the feeling of life carrying on in spite of it all, pulled me out of my neurotic looping and spiralling anxiety, at least for the duration of the walk. But my attempts to keep Magnus safe were also making us more isolated. And the three of us couldn't wander the streets all day. Unlike in the moshpit, where no one was left to fall, we were falling fast. I felt lonely and scared. There was no cavalry coming, no strong arms to lift us up.

It was time to get some help.

Sweet-dreams syrup

Makes approximately 500 ml

This syrup, for children and grown-up children, is a version of
the one I made Magnus when he was suffering night terrors. I'd
give the boys a teaspoon at bedtime, just after we read bedtime
stories and before they brushed their teeth. It contains that
flower of childhood the common lawn daisy (*Bellis perennis*), as
well as chamomile (*Matricaria recutita*) and lemon balm (*Melissa
officinalis*) – all plants I'd find on the banks of the stream behind
my house.

Daisy is uplifting and can heal dulled spirits. Chamomile
and lemon balm are both mild tranquillisers and can help with
sleeping issues.

Ingredients

1 cup chopped daisy flowerheads and leaves
½ cup chopped chamomile flowerheads and young leaves
⅓ cup chopped lemon balm
500 ml cold water
2 cups white or brown sugar

Method

Sterilise a bottle.

Put the chopped herbs in a small saucepan and cover with
the cold water. Heat slowly on a low heat. Bring the temperature
of the water to near-boiling, and then keep there until it takes on
a green colour.

Sieve out the plant matter. Return the infusion to the
saucepan and add the sugar. Cook over a low heat until the
sugar has dissolved and then simmer a little longer until the
syrup thickens. Pour into the sterilised bottle and label.

The syrup is shelf-stable but I keep my tinctures in the fridge
door so that I see them often – it reminds me to use them.

CHAPTER 14

Take it to the trees

Kawakawa

Through Magnus's kindergarten, we got a referral to the local special-education department. Fraser and I filled in a lot of forms. They ran a lot of tests. I was torn; I wanted to be as honest as possible to get help, yet I found it hard to tell them the true extent of how difficult things had become at home. I felt like a failure as a parent. I knew Magnus was very speech-delayed and was exhibiting some unusual behaviours, but I imagined with some expert help he would 'come right'. Fraser wasn't as concerned as me, but he was at work all day so wasn't seeing the extent of what I saw.

The kindergarten was the fourth early childhood education centre we'd enrolled Magnus in. We'd tried and left a Playcentre, a Steiner kindergarten and a high-decile kindy. Joining these preschool communities, with their claims of inclusivity, only to find them unsupportive had left us scared and exhausted. The fourth kindy, low-decile and just around the corner from our house, was the first one to try to help us address Magnus's developmental delays.

Norah, the special-education advisor, came to our house to tell Fraser and I about the test results and to discuss her observations of Magnus at kindergarten. Fraser had come home in his lunch hour for the meeting. Despite everything we'd been through, nothing prepared us for the results of her assessment.

She sat across from us in our living room and said gravely, 'Look, I'm not qualified to diagnose. You have to go to the paediatrician for that. But I'm fairly sure Magnus is on the autism spectrum.' She could see from our faces how shocked we were, how deeply in denial we'd been. 'Try to think of this as a good thing,' she continued. 'A beginning. The point where it all turns around. Once you know what's going on for Magnus, you can help him. And once you have a diagnosis you can access support.'

But we weren't ready for that perspective, however helpful it might have been. We were upset.

Norah gave us a stack of leaflets and a list of appointments we'd need to make. I stared down at the leaflets. They were so reasonable and coolly phrased. *Someone with ASD may have difficulty with communication and interactions with other people. They may have restricted interests and repetitive behaviours. Their ability to function in school, work and other areas of life may be affected.*

Interactions with other people? Ability to function? What did any of it mean? What kind of person was Magnus going to grow into? I hated the flat, clinical language.

I walked Norah to the door. I couldn't feel my legs.

She put a hand on my shoulder. 'Remember, Helen, this is a beginning, not an ending.'

I watched her walk off down the driveway. I wondered how many times in the course of her workday she had to deliver troubling news to parents.

Fraser was pulling on his jacket. As he picked up his cycle helmet and reached for his bag, I stared at him, aghast. 'No, Fraser! You can't go back to work after this! Are you crazy? You can't leave me here.' I started crying, almost begging. 'Please don't go back to work today.'

I was scared to be left alone with the weight of the news. Fraser looked at me blankly, his face pale. It occurred to me that he was in shock too.

He rang his work to let them know he wouldn't be back that afternoon.

Magnus played around our feet, oblivious.

After Fraser put the phone down, his bicycle helmet still on his knee, he said, 'Okay, what now then?'

It was a big question that needed a small, practical answer.

'Let's go for a walk … the valley … the river. There's time to go before we need to pick Willo up from school,' I said.

We needed to tell our families – they'd known about the looming appointment – but I couldn't face it. The day had split in two, fracturing our future as we'd imagined it. Our families could wait. We had shock absorbing to do.

Fraser and I both love the Pohangina Valley, under the Ruahine Range, with its green rolling hills and wide river. It's often covered in a soft mist held by the upside-down bowl the range creates. Fraser describes it as 'hobbit-y'. We go there to relax at times of celebration, to swim in the Pohangina River, and we go there when things are tough.

Not long after we returned to the Manawatū, Fraser lost his wedding ring while swimming in the Pohangina River. I knew then that we'd be staying for a long time.

'You're married to the river now,' I joked.

'I didn't lose it. The river is just where I keep it now. I'll get it back one day,' he said confidently.

The Pohangina River would hold us. We grabbed jackets, bags, snacks for Magnus.

On the short drive from the city, Fraser and I were quiet. Thrown. We pulled up at Tōtara Reserve, got Magnus out of his car seat and started walking. I was stuck in a loop of questions no one could answer, least of all Fraser, who was just as shaken as me.

Will he ever be able to talk properly? Will he be able to go to school by himself or will he need a teacher aide? Will he go to high school? Will he ever have friends? How will we cope if he's still hitting people when he's an adult? Will he need to live with us forever? Will he be happy? Will he be okay?

Will we?

We walked slowly along the path, at Magnus's pace. While I waited for Magnus, I held on to tree trunks and leaned against them, trying to find support, trying to find deeper breaths, something grounding.

'Water! Water!' Magnus was pointing. He could see the river through the trees.

'I'll take him down,' said Fraser. 'You keep going.'

At the river, Fraser could skim stones. Magnus would throw rocks in the water.

I watched them leave. Magnus's hair so fair it was white. He was fairer than his brother; Willo's hair was golden. Magnus had brilliant blue eyes and a broad, strong back. He was physically confident to the point of danger and, as a result, often peppered in grazes and bruises. He looked like a tiny Viking.

I walked along the path for a while but emotion overwhelmed me and I blundered off into the foliage towards one of the ancient tōtara trees that the reserve is named for. I pressed my back into the tree's trunk and slid to the ground. The strength of the tōtara calmed my thudding heart. I lifted my chin and stared into the tree's canopy. The tōtara had grown there for hundreds of years. I imagined I was not the first person to lean on its trunk, looking for support.

I unfastened the clasp of my hag stone necklace and shoved it deep into my pocket. So much for protection. So much for a portal to the future … and for ancestral support. I felt blindsided. I hadn't seen this coming.

Sitting on the ground helped to steady me, ease the sensation of falling.

Kawakawa bushes surrounded me. I gazed through their lacy leaves, which glowed a brilliant green from the sun shining through them. 'Drink me, drink me,' the leaves called.

I pulled myself back up to my feet, answering the plant's call. The attention required to harvest, to gather, was instantly soothing to me. The deep pleasure I always felt from foraging drowned out my roaring anxiety. It gave me something to do other than freak the hell out.

I pinched leaves off using my fingertips, moving from bush to bush, careful to only take a handful from each to avoid damaging the plants. I looked for the leaves with the most holes, taking care not to harvest from the season's new growth. I carefully stacked the leaves into a neat pile as though they were papers or playing cards and tucked them into my jacket pocket. My fingers smelled like their dense, vibrant oil. I loitered in the forest, unwilling to stray too far from the soothing old-tree energy of the giant tōtara.

I started to find my breath again. I could feel my feet and then the ground beneath them. I squatted down and ran my hands over the ground as though to remind myself it was there.

I returned to the path and followed it down to the river. Fraser was skimming stones. He'd taken his jacket and jersey off in the warmth of the sun. 'This was a good idea,' he said. 'I wouldn't have got any work done. Thank you.'

I had no helpful words. We held on to each other.

Soon it was time to head back and pick Willoughby up from school. Suddenly, I felt grateful for the tether of school bells and meal times. *Just stay in the day and do the next right thing*, I told myself.

The next right thing was to collect Willoughby, to make some dinner, to call our parents. All the glue of family life that holds us in place.

After putting the boys to bed that night, I washed the kawakawa leaves and put them in a large pot of water with some grated ginger. I brought the brew to the boil slowly. The leaves began to release their oils and left a blue-black slick on the surface.

I sat on our back steps, looking out at the vegetable garden, holding the tea. A single kawakawa leaf floated in my cup. I inhaled the vapours. It was the smell of the forest.

I thanked the plant for its medicines, physical and metaphorical. For what does a kawakawa leaf look like but a courageous, damaged heart?

*

The next week, Willoughby saw me crying. We'd done our best to explain to him what was going on with his brother, but he was only small. He disappeared into the garden and returned with a bunch of flowers, ripped off at the bloom, carried in his small, sweaty hand. He held them out to me.

I took the crushed flowers. They had little chance of lasting long. I looked for a saucer, holding them up for his approval. 'The grey one? Or the yellow one? The yellow one? Okay.' I filled the shallow dish with water and floated the flowers on the water's surface. I put it in the centre of our dining table. A small, tattered gift, but more meaningful to me than any plastic-wrapped florist flowers.

'Thank you!' I kissed his flushed cheek. 'Mummy loves flowers.'

He looked relieved that I'd stopped crying. 'When will Magnus stop being autistic?' he asked me.

I told him that Magnus would always be autistic, but that I hoped, as he grew older, he would learn and change and be able to communicate with us more effectively.

Willoughby looked thoughtful and then said gravely, 'Mummy, if we do get chickens, can we get Magnus an autistic chicken?'

*

As we went through the diagnosis process, we learned Magnus was a 'sensory seeker'. While some autistic children are overwhelmed by lights, noises and harsh sensations, Magnus was the opposite. The way his senses cognitively processed meant that he needed increased sensory input just to feel them at the 'normal' level. This was why he broke things and sought out noise and chaos. It was a relief to learn there was a reason he behaved as he did. He wasn't just extremely naughty. The paediatrician told us that as Magnus's communication improved and he learned to express his needs, the violent behaviour would hopefully diminish.

There was a sweet kid in there. When he was not being terrible, he was creative and eccentric and funny. Even on the worst of days, we weren't immune to his charms. He liked to dress up in costumes and frequently fell asleep in the dress-up box curled up like a cat. He made his slightly timid older brother braver and more adventurous with his wild ways. At his best, he could make us, a rather earnest trio, all laugh.

My levels of irritation with him were matched by a deep and abiding affection. In my own graceless and grumbling way, I was devoted to him. His pale blue eyes like little speckled moons, his round face dear and doll-like. After long days of chaos, when he slept he looked – as most toddlers do – like an angel.

I felt so alone. My friends were doing their best to support me, but they were busy with their own young families. My parents lived three hours' drive away. Referrals to specialists were a mixed bag: some helped, but we didn't appreciate the levels of scrutiny (parent-blaming, victim-shaming) that we sometimes endured. When you have a violent child, the whole family goes under the microscope.

I'd always tried to live the community values I'd learned as a kid and as a young anarchist. When people were wobbling, it was everyone's job to hold them steady. But here we were, feeling like social pariahs just when we needed people most.

We got through by focusing on one day at a time. As long as the boys were warm, fed and loved, I called the day a success.

Slowly, I was able to see Magnus as my baby boy again, to stop being blinded by his diagnosis when I looked at him, and to appreciate and celebrate his personality and abilities.

Norah had told us that autism was hereditary and suggested that we look back up the family lines for any clues. Between all the generations of Fraser's family and mine, we were a quirky bunch. Maybe all families are, though? Fraser had obsessive tendencies and could happily live the life of a monk without my constant efforts to bridge him to community. Then there was me: equally obsessive in different ways, talking to herbs and birds. Peering through the hag stone hole when I needed guidance. Feeling the personalities of plants and trees as though they were people.

I was aware that, in my own way, I was a sensory seeker, too.

Kawakawa soother tea

Makes 100 g

Kawakawa (*Piper excelsum*) is known as the pharmacy of the forest because of its potent healing properties. Long a treasured plant of rongoā rākau, in recent years kawakawa has risen in popularity in Aotearoa. Its distinctive holey leaves are frequently used as a style motif in art, design and jewellery.

While you can use fresh leaves to make kawakawa tea, this is a method for drying the leaves to make a big batch that will keep longer. I make it in large batches and take bags of it along to my local crop swap, leading to my reputation as 'the tea lady'.

Kawakawa has revitalising and invigorating qualities and a dense, slightly peppery flavour which pairs beautifully with ginger. Both kawakawa and ginger are good for digestion, and the lemongrass adds another pleasant flavour note and scent.

I grow lemongrass in my greenhouse because it needs year-round shelter and warmth. You can dry your own lemongrass at the same time as you dry the kawakawa leaves. Otherwise, small bags of dried lemongrass can usually be found at health food shops. If you can't find lemongrass, lemon verbena is a good substitute.

Using ground ginger will mean the tea is a little cloudy in the cup, but it's worth it for the pungency of flavour.

I found a great pair of herb scissors at the op shop. They look like regular scissors, but they have four blades instead of two. They are fantastic for chopping up herbs into a fine tea blend. You find them in kitchen specialty shops. If you make a lot of teas, I recommend finding some. They're a game changer.

Ingredients

100 g kawakawa leaves
25 g dried lemongrass
2 tablespoons ground ginger

Method

Dry the kawakawa leaves using your preferred method: solar heat, in front of the fire or in a dehydrator.

Chop up the dried kawakawa leaves with scissors. (Chop the lemongrass at the same time if you've dried your own.) It doesn't need to be as fine as loose-leaf black tea, so don't go overboard. Just fine enough to be able to spoon it into a teapot.

Put the herbs in a large bowl, then add the ground ginger. Mix the blend with your hands for a couple of minutes. Put it into a clean, airtight jar and label it.

Brew to your preferred strength. A general rule for herbal tea is 1 teaspoon for a cup, 1 heaped tablespoon for a 600 ml teapot.

Harvest + Compost

CHAPTER 15

Tendrel

Wildflowers

The feeling I'd always had, that I was fundamentally held by life, supported, faded from me. I was done with the metaphysical for a while. I had enough going on with the here and now. I wrapped up my hag stone necklace in a piece of silk and hid it in the back of my sock drawer. It had started to feel more like burden than balm, a symbol of a younger, more naive self.

We'd always holidayed with our friends – families together, kids playing and running around in a pack – but Fraser and I began to feel like our family was a liability on a shared trip. The constant need for damage control and hypervigilance was draining. For the wellbeing of everyone, we started to stay home. At home we could centre Magnus's needs and keep everyone safe, and I didn't have to apologise to anyone.

I discovered a ferocity inside myself I hadn't known was there. I had to advocate strongly for Magnus, for our family, and it took more guts than I had ever had to use before. I named this new, ferocious version of myself 'wolf mother', because I could suddenly spring in front of my child and growl at anyone who threatened his wellbeing, or suggested our home life might be a factor in his behaviour. When children behave violently, people sometimes assume they are modelling behaviour they have witnessed at home. In some appointments, I had to answer questions about whether there was any 'violence in the home'. Each time it happened I grew more enraged.

I became a human shield. I was Magnus's interpreter and translator, reading his needs through his facial expressions and mother-knowing then explaining them to the world. Even the most well-meaning experts could mishandle interactions, so I had to speak up for Magnus and his potential. I became decentred from my own life; Magnus's needs came first in every situation.

I embroidered a brooch to wear to medical and care appointments. It was black, with a wolf baring its teeth and breathing flames. An amulet of protection.

*

When Magnus was nearly five, we found a school that had a special unit for ASD children. A school visit and a long meeting with the unit's staff gave us some hope. Instead of focusing on what was 'wrong' with Magnus, they began the meeting by asking Fraser and me what his abilities and strengths were, even what his interests were. The only trouble was, it was in a different school zone from where we were living. We had to find a new house in the zone.

After a long and increasingly desperate search, we looked at a 1920s bungalow on a street near the school, walking distance from the city centre. It had shiny wooden floorboards, stained-glass windows and tall trees in the backyard. It felt welcoming. I had a strong feeling of déjà vu as I walked around. I seemed to be able to anticipate how the rooms were laid out.

A word was nailed to the front of the house: *Āhuru.* I didn't know what it meant so I looked it up: to be cosy and comfortable; to nest. I took it as a sign. 'We *need* a safe nest. I think this is the one,' I said to Fraser.

It was beyond what we could reasonably afford, but we were well schooled in how to stretch a dollar. We'd go back to the oats and ramen diet if we had to. We put in an offer and it became ours.

*

On moving day, Magnus and I were the first to arrive. I drove our car over while Fraser drove the moving truck we'd hired. I unlocked the door to the empty house and walked into the kitchen. The house wrapped its arms around us from that moment.

Magnus and I walked out into the backyard. The previous owner had left behind a lichen-covered park bench. I sat down under the large plum tree. There were tūī dancing around the tree's tops. The garden we had left had no mature trees so we didn't get any tūī visiting. Magnus plonked himself into the yard's sandpit and started playing. Tears came into my eyes. I was grateful for the comfort of the trees, for this āhuru house, right at the heart of the place we needed to be for Magnus.

Our challenges weren't over. We were a whole different family from the one who had moved into the previous house. I barely recognised myself anymore. Every day was another

walk through a character-tempering fire. I was functioning
fine, but some part of me was emotionally raw, flayed. Grief
and rage could spill out of me at small, unpredictable things
that seemed to be nothing to do with Magnus. I'd lost my easy-
going faith in people.

I closed my eyes and thought of Norah's face as she told
me to think of the diagnosis as a beginning. I understood why
she'd said it, to stop us tipping into despair, but it wasn't that
simple. The grief from the diagnosis became a thread woven
into the fabric of our lives and it would always be present,
sometimes dominating the centre, other times just a small fleck
at the edge.

*

The boys and I explored our new neighbourhood. There was a
community garden nearby – another place to take the boys for a
run around. Community gardens were less fraught than public
playgrounds, where I would have to hover around Magnus to
stop him hurting the other children or randomly running off.

One summer's day we were at the community garden,
walking around the communal beds where I sometimes
harvested herbs for dinner. There was a man weeding the beds.
I smiled at him but he didn't smile back. He glared at the boys.

As we approached the garden at the end of the row, I could
see strawberries dotted through the green of the low foliage.
I called to Willo and Magnus, 'Look at this, kids. Strawberries!
Who wants a strawberry?'

They ran towards the plants, delighted. They knew about
strawberries from our own garden at home. Willoughby called
them 'straw-bellies'. They reached into the leaves.

The man's face clouded. 'NO, boys. *Don't* pick the strawberries. They aren't quite ripe. Leave them alone, please.'

The boys dropped their outstretched hands, looking uncertainly from my face to his. At home they gobbled up strawberries that showed the first flush of red – even white with a pink blush they tasted good, like sour lollies.

'Sorry,' I said to the boys. I shrugged.

'That's okay,' the man said.

He thought I was apologising to *him*. He crawled along the bed and started talking to me about how this was the problem with community gardens: people harvested things before they were ready. He tried to carry on chatting to me, but I was done with talking to him.

I looked at him. *You're dead to me* flared through my mind. I was furious, my hands shaking. *You're overreacting*, I said to myself.

And yet. These kinds of experiences are death by a thousand cuts to our enchantment with the world. I felt the effect of this small interruption to my children's instincts as if it had happened to me, as it must have happened to me in various ways through the years. Not so much a mental memory as a somatic one.

The earth is our shared playground, yet someone will always claim to own it to the exclusion of others. I couldn't believe that someone would get in the way of children engaging with the world, that someone could say no to small, outwardly reaching hands.

I felt irrational rage towards this man who had taken it upon himself to police my children for such an innocent act. In those days we had so few safe, happy places to be. The community-garden strawberries were *meant* for the hands and mouths of small children, red beads on the thread of connected life.

I gathered the boys up and walked away. At the bottom of the community garden there was an old glasshouse. Someone had left a prickly aloe there in a large pot. Over the years, the aloe had grown so enormous that it had broken through the glass roof and was now reaching out to the sky. It had grown huge – triffid-sized. There seemed to be no way to get it out of the glasshouse without cutting it to pieces. The aloe and the glasshouse were totally entangled. We stood and looked up at it in awe. The aloe seemed to be laughing at humans, with our illusions of containment and control.

Willoughby spotted a desiccated hedgehog in the straw and nudged it with his foot. The hedgehog, what was left of it, had an anguished look on its face.

It was a hot day and I was feeling sensitive to all the sharp things around us: the spines of the aloe, the broken glass, the quills of the hedgehog, the dry grass scratching our feet and legs, the prickly strawberry-guarding man. I felt that familiar flayed feeling again. I was not tough enough for this world of spikes and barbs.

*

A little while after that, I was invited by the city library to teach a children's creative writing workshop in the school-holiday programme. I took Willoughby along.

I set the kids an exercise called poetry potluck. They had to write a poem, using all of their senses, about a favourite dish they liked to eat and would take to a potluck dinner. They all read them out at the end in a shared feast of words.

They wrote about hot, buttery corn, toffee apples, mountains of marshmallows and hairy raspberries. Willoughby wrote, 'I would go to the mountain and fill a big bowl with fresh white snow and put it on the table with silver spoons in it.'

I was moved by this potluck offering, the imaginary bowl of snow. It took me back to all the ways my brother and I had interacted with nature as children. We had chewed on onion-weed stems and fennel seeds, nibbled gorse flowers, licked rainwater off leaves, sucked at the trumpets of orange honeysuckle flowers for a small hit of nectar. Discovering through wild eating, taking the world in.

I couldn't replicate the childhood I'd had for my children but it was important to me to raise them with an understanding of what it meant to grow and find food. To be connected to the land where they lived. I tried to see our garden from a child's point of view. I made low strawberry beds within their reach and put cherry tomato plants in containers next to where they played. I wanted to make caring about food, land and people a happy sell, not a heavy sell.

At our new house, I slowly started to build another vegetable garden, my fifth in ten years. A pocket of wildness in the central city. I wilfully fostered the weeds so that I could 'forage' in my own small yard. I strew around seeds for things that other gardeners were weeding out of their plots: nasturtium, violet, nettle, dandelion, magenta spreen and malva. I grew annual vegetables, too, but it was my dream to be able to step out of my door into a weedy wildness of food and habitat, for us, for the birds and for the bees.

I put cardboard down over the lawns to smother the grass. We would use every bit of the little land we had. I read *Jack and the Beanstalk* to the boys and suggested that we plant magic beans too.

One day, walking down a neighbourhood alleyway, I saw someone had dumped the rusting innards of an old wire-sprung mattress. The fabric of the mattress was long gone so only the metal spirals of the springs remained. It was an aesthetically pleasing object, an accidental sculpture. It made me think of the sculptures that English artist Derek Jarman made from the junk that washed up on the beach near his cottage in Dungeness.

It was large and unwieldy, but we were only a few blocks from home so I put it precariously on top of Magnus's buggy and gingerly pushed it home. Fraser stood shaking his head when he saw us walking up the driveway, but he helped me install it between a couple of wooden poles.

I put a wheelbarrowful of compost at the base. Then I led Willo to the bottom of the frame with a packet of bean seeds and poured a few into his hand. 'These are scarlet runner beans. If you plant them here, by the end of the summer the plants will creep up the wires and you'll be able to pick the beans from on top of your fort.'

He gazed at the fat purple-and-black-speckled seeds in his hand. 'But they are purple.'

He had a good point. Why *are* the seeds of scarlet runner beans purple?

'You know, you are *so* clever. I hadn't even thought about that. I don't know why the seeds are purple when the flowers are red. But the beans will be green when they grow.'

Together we pushed the fat, shiny beans into the soil with our thumbs.

When the beans grew, he harvested them each day in his red colander, the proud bean steward of Āhuru.

Willoughby and I liked to make tepees out of bamboo that we foraged from a nearby reserve. In the reserve, bamboo was a pest, but cut and dried it was an asset in our garden, a free resource. We grew peas and beans up the tepees and on hot days the boys would hide inside their shade.

One day I was planting out some pea seedlings that had been getting leggy in the greenhouse. I wound some string around the base of the tepee we'd made so the pea tendrils would have something to hold on to.

Squatting beside the plants, I caught the tender ends of the seedlings on my index finger and gently lifted them up from where they were lying on the soil surface to curl around the string. I held my breath, focusing hard on the task, in case my exhale caused me to yank the plant and snap a tendril.

I felt like I was holding hands with the peas, a gentle task that couldn't be rushed or hurried, like walking along a footpath with a small child. If I rushed, the tendrils would break and the plants would flop back on to the hot summer soil and wilt away.

There's a Tibetan word that sounds the same but is spelled differently, a Buddhist word: *tendrel*. It means 'interconnectedness of all things'.

*

We were still feeling pretty isolated, but I took some comfort in getting to know the neighbourhood people passing by. Small exchanges at the letterbox or gate topped me up.

One day a man knocked on our door. 'Would you folks like a community seat?' he asked. His name was Tomo and he told us about his various projects to enhance the neighbourhood.

He made the seats in his shed. They were low, sturdy benches that seated about three people.

'If you'd like, I'll bring one and bolt it to your front fence,' said Tomo.

'Yes, please,' I said.

Soon he installed the bench on the path out the front of our house. It amused me to see he had painted the words COMMUNITY SEAT on the community seat. Our living room looked out over it. The street was busy and so there was a constant stream of people walking past. For the first couple of weeks the installation of the seat was local news. I heard people saying to each other, 'Oh look! A new seat!' as they walked past. It made me smile. Humans are so endearingly daft sometimes, stating the obvious, surprised by such small things.

No one sat on the seat for a while. Then one day I looked out and a woman was sitting there. There was a supermarket at the end of our street and she had taken a seat with her bags of shopping, having a rest on her walk home. I felt ridiculously pleased. The seat was useful! A triumph! I considered phoning Tomo to tell him, but then decided that was silly. From then, people used it more and more.

I tried to make the seat more inviting. I put large terracotta pots of red geraniums on either side. These lasted about six months, then one morning when I checked the mail I noticed that they had disappeared into the night.

Our vegetable garden was on the front lawn because that was where the sun fell; the back was too shaded by the mature trees. People said to me, 'Don't people steal your vegetables?', but they never did. Lots of people stopped on their walks to chat to me if I was standing in the vegetable garden. They complimented me on the vegetables, or the older people would try to give me advice on how to 'tidy up' the garden.

Gardens are political and cultural statements. Just as you can tell a lot about a person from how they dress, you can guess a lot from how they tend (or don't) to their green spaces. Fraser and I tried to make our yard more of an *approach* than a *retreat*. We wanted to invite a dialogue with the neighbourhood.

The boys and I would watch the community seat from the window. We got to know some of the local characters. There was a scarecrow-like man who dressed in baggy brown clothes so filthy they looked like they were slowly turning into oilskin. He had wild ginger hair and carried a tatty leather satchel. He'd sit on the seat and smoke rollies while gazing over the citrus trees we'd planted on the verge.

There was Meena, who owned the dairy down the road. She would walk past our place each day. If she spotted me gardening, she'd stop, kneel on the seat and look over the fence at the vege garden to ask me what was growing.

She said, 'I don't have time to grow vegetables but I like seeing yours.' I'd try to foist vegetables on her but she'd wave her hand at me and laugh. 'Oh, I don't have time to cook it, dear. Give it to someone who would eat it.'

There were high school kids playing tinny music on their phones, who'd sit for a bit on the way to or from school, pulling lemons off the trees and biffing them at each other.

The community seat became a site of exchange. We'd offer up our garden gluts. In autumn I'd put a big sign saying *Freejoas!* above the seat. Apples, bunches of silver beet, herbs. Other people followed our example and left their own produce to share.

We never knew what we might find. One day there was a *SpongeBob SquarePants* magazine with a post-it note, written in a child's hand-writing, that said, *Look Free Book Everyone!*

When we gave away fruit we'd sometimes find a gold coin in our letterbox. Before long we felt like proper locals.

*

Every day Willoughby, Magnus and I would walk to the boys' school past a decrepit student villa on Pascal Street. The verandah was at an angle, sinking into the earth, the paint flaking off, the roof iron dented. But the bones, the last flourishes, of a once-beautiful garden remained: abundant citrus trees, standard roses along the verandah and a lilac hedge along the front fence that came back to life in spring with great energy.

I wondered how old the lilac hedge was. The house looked to be at least a hundred years old. The delicate purple cone-shaped flowers smelled like a portal to the past, to a world of grandmothers. In spring I picked a bunch to bring home. An Agee jar of lilacs was such an old-fashioned, romantic thing.

One day, as we walked our usual route, we were stopped in our tracks. The student villa was gone. The garden had totally vanished. All that remained was churned mud. I stood at the fence, horrified.

The enormous grapefruit tree was gone. The roses were gone. Most devastatingly, the old lilac hedge was gone. Bulldozed. The wrecked yard looked like a battleground where my side had lost.

My side was the guerrilla-gardening side, the seed-bombing side, the community-garden side. The urban-foraging, plant-medicine-making, heritage-variety-saving side. My side cared about old trees. Too often it felt like my side was losing. It was hard to look at the devastation.

The lilac hedge was not the only neighbourhood plant I grieved over the school-run years. The neighbourhood became dotted with ghost trees. Trees we'd enjoyed, purloined the fruits of, sniffed, admired, photographed. Trees chopped down as the central city's urban sprawl swallowed the old houses.

I missed the elegant plum tree on Featherston Street, which had sweet, small, purple fruit. The giant elder tree outside the BP station on Botanical Road. I could no longer pick its flowers for cordial, or its berries for winter elixirs. The bright dahlias along the side of the hairdressers on Chelwood Street, which had flowered brilliantly every late summer, were tar-sealed over and turned into car parks.

As I walk past all the ghost trees of Takaro, I say a small, sad hello to them in my mind.

Enchanting wildflower activities for kids

Wildflower ice blocks

Makes *6 to 8 ice blocks depending on mould size*

Begin by taking the kids foraging for some edible flowers in your garden or a nearby park. You don't need many – a small bowlful will do. They are for decoration only (you don't want big mouthfuls of petals as you eat the ice blocks).

Here's some commonly found edible flowers: borage (*Borago officinalis*), calendula, chamomile (*Matricaria chamomilla*), chrysanthemum, fuchsia, honeysuckle (*Lonicera* species), lavender (*Lavandula* species), marigold (*Tagetes* species), rose (*Rosa rubiginosa*) petals, violas and violets. Lavender has a strong flavour so use it sparingly. Don't use nasturtium flowers for sweet dishes like this – they have a strong peppery flavour.

Butterfly pea flower tea has a gentle, earthy flavour and is a lovely shade of blue. It turns purple when lemon juice is added. You can use it to create the bright colours that children like without synthetic food colouring. It might not be available in local shops, but many online tea specialists and health stores stock it. If you don't have butterfly pea flower tea, 1 tablespoon beetroot juice or the liquid from tinned beetroot can be used to give the ice blocks a lovely purple colour.

You'll need
½ cup butterfly pea flower tea
4 cups boiling water
1 small bowlful edible flowers
½ cup lemon cordial syrup
ice-block moulds
blueberries (optional)
fresh mint (optional)

Method
Put the butterfly pea flower tea and boiling water into a teapot. Allow to steep for about 20 minutes and then strain out the flowers and leave to cool.

Gently rinse the edible flowers. With dry hands, pull the petals off the larger flowers.

When the pea flower tea has cooled to tepid, pour it into a large glass jug and add the lemon cordial syrup. The blue tea should turn purple.

Sprinkle a variety of edible petals (a big pinch per capsule) into each ice-block mould. Add a few blueberries and a ripped-up mint leaf to each, if using.

Pour the cordial and tea mixture into the ice-block moulds. Freeze overnight. The ice blocks will be ready to eat the next day. (Make sure you let kids know they can eat the petals and mint.)

Smashed flower-print bookmarks

This activity could not be simpler and it's fun for preschool-aged kids right through to teenagers. (I still enjoy doing it myself.)

It's a good idea to have a range of different pounding objects on hand to experiment with, as different surfaces and weights can produce different results. I suggest a flat-edged hammer, a mallet or a heavy pestle to start with.

Set up the activity on a flat surface that can take some hammering – outside on a deck or outdoor table would work. If you're doing the activity with older kids you can do it inside at a dining table but, in my experience, younger kids usually bang pretty hard at first until they realise they don't need to use so much force.

Before starting, take the kids foraging for interesting plant materials, like flowers and leaves, in your nearest nature spot.

You'll need
> thick watercolour paper
> foraged plant materials
> waxed lunch-wrap paper or greaseproof paper
> a flat-edged hammer, a mallet or a heavy pestle
> a pair of tweezers (optional)
> fixative or white vinegar

a ruler
scissors
a hole punch (optional)
ribbon or yarn (optional)
oil pastels or crayons (optional)

Method

Lay down a sheet of watercolour paper on a flat surface.

Place the plant materials on top of the paper. You can arrange them into patterns if you like or sprinkle them at random. Flowers should be face down.

When you're happy with the arrangement, cover the whole sheet of watercolour paper with waxed paper. Gently hammer the plant material. You want to use enough force to make the natural pigments come out, but not so much that you destroy the watercolour paper. (Younger children may need some guidance!)

When you've hammered everything and can see that the colours have transferred, remove the wax paper.

Use your fingers or tweezers to lift the plant material off the watercolour paper.

If you'd like more colours, add some more plant materials and repeat the process.

When you're happy with the print, spray with fixative or white vinegar to fix the colours.

Choose some pretty parts of the print, and then cut out strips measuring 4 centimetres by 15 centimetres. If you like, you can use a hole punch to add a hole at one end and thread through a piece of ribbon or yarn.

Younger children might like to add extra drawings with oil pastels or crayons.

Cress-head creatures

I have done this project many times with the boys. It was a favourite during the school holidays when we were at home more often and could enjoy watching the progress of the tiny plants unfurling. The idea is that, as the cress grows, it looks like the hair of the cress-head creature.

You want to crack the eggshells near the top, so about two thirds of the eggshell is still intact. (It's a good idea to make omelettes for breakfast on the day of doing this project.)

If you don't have eggcups, you can sit the eggs in an egg carton with the lid cut off.

You'll need
    eggshells
    permanent markers
    cotton-wool balls
    cress seeds or any fine sprouting seed mix, like broccoli or alfalfa
    eggcups

Method
Gently rinse out the eggshells with water.

Ask the children to carefully draw faces on the eggshells with the permanent markers, above the level of the eggcup.

Dampen the cotton-wool balls in water and insert one into each eggshell.

Sprinkle 1 teaspoon of seeds on to each cotton ball.

Put the eggshells into the eggcups and then place them on a well-ventilated windowsill that gets natural light.

Leave, and enjoy observing for the next week! You may occasionally need to spray a bit of water on your creatures if they begin to dry out.

The seeds will show signs of sprouting after a couple of days. After about 4 days they will look like tiny plants. After around 6 or 7 days, they should be upright and bright green. You can cut them off with scissors and add them to the kids' lunches. We called this haircut day, and the boys enjoyed snipping the sprouts off their own cress-head creatures.

CHAPTER 16

Radical reciprocity

Apple, fennel and dock

Back home in Taranaki, Borthwicks was bought out by a large international company and gutted of its processing chain. Hundreds of people were laid off. It was a big shock for Waitara. The freezing works had been a central part of the town's culture and working life since 1885. After thirty-five years' labour, Dad was made redundant. He was thrown totally off course and floundered for months, trying to find his feet again.

Then, after a big effort, Mum achieved something no one thought was possible. She persuaded Dad to move out of Taranaki to start afresh somewhere new. Dad had always said that nothing would lever him out of Waitara, his beloved hometown, but he hadn't anticipated how the works' closure would decimate the life of the town. People were reeling.

Mum and Dad had always liked the tranquillity of Lake Taupō. They spent holidays there when they could. Dad loved trout fishing in the rivers and streams near the lake.

So my parents took a sea-change leap: they bought one of Taupō's oldest houses, near the town centre, and moved out of Taranaki. After Dad had a good rest and got used to this huge, unexpected change, his vitality slowly returned.

It was great to see him happy and excited about new terrain to explore. But when I visited them, it didn't feel like I was going *home* anymore, rather I was going to visit their new life. What did 'home' mean now?

*

I'd emerged from the years around Magnus's diagnosis feeling burnt out. One day I was listening to a podcast and the host read out a quotation by Brother David Steindl-Rast: 'Sometimes the cure for exhaustion is not rest, but wholeheartedness.'

Something about the idea resonated with me. The weariness I was feeling would take more than just rest to soothe and solve. I needed to apply my attention to something for myself, to reclaim parts of me that had been dimmed during the wolf-mother years.

I signed up for a local permaculture design course. I hoped it would be a way back into a feeling of community, to the sense of belonging I'd been pursuing since I left home at eighteen. The course was run by Slow Farm, a smallholding on the edge of Ashhurst, near the Pohangina River. Unlike many permaculture courses that cater to people who can travel to month-long intensive immersions, the Slow Farm course focused on teaching locals over a couple of years so the knowledge had time to sink in. The course was very grounded in place, and was designed to encourage relationship-building among the students, the teachers and the land of the Manawatū.

215

Slow Farm's owners and permaculture teachers, Sharon and Phil, had spent years doing community-resilience work in the valley. Sharon had a passion for social permaculture, which focused on connecting people to place and each other in mutually beneficial ways. Phil was a skilled farmer who lit up with pride when he showed us around their farm; he knew each tree and every bump in the land. They'd turned bare paddocks into orchards and edible gardens, and they had a large flock of free-ranging chickens and ducks. Sharon and Phil had a gentle, optimistic way of teaching that instilled a sense of possibility and confidence in their students. I was in awe of how measured and grounded their work was.

Permaculture is a philosophically informed design system that can be applied to any project; it's not merely a formula for self-sufficient gardening, as people often assume. The ideas I learned from the permaculture course gave me the courage to be even bolder with our yard in the city. I used the garden as a playground for applying permaculture theory. I planted a kind of controlled wildness and let it spill out further on the street to invite acts of urban foraging.

Sharon's teachings showed me that I had lived social permaculture and the 'circular economy' in my upbringing – it was like being back at university when I learned about green dollars. 'The circular economy' was more new terminology for the way I'd been raised, fresh language for old ideas.

Sharon set our class an assignment to record any time we were supported by the community, in tangible ways, like shared food, and less tangible ways, like childcare, skill-sharing or emotional support. I kept my record in a small notebook that I labelled *The Radical Reciprocity Project*. It lifted my banged-around spirits and began to restore my faith in people.

I remembered what I'd known before and forgotten for a while: radical reciprocity is a living force ... in nature and in community.

Radical reciprocity is non-transactional, circular rather than linear, unpredictable. It isn't about charity or philanthropy. It means sharing when you have enough to spare, giving with no expectation of return, and knowing that helping others flourish contributes to your own flourishing.

It captured how I'd always tried to live, through ideas learned along the way: childhood, punk culture, motherhood, permaculture, foraging.

With this revived inspiration from the Slow Farm course, all the forms of moneyless exchange around me took on a deeper meaning: the free clothing rack at the community arts centre, community fruit harvests, giving and taking books from 'little libraries' in local parks, gifting to seed libraries, using tool-share groups. Fraser and I would pitch in at 'permablitzes': backyard working bees where groups of friends showed up to work on a garden project for an afternoon in return for a feed at the end of the day. I helped set up a local monthly crop swap. Enchanted once more, I began to remember the radical reciprocity all around me.

Sharon asked, 'What if money is the least interesting way to be "paid"? What if "payment" comes in myriad tangible and intangible ways?'

This made so much sense to me. Through the years, I'd been paid in honey, vegetables, clothing repairs, soup, fallen fruit, bags of hand-me-down clothing. Paid in boxes of pantry leftovers when someone packed up their house and left town. Paid in handmade soap, in house-sitting opportunities when we couldn't afford holidays. Paid in seeds, in hugs, in art. Paid in having my good qualities reflected back to me from the people I loved.

Reflecting on this helped remind me of all the ways I was lucky – privileged, even. It helped me reach towards people after years of hunkering in a protective stance.

*

I tried to learn more of the details of the Manawatū's wild year. The calendar's dictation of when the seasons shifted, one into another, bore little relation to what I observed of the seasons on the land. The seasons were signalled by many small changes – in the quality of light, subtle clues from the foliage, fruits and blooms.

In the Manawatū, spring begins in mid-August and is long, continuing through to December. Summer is brief, autumn is settled and golden, and the winters are becoming warmer, with fewer frosts each year. The waning frosts mean that the behaviour of plants and soils that rely on the freezing cleanse of a hard frost is changing too.

In French culture there is a phenomena called *terroir*, which refers to the particular flavours and qualities of foods grown in a particular locale. I became an obsessive locavore, dedicated to sourcing as much of our food locally as I could. Eating wild foods from my local terroir extended my palette. I could eat bitter things, stringy things, plants with rough or furry textures.

*

One permaculture principle, 'capture and store', led me to step up my efforts to capture harvests. This often involved committed labour. Sometimes it was aesthetically pleasing and sensuous work – making raspberry jam, soaking in the sweet scent of elderflower cordial on the boil – and sometimes it was unglamorous and sweaty – pickling onions, slaughtering and butchering animals.

'Abundance' is such a pleasing word, something we all hope to cultivate. It brings to mind overflowing bowls and baskets, a bounteous burgeoning, a happy torrent. For people new to gardening or foraging or food gathering, an abundant harvest is the stuff of happy daydreams. Abundance sounds nicer than 'glut', which conjures 'gluttony' and conveys excess, too-much-ness, a problem.

But anyone who has stood in a kitchen for eight hours in the heat of summer, bottling plums or peaches or stirring large cauldron-like pans full of pickles or sauces, redolent with hot vinegar as sweat drips in rivulets down their back, soaking the third T-shirt they've put on that day, knows that abundance also means perseverance, responsibility and hard work. To capture the harvest is a commitment.

I enlisted our whole family in capturing the harvests. I'd set up a production line, giving everyone a task suitable for their age and ability. Willoughby had always been a willing kitchen helper, and as Magnus got older he became great at persisting with long tasks, particularly if they met his sensory-seeking needs in some way. If we had a large box of walnuts on the table, it was Magnus who would still be sitting there some hours later, cracking the walnuts with a small hammer, doggedly emptying the box long after the rest of us had wandered off.

Magnus loved food and was always obsessed with what his next meal would be, so planning the week's meals became a family event. We wrote the dinner plan on a large blackboard in the kitchen. We'd make and eat dinner together and then Magnus would cross it off on the blackboard as soon as he'd swallowed his last morsel.

Bringing the boys along to community food-sharing events felt like a way to give them experiences similar to those I'd had as a kid. One autumn, our local chapter of Community Fruit Harvest got a phone call from a farmer. He had a paddock full of buttercup pumpkins he couldn't use. There had been such an abundance in pumpkins that year that the price had dropped on the wholesale market to the extent that it was no longer worthwhile harvesting them to get them to market. Many farmers chose to plough or compost their crops rather than risk diluting the market by giving them away, but some growers chose to share the produce they couldn't sell with the community, inviting the old tradition of gleaning.

The pumpkin farmer told us we had one weekend to access the crop. After that he would have to plough them under to make space for the next planting. The call went out on the permaculture phone tree and a convoy out to the farm was organised. 'We're going pumpkin picking!' I said to the boys.

People of all ages came. By the end of the day, the local food-rescue van, the boots of family cars and even some trailers hired for the day were filled with mounds of shiny green buttercups. Seeing kids running around in bare feet holding pumpkins above their heads was an adorable sight.

We drove the pumpkins back to the city. Some went to the local food rescue, some to foodbanks, and the rest were shared among the families who'd volunteered their labour. A friend from the permaculture community, Emilie, drove slowly along the suburban streets yelling, 'FREE PUMPKINS!' out of the car window. Her children sat on the trailer, handing pumpkins to people off the back.

We were euphoric, both from the mammoth scale of the harvest and from the delight of sharing pumpkins with everyone we knew and many people we didn't. The simple pleasure of sharing radiated out for days. Magnus found a recipe for pumpkin pie on YouTube and I helped the boys make it. It grinned back at us with a pastry jack-o'-lantern face.

*

Richard Mabey calls foraged food 'inconvenience food'. Wild foods and homegrown foods are the ultimate in inconvenience foods. Every part of finding them or growing them is slow and laborious. So is processing them for eating. But what they lack in convenience they make up for in being rewarding and empowering.

An unexciting harvest can test the resolve of the thriftiest forager or gardener. People don't tend to get excited about leafy greens, nettles or bitter, stringy things the way they do the sexy excess of peaches or glowing heaps of plums. Foragers tend to have an appreciation for overlooked fruits. I've learned to appreciate things like japonica apples, nashi pears and rosehips. I make jellies, syrups and dried fruits from these muted stars.

It can all be quite a lot of work. I try to frame it as a commitment rather than a burden. There's mindfulness to be found in the slow, repetitive tasks of food preservation – shelling walnuts, pulling dried herbs off their stalks, separating tiny seeds from hulls and husks. I allow my mind first to settle, then to slowly roam the realm of rest. Many of these tasks are great for kids; they get to feel like they're helping the grown-ups while learning things along the way.

'Capturing the harvest' is work. But it's also a privilege denied to many who can't take time away from the hustle of their survival to wind down to a snail's pace – or to a nut-cracking, apple-peeling, seed-saving pace. Gentle tasks that can offer some respite from the hectic asks of the world.

*

On the first few visits to Mum and Dad in Taupō, it was disorientating seeing their familiar faces in a strange setting, my small-town dad living in a slick tourist centre. But they were settling in quickly. They'd begun volunteering at the local library, delivering books to housebound elderly people. Dad was teaching local children how to fish at the Tūrangi trout hatchery. Mum knitted and sewed for kids needing a hand-up. Dad fished every day and soon learned the ways of the new rivers and streams, making friends among the local fisherfolk as he went. And he was teaching local children how to fish at the Tūrangi trout hatchery.

At the new house, Dad's shed faced the street. He smoked his trout there and, once people learned he was a retired butcher, he began to butcher venison, wild pigs and hoggets for his new friends. Soon his shed was full of hanging dead creatures again, just as it had been back home, with people stopping in to chat to him while he worked.

One autumn when we were visiting, Mum mentioned that she'd seen a big walnut tree in a nearby playground. After lunch we all jumped in Dad's ute. While Willo and Magnus played on the swings, Mum, Dad and I stood in the autumn sun, chatting and collecting walnuts, throwing them into cardboard boxes. I could see that Mum and Dad were bedding in to the land and the local community, just as they had in Waitara. After gleaning those walnuts in the park, my disorientation settled. They were happy.

*

At permaculture class on Saturdays we shared long potluck lunches full of homegrown, home-preserved and foraged delights. They were jovially competitive. How many homegrown, foraged or locally sourced ingredients could we cram into our potluck dishes? No one takes local food more seriously than a bunch of permaculture nerds.

There were frittatas made from eggs laid that morning, 'weedy' pies full of foraged greens served with homemade labneh, jars of nasturtium capers, pickled burdock stems, dock and fennel seed crackers. Crusty sourdough loaves made from wild yeasts, venison meatballs from meat hunted in the nearby Ruahine Range served with a pungent sauce made from wild hawthorn berries, chocolates decorated with edible flowers. Every Saturday saw another array of locavore delights arranged on the table with great pride, followed by quizzing about provenance and requests for the recipes.

I loved spending whole days steeping in the company of people who shared my community-resilience aspirations, and getting some respite from the demands of the boys. My permaculture friends didn't know me as 'mother of Magnus, that hitting kid'; I was just Helen – herb nerd, permaculture student and passionate forager.

One autumn day, a young farmer, Duncan, brought in two large baskets of gleaming apples of four different heritage varieties – enough for everyone to take some home to taste. Everyone on the course was passionate about finding heritage fruit-tree varieties. In fact, people were passionate about everything, from land tending to global politics. A discussion before lunch on how best to use permaculture to mitigate climate change had got quite heated. Being aligned in values didn't mean that we always agreed on everything. Things had got a little tense, but at lunchtime we sat around munching on Duncan's apples.

That they were the sweetest, crispest and freshest of apples was something we could all agree on.

Dock and fennel seed crackers

Makes approximately 16 medium-sized crackers

These aromatic crackers are great with cheeses and dips, or just on their own.

Autumn is the time to harvest dock (*Rumex crispus*) seed and fennel (*Foeniculum vulgare*) seed. Both plants are usually abundant along waterways and other edgelands.

Curly dock seed is easy to harvest and, as a relative of buckwheat, it's gluten-free. The seeds can be ground whole with their chaff to save the fiddly work of winnowing the chaff off the seed. Dock seeds appear in late summer or early autumn. Harvest them on a fine day when the plant is very dry, brown and crinkly to the touch. Using secateurs or strong scissors, cut the stems low down on the plants, then strip the seeds off by running your fingers along the stem over a bowl. Sift the seeds through a colander to get rid of any bugs or detritus, and then grind them into flour using a spice grinder or food processor. Dock-seed flour can be kept for a couple of months in an airtight jar.

The liquorice flavour of fennel seeds acts as an instant mouth freshener and its pungent scent is uplifting. To collect wild fennel seeds takes a bit of vigilance because birds love them. Take a large paper bag and some scissors with you on your walk and look out for healthy-looking dry seedheads with large seeds. Cut off the seedheads and drop them into your bag. Once home, get a large bowl and remove the seeds from the seedhead with a swift rubbing motion. Remove any detritus from the seeds and store them in an airtight jar. If dried well, they'll last a couple of years.

For a gluten-free version of the recipe, use a gluten-free flour. For a dairy-free version, use 2 tablespoons of brewer's yeast instead of cheese.

Ingredients
   1 cup dock-seed flour
   1 cup strong flour
   ½ cup finely grated Tasty or Parmesan cheese

1 tablespoon fennel seeds
¼ cup of olive oil
warm water, for mixing
sea salt

Method

Sift the flours into a large bowl. Add the cheese and fennel seeds, then mix everything together. Rub in the oil, and then slowly add small amounts of warm water to form a firm dough.

Roll out the dough to about 5 millimetres thick, then sprinkle with sea salt. Cut the dough into rectangles and transfer to a well-oiled tray. Bake in a hot oven, 200 degrees Celsius, for 10–15 minutes, until brown and crispy. Keep an eye on them towards the end.

When the crackers have cooled, store them in an airtight container for up to 2 weeks. (If they go soft, they can usually be brought back to life by heating them in a low oven for 5–10 minutes.)

Apple-scrap vinegar

Makes approximately 1.5 litres

Apple-scrap vinegar is satisfying and simple to make; it just takes three ingredients, a dark cupboard and time. If you've never tried fermenting before, this vinegar is a great introduction to the wild world of natural fermentation. In true apple cider vinegar, the apples are made into cider first and then the cider is fermented. Apple-scrap vinegar skips the cider-making step. The results taste just as good, though.

You don't need to use foraged apples for this recipe – any apples (*Malus domestica*) will do – but it's a great way to use less-than-optimal foraged fruit. You can also make a batch just from apple peels and cores, so if you have a big session of apple-preserving or apple-pie-making, use the mountain of cores and peels to make another product. Use peels and cores, or scrappy apples chopped up roughly, or a mix.

You might have seen apple cider vinegar for sale in supermarkets and health shops with labels that say 'with the mother'. The 'mother' is the strands of protein that contain enzymes and beneficial bacteria that give the vinegar a cloudy appearance. Raw vinegar looks cloudy and may have sediment floating in it. Pasteurised apple cider vinegar is clear and doesn't have quite the same probiotic properties.

I have, for years, substituted apple-scrap vinegar in recipes requiring apple cider vinegar without observing any difference in flavour. Don't use apple-scrap vinegar for making preserves, however, unless you have a way of testing the acidity. Vinegars need an acetic acid level of 5 per cent to be safely used for preserving.

You can use white sugar or honey in this recipe. Honey is a little slower to ferment than sugar, though, so be prepared to wait a bit longer. Sugar is needed for the fermentation process to work.

Ingredients
   enough apple scraps to fill a 3-litre jar, rinsed
   white sugar or honey, 1 tablespoon per 1 cup water

filtered water (chlorinated water can interfere with fermentation)

Method

Fill a 3 litre glass jar or ceramic crock with apple scraps. (Don't use a metal vessel – vinegar corrodes metal.)

Make a sugar or honey solution, enough to fill the jar, at a ratio of 1 tablespoon of sugar or honey to 1 cup of water.

Pour the sugar solution over the apple scraps until they are totally covered.

Use a saucer, small glass jar or fermentation weight in the top of the jar to ensure the apples stay submerged. Cover the jar with a small cotton cloth held in place with a rubber band. Put the jar in the back of a dark cupboard for 4 to 6 weeks. (Check it occasionally to make sure all the apple scraps are still submerged.)

After this first fermentation, strain out the apple scraps (the strained fruit is great for composting or feeding to chickens), then pour the vinegar into a bottle and put it back in the cupboard for another month.

After the second fermentation, check the flavour. If it tastes like apple vinegar, it's ready to use and will keep in the fridge for a year. If the flavour isn't quite there yet, put it back in the cupboard for another few weeks.

Your vinegar may develop a rubbery blob floating in it; this is a mother. You can remove it, leave it in or put it in a small jar full of vinegar to add to your apple-scrap vinegar as a 'starter' next autumn. Having a bit of the mother will speed up the fermentation process.

CHAPTER 17

The butcher's daughter: four dead-bird stories

Free-range eggs

I seem to attract dead birds. In my favourite photograph of myself as a child, I'm about three years old and clutching a dead quail to my chest.

The family story goes that Dad had shot the quail while out duck hunting and laid it on our front porch while he plucked the ducks in the shed. I came out of the house, found it lying there, decided it was 'sleeping' and claimed it as my new pet. I would not be separated from it. I carried it around, talked to it and tucked it into bed beside me at night. Mum and Dad indulged me for a couple of days until the bird began to smell, when they liberated it from my clutches and buried it in the garden. In the morning, they told me it had 'flown out of the window' in the night. I was bereft.

*

There's a T-shirt slogan: 'It's not a hobby, it's an apocalyptic life skill.'

A joke, but it's sort of how I think about foraging and wild food. If I got lost, I would – hopefully – be able to fend off starvation for a few days. Lots of things I've chosen for pastimes could fall into the category of 'apocalyptic life skills'. They're ancestral skills. Skills like growing, seed-sowing and seed-saving, fermenting, preserving ... and learning how to butcher chickens.

Since joining the permaculture community through Slow Farm, I'd started getting invitations to some interesting gatherings: crop harvests, sourdough-baking lessons, seed-saving afternoons (we'd sit around with dried seedheads and paper bags, learning to do archaic-sounding things like *threshing* and *winnowing*), a scything-skills workshop, and mass rooster culls – a somewhat less quaint way to spend an afternoon. Always keen to learn more, I tried to go to as many skill-sharing sessions as possible.

Those with free-ranging chicken flocks invariably end up with an excess of roosters, and roosters don't lay eggs. They are also territorial and tend to start fighting among themselves once they mature, disrupting the peace of the flock. Once there are a few roosters around, it's time to rehome them or do a cull – a polite word for what is essentially a mass killing.

A rooster cull was an opportunity to learn or practise basic butchering skills with the added bonus of sharing in the meat from the day's labour. When I got my first rooster-cull invitation, though, I hesitated. Was I capable of it? I wasn't squeamish, but, while Dad had taught me knife skills and about different cuts of meat, I had never killed and butchered an animal myself from go to woah. It had been many years since that traumatic possum incident.

I would never be a skilled hunter or fisher like my father and brother, but I decided I wanted a tangible experience of butchering if I was going to eat meat and dedicate myself to local food. Besides, I wanted to earn my stripes as a butcher's daughter.

Fraser was keen to come with me. He'd started to get more interested in hunting and butchering. Dad and Roy had recently taken him on a hunting trip in Waikura in the eastern Bay of Plenty. They'd spent the last day of the trip butchering a deer back at base camp. Fraser had learned a lot.

The first rooster cull I attended was at Emilie's farm. Emilie, a friend from the permaculture community, had recently bought a piece of land in Tokomaru and was learning to tend it as she went. She had nine roosters to cull but said she'd be happy if we got at least six done that day. There were five adults – me and Fraser, Emilie, and Nic and Jacquie, two friends who lived nearby – plus all our kids. Nic and Jacquie had come along because they'd been offloading their own roosters to new homes and they wanted to learn how to turn them into dinner. Both of their partners had turned down the offer to join. Emilie scoffed. 'Women give birth. That means we know death.'

Fraser stared at the ground.

We all contemplated her statement in silence while she strode off to get her roll of lethally sharp butcher knives.

Nic said, 'Is anyone scared?'

Jacquie and I raised our hands. Fraser said, 'I'm not scared, but I'm not looking forward to the killing part either.'

That summed up what I knew from growing up around farmers in a hunting, butchering family. Nobody *enjoys* killing animals. It is usually done with gritted teeth, a solemn expression and held breath.

Our collective inexperience showed when it came to culling time. Emilie took us to a large round of wood that served as her kindling chopping block and handed Fraser a large, sharp axe. He was dubious. 'Shouldn't we hang them upside down beforehand so they can't run around afterwards?'

If you hold a chicken upside down it goes limp and compliant immediately.

'No need,' said Emilie. 'We'll just hang them upside down right away and let them bleed out for a while.'

We sent Willoughby, Magnus and Emilie's kids to do some rooster-catching and stood ready by the chopping block. Once the kids caught a rooster, Emilie and I held it down on the block and with a big *whack* Fraser beheaded the unfortunate creature. The rooster surged off the block and began to run around with blood spurting out of its neck.

Emilie and I ran after it. The children yelled, 'Zombie chicken! Zombie chicken!'

Eventually Emilie grabbed it, and I tied a thin rope around its feet and strung it up from a large nail on the side of Emilie's wood shed. It poured blood.

We'd botched the culling of the first rooster, but we did better with the subsequent ones – by hanging them up before their heads were cut off.

Emilie set up an efficient production line for plucking and gutting. The drained carcasses went into a large pot of boiling water to be scalded, then we plucked off the feathers while the carcass was warm from the hot water. The heat made the feathers come off more easily.

I was on the plucking station and was soon covered in

feathers and down. The wet feathers had a peculiar oily, inky smell and took some force to pull out – even after the scalding they didn't yield easily.

After plucking, the roosters were passed along for Emilie to gut. Gutting was messy and time-consuming – not a job for someone who didn't know their chicken anatomy.

It was absorbing, if macabre work. After a few hours, Emilie's mother appeared with a generous lunch that was, mercifully, vegetarian. The morning's activities had squashed any appetite for meat. I felt immersed in Tennyson's description of nature as 'red in tooth and claw' – only in this instance I'd been the predator. We gratefully ate the cheese-and-leek quiche on the lunch table.

By the end of the day, I'd reawakened some long-dormant memory of chicken plucking, Willoughby had invented an elaborate song about zombie chickens, and Nic had declared she was returning to vegetarianism.

That night I looked up the Ministry for Primary Industries guidelines on home-kill animal welfare, curious to see if there was anything to know for next time. It boiled down to one line: if you kill an animal, you are responsible for ensuring that it does not suffer 'unreasonable or unnecessary pain or distress'.

I tried to push the image of the frantic, running headless rooster out of my mind.

Emilie had sent us home with two rooster carcasses in a chilly bin. I put them in the freezer, but somehow they kept getting shuffled to the very bottom.

*

My second invitation to cull roosters came from Phil, my

permaculture teacher. Sharon had put a moratorium on helping with the farm's rooster culls, weary of it after many years of being a 'hen wife', so Phil had put the call out for volunteers. This time I was determined not to shy away from the viscera of gutting work like I had at Emilie's.

We started early. Fraser opted for a sleep-in rather than another Sunday spent killing roosters, so it was just Phil and me. I knew I was in for a long day, but Phil had his systems well organised. He'd done all the rooster-chasing the day before and isolated them in a holding pen overnight. We grabbed them out of the pen one by one. I held each one upside down while Phil tied its feet together and then hung it in a tree. The roosters quickly went limp and compliant. Once a rooster was still and calm, Phil would decapitate it in one quick motion with a pair of bolt cutters. Soon there was a gruesome, blood-stained confetti of twelve rooster heads scattered around our feet.

We were working hard, but it was fiddly work and there was a lot to do. When Sharon saw how slowly it was all going, she relented and came out of the house to help on the plucking station. We filled old stock-feed bags with the feathers, which Phil and Sharon would add to their giant compost heap.

With Phil's help, I had a go at gutting two roosters. He patiently talked me through the cuts I needed to make and how to pull the guts out of the bird's body. I learned a lot, but I was slow and tentative so after a while I handed the knife back to Phil. I felt like I was holding up progress on the production line.

Phil set me to carving out the roosters' crops and cutting apart the gizzards. The crop is a fleshy bag filled with whatever the chicken has been eating before it is digested by the gizzard, a tough and gristly muscle full of small stones that the bird swallows to become the grinders – 'teeth', essentially – of its digestive system. Slitting each crop gave me an archaeological cross-section of the chicken's grazing history over the last few days. The food was unchewed, a dense green plug of compacted grass and weeds, a few insects and pellets of chicken feed.

I'd make a slit in the gizzards and then turn each one inside out, causing the stones and grit to fall out. This exposed the white ribbed interior of the muscle. In nose-to-tail cultures, which eat every part of an animal, the gizzards are cleaned and made into stews. Liquid and slow-cooking will eventually make them tender. Phil offered me some gizzards to cook, but after spending so much time examining them I was not tempted.

A free-range rooster is nothing like the plump, hefty chickens at the supermarket. They are strong and lean. Their flesh is a different colour too: darker, with a range of greys, yellows and blues. Once plucked and dressed for the pot, the roosters looked scrawny, sinewy and not especially appetising.

Phil had offered to cook me a roast dinner at the end of our day's labours. As Sharon and I cleaned up the yard, he put a couple of roosters on to roast on a bed of onions, surrounded with pieces of red kuri pumpkin and potatoes. I washed up, spending a long time trying to scrub the death smell off my hands, and sat down at the table. I was ravenous after the physical and oddly emotional work. I knocked back most of a bottle of beer in one long, thirsty gulp.

Phil lifted one of the birds on to a wooden chopping board. It had gone a dark jaundiced yellow. Rebellious to the very end, the rooster refused to be carved. The roasting had tightened all of the small beast's sinews and muscles. Phil's knife failed to make an impact on the meat's tough surface. The rooster slid around the roasting dish, evading his blade.

'Mmm … rubber chicken,' I joked.

Phil snorted. 'A bit. Maybe I should go and get my hatchet?'

I filled my plate with roast veges and reached for a second beer.

I got home from the Slow Farm session smelly, tired and carrying another refrigerator bag full of skinny chicken carcasses. Fraser eyed them without excitement. 'We haven't eaten the ones from Emilie's yet.'

'This week. I'll cook them this week. I promise,' I said.

There was no point in learning to cull roosters if we weren't going to eat them. Over the week, I defrosted Emilie's roosters and slow-cooked them with Phil's in our electric crockpot with onions, celery and herbs. It made several litres of a rich, dense chicken stock. Eventually, the rubber chickens cooked down enough to yield up their stringy meat, which I then scraped off the bones with a fork, chopped up and made into a large casserole.

Fraser and the boys ate it without much enthusiasm – lacking sufficient appreciation for my farm-to-table labours, I thought.

*

A while after rooster-culling season, my friend Anthony texted me a photograph of a dead tūī he'd found while tramping in the nearby Ruahine Range.

Do you want this?

What made you think I'd want that? I texted back.

Do you?

Yes.

There you go. It's in my freezer. Come and get it next time you're over this way.

Most dead native birds are given to DOC, who give them to tangata whenua for cloak and jewellery making, but Anthony had tried DOC first and they hadn't wanted this one. Their freezer was full up.

I picked it up from Anthony's and brought it home. I showed Fraser.

'Very pretty. And what are you going to do with that?' he asked.

'I don't know yet.'

Even dead, the tūī was exquisite. Perfect, with no visible sign of injury. I'd thought of tūī as being black, but close up its wings were a wide range of greens, blues and iridescence. The fluffy white throat feathers had a kind of lacy scribble around them of finer white feathers.

'How did you die?' I ask its frosted body, closing my eyes to see if anything appeared in my mind. No images of violence came. 'Maybe old age?' I said to it.

It felt like such a gift. I wanted to honour it in some way.

I put it in a Ziploc bag in my freezer while I pondered its fate.

Several months later, one hot January day, we were defrosting our chest freezer when I found the tūī again. Fraser suggested it might be time to move it along. He is long-suffering of my eccentricities but not infinite-suffering.

'This is not going back into the freezer to haunt us for another year,' he said.

I dithered a little longer and then a memory of something that had happened earlier in the summer helped me make a decision.

I'd been at a summer solstice party on my friend Anne's farm. It was a colourful gathering; she had an interesting mix of friends from all walks of life. While I was standing outside at the potluck dinner table, a man looked intently at me. He looked to be in his sixties or so, had massive, earthy hands and was wearing a fringed leather vest.

He introduced himself. 'I'm Bear.'

'That's an unusual name,' I said.

'It's my shamanic name,' he replied, totally without irony.

I wondered if he was one of those self-appointed 'shaman' or if he'd been gifted the role by his community, in the way I understood shamanism to work.

He appraised me from underneath his felt hat. 'Are you from Taranaki by any chance?'

I was taken aback.

'Yes … ' I said tentatively. How did he know?

'Ha, I thought so. Y'see, Pākehā from Taranaki have a real heaviness around the neck, especially the throat. A loaded energy. It's an ancestral inheritance. A bit hard to explain. It's like, it is yours, but not yours *personally*.'

I thought of the land wars. It made sense to me that there might be a karmic load from such history. He waved the hand not holding a plate around his throat. 'You'll need to find some kind of throat practice to move it through so it doesn't get stuck and cause you problems.'

'A *throat practice*? What do you mean?' I was irritated by this unsought-for diagnosis but also intrigued. I put my hand on my throat in a searching way.

'Yeah, you have to move it through you. Find a way. Singing. Chanting. Screaming. Something.'

'Huh,' I said. 'What about writing?'

He shrugged, losing interest. 'Maybe. I guess it's a kind of speaking.'

He plopped a large spoonful of hummus on top of his salad and wandered back down the porch steps into the garden. I wanted to follow him and ask for more details, but it seemed like bothering a doctor at a party to help with a backache. I quashed the urge.

When things like this happen, I always have to negotiate the opposing voices inside me. The logical, analytical part is sceptical and will quickly squash the world's magic with overthinking. The part of me open to the ideas of signs, symbols and messages is delighted.

I decided to park the incident on a shelf at the back of my brain. Maybe it would be one of those things that made sense in time?

Looking down at the beautiful tūī and remembering the potluck shaman and his warning about throats, I took out a pair of eyebrow tweezers. I carefully plucked the tūī's white throat feathers, so evocative of its song. I put the feathers inside a copper locket and put it around my neck. It was the first talisman I'd worn around my neck since I'd taken off my hag stone. A tentative return to the world of incidental magic. The power of the tūī's throat could sit at my throat.

Taking the throat feathers felt like enough of a gesture to honour the gift of the tūī. I didn't feel the need to do anything more. I wrapped it in a green silk scarf and buried it deep at the back of my garden with a Pohangina River stone on top.

Maybe the throat feathers would help me express myself more clearly in my writing, or when I needed to find extra courage to advocate for Magnus? I was open to welcoming potential support in any form.

*

A while later, Dad came down to visit with a large box of food for us from Taupō: smoked trout, wild venison and, unusually, a wild turkey. A friend of his had shot the turkey on his land. The turkeys had been living in the bush edge, grazing his paddocks during the day, eating precious pasture. Dad had plucked and dressed the turkey for eating but had kept the bird's wings intact for me.

We sometimes laugh at turkeys for their wobbling red wattles and gobbling cry, but their wings are stunning – large and strong, with feathers in all shades of brown, white, grey and black. Dad and I stood on my porch admiring them, slowly opening and closing them like macabre fans. The architecture of the wing was magnificent. I wanted to keep them, but the spot where Dad had cut the wings off from the body was bloody and meaty.

'This part will go bad, won't it?' I said to Dad.

'Yeah it will. If you want to keep them, you'll have to salt-cure them,' he said. Over the years Dad had tinkered with leather crafts and had made many interesting adornments out of bones, feathers, leather and claws. His favourite leather hat had a cat's skull and a bound kārearea claw sewn to its front, both pieces he'd preserved from creatures he'd found in the bush.

He hung up the wings from the rafters of the porch. After he'd gone home, I watched some YouTube videos on how to salt-cure wings. It was a relatively simple process; it just, like many preserving chores, took a lot of time.

After a long soak in a strong salt brine, followed by a long time drying on the porch, the butchered edge went dark, dry and clean. It was leathery in texture. The feathers retained their glossy glory.

I propped the wings on a shelf in my study and used them to waft incense into the corners of the room before I sat down to write. I looked up the bird's spiritual meaning. I was moved to read that the turkey is the animal of the hearth, of motherhood, family, sharing, abundance and earth-tending, and, yes, thanksgiving and gratitude. That the turkey wings had been gifted to me by my father, to become part of my hearth-bound family life, felt just right.

Besides, through this latest dead-bird happenstance, I'd learned how to salt-cure bird wings – another apocalyptic life skill to add to my list.

Caro's black eggs

Makes 12 eggs

Rather than a rubber-chicken recipe, here's a delicious marinated-egg recipe from Caro, a friend from my permaculture community. Caro often brings this dish along to potlucks. It's a great potluck dish because it doesn't need reheating, it can be transported in a jar, and it feeds a lot of people.

The recipe is super flexible, so you can get creative and add extra flavours of your choosing – any of your favourites.

Ingredients
    12 free-range eggs
    ¾ cup water
    1 cup soy sauce
    2 tablespoons sugar
    a splash of vinegar (any except balsamic)
    flavourings of your choice, e.g. garlic, sweet chilli, star anise
        or black pepper

Method
Hard-boil the eggs and peel them. Set aside.

Add the water, soy sauce, sugar and vinegar to a small saucepan and bring to a gentle simmer over a low-medium heat. Simmer, stirring occasionally, until the sugar has dissolved. Take off the heat.

Add the peeled eggs to the marinade. Let them sit for around 5 minutes.

Shove the eggs into a 1 litre Agee jar (or similar). Pour the marinade over top. Add any extra flavourings.

Store in the fridge. Eat within 3 days. (The eggs will start to go rubbery after that.)

CHAPTER 18

Sometimes the plants find you

Plantain and rosemary

Āhuru had become the nest we needed. Magnus was beginning to do well at school with a teacher aide and the proper support to help him learn to communicate. He started to be able to speak and his echolalia eased. He became more settled and calm, and, by the time he turned seven, his hitting gradually stopped altogether. The relief I felt about the end of the hitting took years to ripple through me.

Once Magnus was starting to do better, I found the capacity to work on my writing again. Around that time there was a New Zealand arts podcast I listened to. The host had a habit of saying to women artists and mothers something along the lines of: 'So you released that album/book/film, and it did pretty well, but then you kind of *disappeared*.' Every time he said it, it made me a little angrier. The absent woman artist. Where *did* she go?

She didn't go anywhere. She was the axis of her family, holding down the fort, compromising her career to care, with the foresight to know she couldn't be at the centre for a while and that was okay; there were larger webs being woven. The absent woman artist is never absent from her own life. She's the strong connective tissue of her family, her community. If you were to ask them where she was, they'd say she's right there, looming large and glowing brightly.

I thought back to how, when I'd left England, I'd planned to publish a book before I was thirty. Twelve years of road bumps and curve balls later, my first book, a volume of poetry, *The Comforter,* was published just as I turned forty.

At the book's launch, I made a giant bowl of pink punch and floated borage and calendula from my garden in it. I made a dip from Dad's smoked fish, served on the permaculture-course crackers, and a huge carrot cake covered in foraged flowers. The launch party felt less about the book and more a celebration of putting myself back together after the shattering I'd experienced through my thirties. I felt at peace. Publishing the book settled the tight yearning I'd been carrying since my twenties.

*

I'd turned our small yard into an oasis of biodiversity in a street where most gardens were tightly controlled and nature was more fought against than flowed with. Our garden was wild, haphazard and random; I loved it. It wasn't a park-like effort, with organised flower beds and an abundant vegetable bed neat enough to make an old-fashioned grandad proud. All gardens are just attempts to rein in nature. We hang on tight in the face of nature's rampant forward-galloping but our hold on the reins is always tenuous. Whenever I felt like I'd been neglecting the garden, it would laugh at my fretting and say to me, 'Look at me. I'm doing just fine. Take a breath. Don't bother tidying me up, don't weed, don't worry.'

I foraged from my own yard: chickweed, bittercress, violet flowers, nasturtiums, plantain, fat hen, red clover, mallow. These plants regenerated year after year without any interference from me. I also had tradescantia, oxalis and convolvulus – less welcome 'volunteers', although, as Madz had taught me all those years before, oxalis leaves were edible.

I tried to let one plant in each vegetable crop go to seed. Partly so the plant could have a chance at self-regenerating and partly so I could observe what it looked like through all of its life stages. Some plants were astonishing at their full expression: alliums, like leeks and onions, grew tall sculptural spindles with Hundertwasser-like turrets on top that eventually exploded into large purple pom-poms. Parsley seedheads looked similar to those of their wild cousin, Queen Anne's lace. Lettuces grew into tall towers with frilly and brilliant blue flowers.

Ours was a small patch of earth, and not really 'ours' but somewhere for us to be custodians as long we lived there – with 'all our relations', as some Indigenous American cultures say of the more-than-human world.

Mum always calls my yard 'your weedy garden'. We have differing views on weeds. Her weedy is my wild. I don't see a mess; I see joyous, romping life.

*

Another permaculture principle is 'observe and interact'. As my plant vocabulary increased, my interest in wild medicines and folk herbalism grew, too – a bit of urban hedgewitchery. On my walks along the Manawatū River, plants with more medicinal than edible uses began to step forward. I found yarrow growing in abundance, angelica, nettles, red clover and shepherd's purse, all herbs that are great for women's health in particular. I started making more folk medicines – elixirs, tinctures, oxymels and herbal oils.

When I was out on a gentle walk with a friend while I was recovering from a bout of pneumonia, she pointed out mullein to me. It's such a distinctive plant, tall and silvery with furry leaves, that I couldn't believe I'd never noticed it before. It's known as the candlestick plant because its long, strong central stem with a yellow flower resembles a burning candle, and also because it was once used as a candle – dipped in beeswax, its slow-burning stem a natural wick.

My friend pointed it out to me because it's a plant that opens up the lungs. A strong respiratory tonic, it can help to ease coughs. I harvested a bag of the young leaves, and when I got home I brewed a strong tea with it. The tea did ease my laboured breathing.

Learning to make medicines for my family was empowering. I'd always suffered from bad periods, but now I could chew on yarrow leaves and drop a shepherd's purse tincture down my throat to help with the pain. I took drops I'd brewed from foraged chamomile, lemon balm and catmint to help me sleep. As we headed into winter, I'd make my family take spoonfuls of fire cider – a spicy brew of garlic, herbs and spices steeped in apple cider vinegar. It boosted our immunity to help fend off winter colds.

I made tea blends from foraging walks and the garden as seasonal snapshots, dictated by what was blooming at the time of harvesting. I dried the plants and then noted the season on the label. 'High summer: yarrow, lemon balm, verbena, mint, nettle.'

When I foraged while I travelled, I'd note the provenance on the tea's label. 'Raglan kawakawa tea.' It was a way of bringing a little of the place I'd visited back home and also an experiment in terroir. Was Raglan kawakawa different from Manawatū kawakawa? Yes, a little bit. The leaves were much larger and the tea seemed more peppery. It could be a bit frustrating if a brew was particularly delicious, as it would never be exactly replicated, but there was something of this ephemerality that I enjoyed, a reminder to be here now.

Folk herbalists recommend close, consistent exposure to the plants you're trying to learn from. They advise wearing the plants – in pockets, around your neck, in your hair. As adornment, the plant becomes a companion – to sniff, to hold, to gaze at and to be with. Just as we like to be with people we're befriending. I took to this idea and soon most of my pockets were full of drying plant bits. Interacting with plants in this way – befriending, foraging, making medicines – heightened a kind of sense memory in me, old ways for urgent days.

Wild 'weeds' and herbs have been so long overlooked, disregarded or forgotten. What does it say about humans that these medicinal, highly nutritious plants, once so prized by our ancestors, are now so diminished and regarded as pernicious pests? In the humblest of places, invisible to all but the curious, the wild weeds are beacons … trying to catch our attention and call us back.

*

As I learned more about the medicinal properties of the plants I was foraging, I grew more courageous about sharing my knowledge. One day, I was out in a favourite foraging spot looking for dock seeds for my permaculture crackers. I couldn't see any dock. I wandered off the main path, turned to my left and saw a thin desire line. The fennel growing either side was over eight feet high and the bright yellow seedheads were leaning to touch and intermingle, forming a natural arch of verdant green topped with gold – a tunnel of fennel. *Fennel tunnel, fennel tunnel.* The incidental poetry pleased me and I repeated the phrase to myself as I followed the desire line. The fennel smelled like sun-warmed liquorice.

I popped out of the tunnel and saw in front of me a bright patch of plantain. Plantain usually grows fairly low to the ground, a consequence of being frequently mowed, but this patch was tall, vital and thriving. I kneeled down beside the patch, admiring how thick and healthy the plants were. I took out my scissors and delved into the centre of the plant to harvest a big handful of the largest, healthiest-looking leaves. I picked one of the long stalks from the plant and used it to tie up the fat bundle. Plantain is a skin-soothing and skin-healing plant. I'd make a salve with it, given it had announced itself to me with such vigour. I tucked the bundle into my bag and carried on.

I headed back to the main river path and saw a young woman calling to her child, straggling behind her. 'C'mon! If you hurry up we can go and get some food!'

Her wee boy was barefoot and looked hot and hōhā. He ran towards her across the thick grass dotted with white clover. Then he fell to the ground, grabbed his foot and let out a wail.

'Oh no! Did you get a bee sting?' the mother called. She ran towards him. He was crying and holding his foot.

'It's okay. Let me look,' said his mum. She spat on his grubby foot to try to clear a space through the grime to look.

It was an intimate scene. I'd been in the same position many times with my own boys, caught short somewhere by some random occurrence with a distressed child, feeling ill-equipped to deal with it. I believe in the 'village to raise a child' idea but I know not everyone else does; sometimes an offer of help can be met with suspicion. But I was also aware that just a few minutes earlier, plantain had appeared to me, seemingly out of nowhere.

The boy was wailing. I wrestled with whether or not to offer help and then I thought, *It's not about you, Helen. Honour the plants.*

I pulled some plantain leaves out of the bundle in my bag and walked carefully up to the pair. 'Hey, do you mind if I try to help?'

The mother looked at me. She was tired and anxious but she didn't refuse. I knew I was probably going to seem like a nutter but, given she hadn't told me to go away, I gave my attention to the little boy.

'Do you see these leaves? They are a kind of medicine that can help your bee sting. Can I put some of the leaves on your sore foot?' He stopped wailing and gave me a tentative nod. With one hand, I vigorously rubbed some plantain leaves, trying to get some of the juices out. With the other, I handed the mum a few leaves. I said to her, 'It will work best if it's chewed up, but you probably don't want some stranger's spit on your son. How do you feel about trying it?'

'Are you sure?' she said.

To prove she wouldn't die, I put a leaf in my own mouth and started chewing. Reassured, she mirrored me.

The sting was red and swollen but not too bad. I dabbed the little plantain juice I'd managed to squeeze out of the leaves gently on to the sting. The boy yanked his foot back and started to cry again.

'Hey! The lady is only trying to help you!' the mother said.

'It's okay. It's all a bit scary, eh?' I said to him, then to her, 'When you can feel the leaves are broken down, spit it into your hand and put it on the sting and hold it there as long as you can.'

She gingerly spat the green mush into her palm.

'Give me your foot, baby, I'm going to put the medicine on,' she said to the child.

He rested his foot on her thigh and she held the green wad on to the sting. The boy was still whimpering but after a while his grizzling subsided. He became less worried about his foot and more curious about me. The plantain seemed to be doing it's soothing work.

I got up from where I'd been kneeling beside them. The urgency had passed and now I felt awkward, intrusive. I wasn't quite sure what to say.

'Best of luck. Hope it feels much better soon.' I walked away, cheeks burning.

The mother called after me, 'Thank you! Thank you so much!' She pulled the boy into her lap and sat rocking him while pressing the poultice on to his foot.

I exhaled. She'd said thanks. Maybe it had been an okay thing to do?

I put my hand on the plantain bundle in my bag and said to the plant, 'Thank you. *How* did you know?'

Hedgewitch herb bundle

Makes 1 cleansing stick

Go into any crystal shop or New Age store and you'll probably find an imported 'smudge stick' made from dried white sage, most likely harvested from a desert plain in New Mexico or some other desert terrain of the US. Smudging is a unique spiritual practice belonging to some tribes within the Indigenous American peoples, a ceremonial practice unique to culture and place, and ought to be respected as such.

Many cultures around the world use herbs for 'smoke cleansing' in their dwellings or during rituals. In European cultures, herbs used for smoke cleansing include yarrow, sage, lavender, rosemary, rose and mullein.

Rosemary is one of my favourite incense herbs and is used a lot in urban landscaping (city councils seem to adore it), making it an easy one to forage. The oils in rosemary assist with mental clarity, giving rosemary its reputation as the herb of remembrance.

European superstition says a rosemary plant near the entrance door of your house will ensure that anyone who visits remembers you fondly, and UK folklore has it that 'Where rosemary grows / the mistress is the master' – good motivation to encourage rosemary plants to thrive!

Don't use a fibre with any synthetic or plastic in it to tie your herb bundle. You will be burning the string and you don't want to inhale the burning plastic – it could potentially be carcinogenic. Instead, use a natural fibre like cotton, linen, wool or harakeke.

Ingredients

locally sourced herbs, any combination of yarrow, rose petals, lavender, mullein, sage, rosemary, lemon balm and fig leaves

a thin string or cord made from a natural fibre

Method

Give all the herbs a very quick rinse and shake to get rid of any dust and insects. Allow to thoroughly air dry in a patch of sun until there is no moisture from the rinsing process visible on the plants (this should take an hour or two).

Cut the plants into lengths of about 20 centimetres. If you're using rose petals, you will be able to tuck these in at the wrapping stage.

Assemble your herbs into a tight 'wand' shape.

Tie the herbs tightly with a strong knot at regular intervals along the bundle. It's important to take your time with the tying. When you burn your bundle, you will be burning through the string or cord also, so regular knots are vital. Tie a tight knot at the top, then wind down the bundle a few centimetres and tie another tight knot. Continue this all the way down the bundle. Hold the bundle together firmly and tie the knots as tightly as possible, so that once the herbs have dried the bundle will remain dense and tight enough to burn continuously. (Note the herbs will shrink as they dry.) Tying the bundle this way also means that you will be able to snuff out your wand once you've had enough of the smoke and reignite it later.

If you're using rose petals or other flower petals, tuck them around the outer layer as you wrap the string around your bundle.

Once you're satisfied you've tied your bundle as tightly as you can, put it on a wicker tray or a metal tray with holes in the bottom. Leave in an airy, sunny, warm spot to dry. Because the herbs are so densely packed, it will take some months for them to dry adequately. Keep checking until they sound crispy and crackly when you squeeze them.

To use a herb bundle, set a match to one end until the herbs catch alight, then blow out the flame. Blow on the glowing ember, and then waft the herbal smoke wherever you'd like to cleanse, perhaps around your body or around the corners and edges of your home.

CHAPTER 19

Springtime can kill you

Comfrey

Parenting a child with special needs puts a huge strain on a couple. Around sixty per cent of couples who have a child with special needs break up.

Fraser and I were plodding along okay, but in my quest to put my heart back together as I emerged from the isolated years, I had thrown myself into community-facing activities, permaculture, urban foraging and community-resiliance projects. I was also frantically trying to write a second book. After work, kids and my various projects there wasn't much left for tending to our relationship. We were steady enough but perhaps not thriving.

Despite being a gardener, I don't like spring much. There's a Jolie Holland song called 'Springtime Can Kill You', and I get it. Spring flowers are cheerful and the gradual lengthening of the days is welcome, but there's a vulnerability to the season that I feel right to my bones. It's a capricious, trickster season.

In the spring of 2016, I nearly lost Fraser.

I'd been absent from the family for a few weekends, away at permaculture Saturdays and locked in my study finishing my book, so I told Fraser to take a weekend for himself, to have some time to refresh. He decided to go into the Ruahine Range for the night.

It was Fraser's first trip out with his new gun. He'd recently bought a rifle for hunting. Obtaining a rifle in New Zealand is quite a process. Before you can buy the gun you have to get a gun licence and a gun safe, and pass an interview with a gun-licensing officer. They come to your home, check the safe and interview your family.

The officer was an older man, with a long grey ponytail and nicotine-stained fingers. He looked more like an ageing country and western musician than a police official. He was kind, although he told me several times to relax, which had the effect of making me more tense. It was an odd experience sitting across from this stranger, answering intimate questions about Fraser's habits, intentions and mental wellbeing. It wasn't until this interview that the gravity of having a gun in the house truly dawned on me.

Fraser had always been a keen tramper, but he'd become interested in extending the purpose of his walks from leisure to food-sourcing. Like my father, Fraser was motivated by the chance to find food for our family. But he hadn't grown up hunting.

I had mixed feelings about having a gun in the house but couldn't think of a rational reason, apart from some fear, to object. If anything, it made sense as a next step for us greenie locavores. It was just another version of what I got up to in the wilds but hunting beasts rather than plants.

One factor fuelling my unease, however, was that Fraser preferred to tramp alone. I couldn't go because one of us had to look after the kids, but he liked a chance to get away from people. He's not blokey and can feel a bit uncomfortable around the machismo of stereotypical hunters.

While tramping alone has some risks, hunting alone has more. Along with the obvious personal safety risks of carrying a gun, there are practical issues too. It's no small thing to carry huge sides of venison out of the bush alone.

I was a little anxious about this first hunt, and I did a bad job of hiding my anxieties.

Fraser brushed aside my concerns. What else could he do? He was a little nervous, too. Carrying a gun adds a bigger load to a walk in the bush, literally and metaphorically.

When Fraser tramps, he always leaves me a plan of his route. This is tramping common sense, but it can seem a little less vital since the advent of smartphones. Since having a smartphone, Fraser would send me cheerful texts and photographs of where he'd got to as he weaved in and out of range. Sometimes he'd record snippets of bird song and send those.

He likes to travel light and he hadn't packed enough food in the past. I quizzed him about his rations and he assured me he had plenty, in our usual delicate dance between my concerns and his autonomy. I wanted to nosy in his pack to see for myself but I squashed the urge.

The forecast was for cold weather but, for Fraser, this just added to the attraction. He's a man who likes being in a storm. The happiest I've ever seen him was in squalling winds or snowstorms. He often cackles in delight when reading that extreme weather is headed our way.

I put the note with his planned route on the table and waved him off.

I had a couple of texts from him that night. They were happy, casual. The rain was heavy but he was having fun. He hadn't spotted any deer sign yet. I waited for the usual goodnight text. It didn't come but I wasn't too worried. I figured it was his downtime and I shouldn't expect him to be texting me every ten minutes. Maybe he was chasing a deer through the dark?

*

The next day I kept glancing at my phone in anticipation of a good-morning text from Fraser. None came. I made myself a coffee, feeling his absence; he usually brought me coffee in bed. I sat with a book in my lap, trying to enjoy it, but tendrils of concern crept into my mind. Rather than indulging these thoughts, I got up and had breakfast with the boys, filled the washing machine. Kept busy.

He'd said he'd be walking back out after breakfast and should be home just after noon. As the morning wore on, grindingly slow, tendrils turned into brambles of worry. My texts to him increased in urgency. Nothing came back. I stopped hearing the boys when they spoke to me. They had to tug my arm to get a response. I decided to wait until 1 pm and then I would call the police, figuring they probably wouldn't accept he was missing if he wasn't even technically late, despite his lack of phone contact.

One pm came. Still no replies from Fraser to my barrage of texts. I steeled myself and rang the police, ready to persuade them that it was very out of character for him to be out of contact, to not meet the terms of his going. But I didn't need to persuade them. They immediately took it seriously. That he was carrying a firearm seemed to add to the gravity.

The policeman spoke to me very gently and slowly, as if talking to a lost child. He was firm that I shouldn't rush to the track. The best place for me was home, he said, looking after the boys. He told me Search and Rescue would be on the track to look for Fraser within a few hours.

A few hours seemed a good response time, especially considering Search and Rescue is made up of volunteers, but because it was Fraser who was missing, a few hours of more waiting was a unique torture.

While I waited, I called a friend who lived in the Pohangina Valley, on the same road Fraser had driven up to access the ranges. She drove up to the car park to check that our car was still there. It was. There was no sign of him around the car. She walked a little way up the track but it was very cold and raining heavily, so she turned back. I rang Search and Rescue with this update.

The man asked me if I could email him a recent photograph of Fraser. I could barely stand to think about what this might mean. It was hard to find a photograph of him by himself. Most of the recent photographs were selfies of the two of us grinning into the camera, our heads pressed together, on beaches or bush walks. Eventually I found one.

My panic grew by the hour. I knew I had to allow my worst thoughts in so I could try to be present to what was happening. I went to the thing I was trying hardest to push away, *What if he's dead?*, and worked backwards from there.

If he *was* dead, I reasoned, trying to breathe, I would still be alive. I would still be here for our children. It would be unfathomably awful. I would grieve and suffer but live on. Life as I knew it would stop, but life would not stop.

The very fact of life's ongoingness gave me a tiny chink of comfort. *You can survive this*, I told myself. *Even if he is dead, you can carry on.*

My mind seemed to detach from my body, expanding out to the past, future and awful present all at once. We fool ourselves into thinking the people we love won't die because we love them, as if love is a protective veil. The possibility of Fraser's death clattered around my skull like a marble, making my head ache.

Time took on a fractured, grainy quality. I cooked food for the children, but at one stage I put onions on to sauté and then suddenly the room was full of dark smoke and the fire alarm was going off. I had completely zoned out, my mind on repeat. *What if he's dead what if he's dead what if he's dead?*

I called a friend, Miribai, who lived nearby and asked her to come and sit with me. I was finding it hard to stay calm for the boys and thought it would help if I had another adult around. I held off calling our parents. I figured they didn't need the stress and anxiety until there was something substantial to tell them. He might be found soon and *then* I could call them.

I called our old friend Maria. She was steady and calm, helpful. 'Look, Helen, Fraser is the most sensible person I know,' she said. 'They will find him.' Hearing her voice helped ground me a little.

After years of looking for things, in the wilds, at the edges, this heralded the most urgent search of my life.

*

When you've been together for over twenty years, you get comfortable. Comfort was a priority in my life. I worked to make my home feel comfortable, safe, warm – the nest of its name. Winter evenings at our house were often candle-lit, quiet, cosy, punctuated by hot dishes from the oven and warm drinks. We were comfortable. We took comfort in each other when the outside world got too much.

Comfort can lead to complacency, however. Marrying so young, we'd grown up together. Fraser felt like an extension of me, one who would surely always be there. There had been long stretches of time when, with everything we were holding and juggling, it was too easy to stop really *seeing* each other.

The mystic poet Rumi says, 'Don't go back to sleep.' It's an imperative to stay conscious and alert to all the gifts of your life. People call their shocks and traumas wake-up calls. Fraser going missing woke me up like a bucket of ice water being poured over my head. In the window of his potential absence, I felt how huge his presence was in my life, and how bereft I'd be without it.

Search and Rescue called to report that one of their volunteers had been in the area earlier that day and said that, with the sudden rain dump during the night, many of the streams and rivers in the valley had risen considerably. They might struggle to make some of the crossings in the terrain of the search area.

I thought about Fraser losing his wedding ring in the Pohangina River, how I'd joked that he was married to the river. This long-standing joke soured on me. I closed my eyes and brought the river to mind. 'You can't have him. He's mine,' I pleaded with it. 'You give him back to me.'

I paced the living room. I couldn't stop myself firing off texts to him.

Are you okay?

Where are you? Please reply asap.

Bargaining is a stage of grief. It's also a big part of worry. I tried to hold the possibility of Fraser's death in one hand, and with the other hand I made desperate offerings. *If he is okay, I will be a better person. A better partner. I will try harder. I will be so, so grateful every single day. I won't ever forget how lucky I am.*

I curled into a knot under a blanket on the sofa, clutching my phone. Miribai had turned on the TV as a distraction from the weight of our waiting. I stared at the screen, taking nothing in. Staying at home made sense but was also maddening. I wanted to drive to the track right away so that, whatever happened next, I would be close to him.

*

When he was six, Willoughby went through a phase where he liked to add 'of doom' to things for fun, to make them sound ominous. Cake *of doom*. Pillow *of doom*. It was uncanny and cute coming from a small child. This came back to me as we waited. Household objects were attracting doom as my eyes rested on them. Teacups of doom. The pyjamas Fraser had taken off on Friday morning, coiled under his pillow … doom. Phone of doom. Death was suddenly not just an abstraction to contemplate; it was in dark proximity and filling my house.

Then my phone dinged.

comfortable

I replied immediately. *What do you mean comfortable? Are you okay? Where are you?*

But nothing came back. That was it: *comfortable*

He was alive! But *comfortable*? What could that mean?

I sat and stared at that one word on the phone's screen until it burned into my brain. I rang Search and Rescue with the update.

*

An hour after the inscrutable *comfortable* text, Search and Rescue called to say they'd found him. He was okay, wet and cold but not hypothermic, and he had a broken ankle. He'd need to be helicoptered out.

Just like that, death retreated. He was alive. Exhausted, in pain, hungry ... but *alive*. His glasses, first-aid kit and food had washed downriver when he'd broken his ankle crossing a stream and fallen in. It'd happened on Friday night. He'd managed to pull himself to the bank and burrow into his sleeping bag under a tarp. He was out of phone range (apart from that stray, contextless *comfortable* – one of a string of texts he'd sent to me but the only one that had arrived) and he didn't have a personal locator beacon.

Because the rain had been so relentless, the river had kept rising and Fraser kept having to drag his camp higher above the water through the night. His gear was coated in mud. He hadn't slept at all, in pain and vigilant about the rising waters.

I felt guilty that he'd hurt himself fairly early on the Friday night. I hadn't called for help until lunchtime on Saturday.

The helicopter was needed for a more urgent rescue, so the rescue team had to half-carry him out, his arms slung around the shoulders of two of the younger men, his good leg hopping.

Soon, Search and Rescue called to tell me that they were on their way home with him so that I could take him to A & E. I was grateful Miribai was there to stay with our boys.

Half an hour later a car pulled up. There he was on the back seat, shivering, wet and ashen.

I dumped his filthy pack in the laundry then ran inside and gave the gun to Miribai. It was covered in mud. I didn't have time to linger to put it away.

'Can you give this a wipe and put it somewhere safe out of reach?' I said as I ran back out the door towards a long night in A & E. A vegetarian and life-long pacifist, she sat on the living-room floor blinking in shock at finding herself suddenly holding a rifle.

*

He was okay. Had my bargaining paid off? His return felt like a miracle because for a whole day he could have been dead. Schrödinger's cat.

Afterwards, when the accident came up in conversation, Fraser was at pains to point out he hadn't been lost. He had just been *stuck*. He knew exactly where he was.

His ankle was badly broken and needed metal plates. He spent a week in hospital, but over the spring and summer he healed.

Fraser is a keen cyclist and has always biked to work in all weathers. Over the months he was recovering, I noticed how much I missed the sound of his bike leaving in the morning, returning in the afternoon, its tinny rattle. The sound of it had bookended my days for years, since I'd been at home with children. If I was standing in the garden when he got home, he always startled me, flying up the driveway on his bike, quick as a flash. It's the sort of little, particular thing there's no predicting you might miss until it's gone. One of a string of small rituals that become part of life's daily rhythm. Once he was back on his bicycle, a natural order was restored.

Things were different between us after his accident. Nearly losing him to the river put him back front and middle of my life, and it reversed the drift of overwhelm that many parents of children with special needs fall prey to.

Not dramatically different, just more tender, as though the day I thought he might have died now dwells between us, the glimpse of death's door a third entity in our relationship.

Wild first aid

Here's a brief list of some 'wild first aid': common plants that can help in emergency situations. They're useful to know for times you find yourself away from home without access to your usual first-aid kit, like when you're tramping or travelling.

I've only included plants commonly found in New Zealand that are relatively easy to identify, but of course there are hundreds more medicinal plants. Once you begin learning the medicinal properties of plants, it can easily turn into a lifelong quest.

I've left some medicinal superstars off the list because they are easily confused with other plants, such as yarrow, which looks very similar to the highly poisonous hemlock to the uninitiated.

Chamomiles (*Matricaria recutita, Matricaria discoidea* and *Chamaemelum nobile*): as a tea, can act as an antihistamine for seasonal allergies and hay fever; apply crushed flowers topically to mosquito bites.

Chickweed (*Stellaria media*): apply topically to soothe eczema, heat rash and sunburn; can draw out prickles.

Common lawn daisy (*Bellis perennis*): the bruised leaves can be applied topically to staunch bleeding and prevent swelling of bruises and sprains.

Dandelion (*Taraxacum officinale*): the white juice from the stalk is said to cure warts if applied daily for a few weeks; drink as a bitters tonic to assist with headache, mild cystitis and liver function.

Dock (*Rumex obtusifolius* and *Rumex crispus*): apply the leaves topically to treat abrasions and bruises; can also help staunch bleeding.

Eucalyptus leaves: use topically as a poultice for wounds and inflammation; can be brewed as a tea to help a sore throat or mouth infection, like dental pain or mouth ulcers.

Feverfew (*Tanacetum parthenium*): apply topically to soothe insect bites; eating some feverfew leaves can help with migraines.

Kawakawa (*Piper excelsum*): as a tea, can assist with upset stomachs, coughs and colds; apply topically to wounds, abrasions and nettle stings.

Mullein (*Verbascum thapsus*): as a tea, can help with coughs; a tea made from the flowers can help bring on sleep.

Nasturtium (*Tropaeolum majus*): as a tea, can boost circulation (if someone is on the edge of exposure, for example); can assist with mild cystitis; can help soothe colds and coughs.

Pine (*Pinus*) tip tea: strengthens digestion and can help stomach upsets; can help recovery from colds and flus; can help soothe mild cases of cystitis; can soothe headaches and toothaches; can cleanse the mouth if you forgot your toothbrush and toothpaste!

Plantain (*Plantago major*): chew the leaves to make a topical poultice for bruises, bites, grazes and stings.

Red clover (*Trifolium pratense*) flower tea: can help headaches; can help asthma and bronchial issues; can relieve heavy periods.

St John's wort (*Hypericum perforatum*): apply topically for nerve pain; as a tea, can be a mild sedative (useful while travelling, for example); as a tea, can be a mood booster.

Willow (*Salix*): willow bark can act as an aspirin replacement; willow-bark tea can help treat diarrhoea; also good for sore throats and mouth infections.

CHAPTER 20

Drink your bitters

Nettle and elder

Not long after Fraser's tramping accident, I published my second book, *Write to the Centre*, about the practice of journalling. My journal had been my constant companion through the previous twenty-five years. I wanted to share the potential of the practice with other people. By keeping a journal, I'd found a way to keep my creativity alive; it turned out that whole books could be written in distracted ten-minute bursts.

By the time Magnus reached high school, the traces of his gremlin years had faded away. He had learned to speak, write, read – all things I hadn't known if he would ever be able to achieve. He developed a passion for cooking. Our habit of including the boys in meal times – in food-finding, food-growing and cooking – had paid off. Now a teenager, he had confident knife skills and could cook independently.

I still dragged the boys out for nature walks, although they were less keen all the time. I tried to share with them what I was learning about the plants. On our walks, I'd pick things and nibble them, testing what on the large spectrum of 'edible' was actually tasty.

One late summer we were out for a walk. It was hot. The summer holidays had stretched on for too long and we were all ready to get back into routine. The boys were hōhā; they hadn't wanted to come and they were dragging their feet. Sweat trickled down my back. I wanted to just *be*, to relax among the green, but I was distracted by the boys scrapping with each other.

'Taste this,' I said to Fraser, holding out a long leaf of wild mustard.

'Do I have to?' he said, teasing, but after giving it a rinse with his water bottle he put it in his mouth. 'Woah, it's so spicy!'

I liked to test Fraser and Willoughby. 'Hey, you two,' I said. 'What can you see around here that we could eat if we were starving?' They rolled their eyes. We were all sweating in the heat of the day. No one was in the mood.

'I'd order a pizza,' Willoughby joked. 'They probably deliver to the Esplanade.'

But despite the jokes, some things were sinking in. Willo would surprise me by pointing out a plant on our walks, identifying it correctly and listing its properties, when I'd assumed he'd only been half listening.

The previous year, he'd started university and enrolled in a creative writing paper. For one assignment, he had written a poem about picking tomatoes with me. I'd asked if I could read it. He'd been too shy to hand it over but sent it to me by email. In the poem, he described the two of us standing in the warmth of a summer's evening, picking the last of the tomatoes before we pulled out the plants, marking the end of the season.

In this moment it dawned on me that I'd raised a young man who knew that to tend to land and grow food alongside family made for a subject for poetry. Turns out that some seeds, sown early, eventually bloom.

I let the realisation sink in. My most meaningful harvest.

*

To the side of the track, I spotted a parting in the long grass where people had been walking – a desire line.

'Let's go and see what's down there!' I tried to make my voice cheerful. Could I divert us all from our cranky moods?

We ambled through the divided long grass, down a short slope to a small clearing. Just thirty metres or so from the main track, there was a tall wilding peach tree. We'd struck it just at the right moment – the branches were heavy with small, pink peaches. There was evidence of savvy locals in the form of peach pits dropped on the ground, sucked clean. Most of the low pickings were gone.

'Wow, I think they're ripe!' I said.

I pulled off the nearest peach I could reach. The flesh inside was white, and they were intensely sweet. Sweeter than any peach I had ever tasted.

'They're perfect!' I handed one to each of the boys. They slurped them down, the peaches nearly dissolving into juice at the slightest pressure. We were soon covered in peach juice down our wrists and T-shirt fronts.

Fraser said, 'Mmm, and the firm ones taste as good as the soft ones.'

My habit of always carrying a tote bag with me paid off in moments like this. A gesture of openness – if I carried a receptacle, I was inviting it to be filled. Nature abhors a vacuum.

When we'd all eaten enough peaches to slake our thirst, I said, 'Shall we pick a few to take home? Try to find some firmer ones so they don't squash in the bag.'

The boys climbed up into the tree's centre and reached for the fruit unblemished by bugs or birds. I carefully placed them into the bag. When its weight started to pull at my shoulder I said, 'That's enough. Leave some for other folks.' Fraser and I helped them climb back down.

It was a happy distraction from the fractious state we'd all been in twenty minutes earlier. We walked back to the main track and then to the river to wash our hands and mouths. The boys had stopped fighting, and they started looking for the biggest rocks to hiff into the water. Even after washing my hands, the sweet floral scent of the peaches clung to me and I felt calmer, happier.

'How did you know there'd be a peach tree down there?' said Fraser.

I shrugged. 'I didn't know, but the other locals did.'

That night, I looked up the spiritual meaning of the peach tree on a plant-essence website I liked to refer to. It said that the peach tree is known as the selfless mother of the plant world, a balm for soothing irritability and tension, helping us expand our sympathies to the needs of others. It could also help children to get along better with their siblings.

I didn't need any persuading. I'd just seen it happen.

*

Ten years after the first foraging article had appeared in the newspaper, I was contacted by another *Manawatū Standard* journalist, Shilpy Arora. She had a theory that there was an increased interest in foraging because of rising food prices and wanted to talk to a local forager about it.

She asked if I'd take her on a foraging walk, the same thing Bronwyn Torrie had asked Madz and I a decade before. This time I didn't have any small children to wrangle, so I said yes.

I was nervous on the day of the interview. Whenever I take a newbie out for a forage, I always have some anxiety about whether I'll find enough things to capture their interest or to convince them that it is a worthwhile pursuit. But Shilpy turned out to be an enthusiastic foraging companion, genuinely excited by the plants we found. She told me about her grandfather, who had foraged for medicinal plants in the Himalayan mountains to make potions for her family. 'I never paid much attention at the time, though, and I regret that now,' she said.

When the article came out, it was accompanied by a large photograph of me on the path, carrying a basket full of plants and looking slightly bashful. It described what I'd found: 'nasturtium leaves, bright yellow Indian cress blossoms, mustard leaves, fennel seeds and chamomile flowers [...] all free and enough to cook a meal.'

It was strange to be in the newspaper for foraging again exactly a decade after the first article. It made me think about all the ways I was different and all the ways I was still the same. Although my enchantment with the world had taken some knocks, the love of foraging as a way to pay close attention, observe the seasons and find simple wonder had not wavered.

*

As Magnus was finishing high school, I turned fifty. I was neither young nor particularly old, but suddenly there were likely more years behind me than ahead. In Chinese medicine, rather than being seen as the start of a decline, menopause is called 'the second spring', a kind of second adolescence. Just as the first adolescence is full of discovery and exploration (and hormones), so is a woman's midlife, if she chooses to sit with the shadows and embrace the changes.

I looked to my favourite herbal-medicine books for which herbs and plants were helpful at this time of my life. Perimenopause brought new physical and emotional challenges. I read that it was important to increase my 'capacity for bitters': herbs that are bitter and astringent, like nettle and dandelion. These tonic herbs support the liver, and it's the liver that has to flush all the excess hormones.

The Western palette is so skewed towards the very sweet and very salty that at first bitterness can seem unpalatable. In some cultures it's common practice to take a bitters tonic after eating to aid digestion.

I started drinking a litre of bitter infusions of foraged and cultivated herbs each day. Mostly nettles, which make a great all-round tonic for midlife, and also dandelion, yarrow, red clover and shepherd's purse. Eventually I learned to drink it without grimacing.

A strong infusion takes time, so I would set it to brew when I first got up in the morning. Pouring the boiling water over the tangle of fresh and dried herbs and watching the first tinges of green emerge was a way to make a small dedication to myself before I had to be a parent, a wife and all my other roles. After steeping for some hours, the infusions turned a deep, cloudy forest green. Fraser started calling these brews my 'swamp water'.

To me, the idea of increasing my capacity for bitters matched what the midlife shakedown asks of a woman. What things in my life did I need help to metabolise? If I could increase my capacity for digesting my 'bitters', could I cultivate the ground for sweetness in my old age?

Thinking about midlife brought to mind the elder tree. My ancestors knew the elder tree as 'Mother Elder'. In Europe it is regarded as a spiritually protective tree. Elderflowers and elder berries are rock stars of the foraging calendar and among my favourites. Both the flowers and berries possess unique scents, flavour profiles and healing properties that make them much loved and sought after.

The elder tree's two main offerings bookend winter. The berries, rich in vitamin C and excellent cold and flu medicine, appear just as summer descends into autumn. Then the frothy flowers unfurl in spring for summer socialising and celebrations. Elderflower as a flavour heralds summer, appearing just as the mercurial weather of spring steadies into summer's more committed heat. Elderflower sings when made into drinks: fermented fizzes, sweet cordials or elderflower champagne.

Fifty felt significant. Midlife is the portal to that third section of life: elderhood. Canadian grief worker Stephen Jenkinson speaks about the idea that in communities there are 'elders' and 'olders'. He challenges the idea that everyone who ages becomes an elder. Olders are people who just get older, without integrating their shadows or choosing to be of service to their communities and descendants. Eldership is earned. Ultimately, it's younger people who will decide if a person is 'elder' or 'older' through who they seek counsel from and who they respect. This idea resonated with me.

I began to think of myself as a baby elder. It felt important to do the shadow work, release old griefs and make conscious decisions in order to become the useful, supportive, playful, creative elder I hoped to be in the future. I might not get to choose 'elder' for myself, but I could take on a voluntary apprenticeship to try to become one.

The cliches of the midlife crisis exist for a reason, although I prefer to think of it more as a midlife passage, a slow shadow walk, when you take some big questions underground for a while before re-emerging into the light. A time to inspect your accumulated emotional baggage. Over a lifetime things collect and coagulate, like sediment on the psyche. What could be shed? What might be sloughed off? What did I need to make peace with so I could step through the hag stone portal once again into a new form, free from regrets?

I took my hag stone out from where I had tucked it away. I put it on once again and it lay cool on my clavicle. Now I wore it as decoration, a literal touchstone. I no longer imagined it held the secrets of the future, but it reminded me that everything I needed was within me. As much as I loved its origin story, I knew no mystical talisman could deliver more insight than my own intuition.

I'd had a career only in the sense that I'd *careered* from one thing to the next, propelled more by bumper cars of circumstance than any kind of conscious planning or strategic thinking. I'd been a writer, a teacher, a mother, a forager, a gardener and a community activist and the riches from these things had come from the intrinsic peace and satisfaction of living my beliefs.

Foraging, walking, watching and harvesting had given me a consistent green thread to hold on to, whatever else life was throwing at me. I was a forager of many things: meaning and connection, food and medicine.

I'd wound up not so far from where I'd begun, a place where local food and wild food was valued, in a strong, generous community.

*

Somehow, Fraser and I had been married twenty-five years. He asked me what I wanted to do to mark it and I said, 'Throw a huge potluck dinner party in our backyard.' We dressed up as John Lennon and Yoko Ono in bright white suits and got a friend to take a black-and-white photograph for the party invitations. In it, we held up a version of their iconic sign: *War Is Over If You Want It*. We felt like celebrating this milestone; we'd been through a lot and emerged, still together, still in love, out the other side.

Mum and Dad couriered down a box of food for the party: a large chilly bin of smoked trout, frozen pheasant and venison from Dad; a box of pickles, relishes and preserved fruits from Mum. 'In my late seventies and I'm still feeding my kids from the land,' said Dad's note. 'Happy big anniversary, you two.'

We put up wooden trestle tables, hung bunting, prepped a fire pit, threaded coloured lights all through the trees. Friends came from near and far. Fiona from our Bristol days. Sharon and Phil from Slow Farm and our other permie friends. Caro, Madz and the other MAMAs. Maria, her partner, Joe, and their two girls. Willoughby was on drinks duty, pouring wine and keeping the punch bowl topped up. Even Magnus came out for a little while before getting overwhelmed and retreating, demanding that a dinner plate be delivered to his room. Soon the whole yard was full of people lolling on picnic blankets and lawn chairs.

There had been bushfires raging over in Australia for weeks. They had turned our spring skies unusual shades of orange and yellow. The garden had a strange peachy glow.

'Trust you to order up some theatrical lighting from nature,' Maria said.

Fraser peered up at the uncanny sky and said, 'It feels a bit like a party at the end of the world.'

I kissed his cheek. 'You always know how to bring the romance.'

The dining table was laden with colourful potluck dishes. When it was time to eat, I stood on the back porch and rang a loud dinner bell. Our friends lined up in a queue that spiralled out of the kitchen, through the laundry and into the garden. The sight of this long dinner line full of beloved friends holding empty plates to be filled from our collective efforts made me happier than I'd felt in years. Potluck food, friends strumming guitars around the fire, lying on picnic blankets among the romping weeds. Humble, but to me a kind of heaven.

Over dinner, I caught up with a friend who had also recently turned fifty. She had a lot going on. She was leaving everything – her marriage, her house, the city – off on a midlife adventure to find herself. I admired her courage. I wished I were tougher, funnier, braver and not so easily bruised. More acorn than apricot.

We talked for a long time about her exit plans. It was a kind of last supper. She had to leave the party early because she was flying out the next day. After she'd eaten, I walked her to the end of our driveway, hugged her goodbye and watched her drive away.

The odd peachy sky was growing dark. Back at the party, someone had cranked the music up. Probably Maria. Dusk meant that the dancing hour had arrived.

I thought about how my friend was going, leaving it all behind, and I was staying. How there are moments when we look at what we already have and we choose it again. How staying is not the same as not going anywhere.

I have a long way to go, right here.

Foraged herbal infusion for perimenopause

Makes 1 litre

While there are many herbs that benefit perimenopause and postmenopause, most are imported or expensive. This infusion is made from two that can be easily foraged: nettle (*Urtica dioica*) and red clover (*Trifolium pratense*). Nettle is often found in edgelands. The best time to look for it is late winter into spring. I often find nettle growing along fence lines in the shade of trees. Take care while foraging that you are confident you have correctly identified *Urtica dioica*. New Zealand's native nettle (*Urtica ferox*) is poisonous. Consult your foraging guides.

Nettle is a marvellous general tonic for perimenopausal and postmenopausal women. Among its benefits are adrenal support and boosted energy, plus it builds blood. It can protect the heart and bones, assist with hot flushes, and help with the anxiety prevalent at this time of life. A lovely side effect is that it is also good for making hair thick and lustrous.

Red clover is a common lawn plant and can be found anywhere that a lawn is a multi-culture of grass plants, not a monoculture. My most recent harvest of red clover flowers was out at Foxton Beach, where it was growing abundantly everywhere there was grass.

Red clover can help with menstrual issues, heart health, bone density and hot flushes.

Unlike a tea or tisane, an infusion is a very strong brew of herbs steeped for longer than a tea and then drunk over 24 hours or so. It can take a bit of adjustment to integrate the practice of drinking a herbal infusion every day. I make mine in the morning when I make my breakfast. If not refrigerated, nettle infusion can 'go off' after about 12 hours. Try drinking it when you would normally reach for plain water.

The infusion doesn't taste especially great; it has a dense, grassy flavour that I'm used to now but still don't relish. I add a bit of ginger to assist with the flavour.

This infusion is made with three parts nettle to one part red clover flowers.

Ingredients

3 tablespoons dried nettle

1 tablespoon dried red clover flowers

½ teaspoon ground ginger

1 litre boiling water

Method

Add nettle, red clover flowers and ginger to a 1 litre jar, teapot or flask. Pour over boiling water.

Stir with a wooden spoon for a minute or so, then leave to steep for at least 4 hours, longer if possible. The water will go a dark, khaki green.

Elderberry syrup

Makes approximately 600 ml

Elderberry syrup can help with recovery from colds and flus. It contains high levels of vitamin C and antioxidants, plus it tastes very good. Adults should take 1 tablespoon each day that a cold persists, children 1 teaspoon.

This recipe will make enough for a small bottle of syrup; hopefully that should be enough to get you through a winter, but if you have a large family or household you might want to make more. It will last around 3 months in the fridge. As elderberries are an autumn harvest, this means the syrup will last through the winter, when it's most needed.

Ripe elderberries are very small and delicate, making them hard to handle. When very ripe they disintegrate at the smallest pressure. A good trick is to lightly rinse them, allow them to dry and then freeze them before processing. Once frozen, the berries will easily come off the umbels if you 'comb' them with a fork above a wide bowl.

Ingredients

2 cups fresh elderberries
1 cinnamon stick
4 whole cloves
1 teaspoon ground ginger
4 cups water
1 cup honey

Method

Sterilise a dark glass bottle.

Put all the ingredients except the honey into a small saucepan. Bring to the boil and then turn down the heat and simmer for about 10 minutes. Take off the heat.

With a potato masher, mash the berries to extract as much juice as possible.

Strain the liquid into a heatproof jug using a fine sieve or piece of muslin. Compost the berries and spices. Allow the liquid to cool down from boiling. While it is still slightly warm, stir in the honey. If a lot of the liquid has evaporated, add enough boiled water to fill your bottle.

Once the honey has dissolved, bottle the syrup, label and refrigerate.

EPILOGUE

Woman slow walking

I've always done my best thinking while I'm walking in the bush or by the river. But these days my left leg is, to use New Zealand slang, munted.

It started with an injury after a yoga teacher cranked me into a posture beyond the stretching capacity of my fascia, causing my knee to make a gut-churning sound like a dry stick breaking. In spite of years of different physio regimes, acupuncture and sports massage, it's never been the same again. The rehabilitation efforts helped a bit but now I can only walk about five kilometres before my knee gives up and my leg begins to *sproing* out from my hip in a disarmingly elastic way. It becomes a noodle-y, useless leg unless I stop and rest it. If I skip the rest stop, my hip also begins to radiate pain and I start to limp. Nonetheless, for a long time I kept hoping that with time and care my leg might heal.

This injury makes me a frustrating walking partner for my friends and family. I've done a lot of apologetic explaining before walking with new people to give them a chance to bow out. Where once I charged up the Kepler Track and walked for ten hours a day in the long light of the Scottish summer on the West Highland Way, now I am comically, painfully slow.

Then, at the beginning of New Zealand's first Covid-19 lockdown, I was rushing around the backyard in bare feet when I accidentally kicked a large concrete block that we use as a stop for our gate. The pain was immense. I limped to my bed and lay back, crying in agony.

Over the day, my toes swelled up into a purple mess. I'm sure I broke a couple, but the first week of the first lockdown was not a time to bother an A & E department with such a minor injury. I took some painkillers, gingerly wrapped a comfrey poultice around my toes, hopped about a lot and waited for the swelling to go down. I figured that not much can be done for broken toes anyway. Since then, my foot aches with nerve pain if I stand on it for too long, adding to the sad state of my left leg.

There's something of a typical tramper in New Zealand. They are all about speed, efficiency and beating personal records. Even at my fittest, when I tramped with this kind of walker I didn't enjoy it very much, always wondering what the hurry was. They are Edmund Hillary-style trampers – they want to 'knock the bastard off', whatever the 'bastard' of the day is.

I don't want to knock any bastards off. I want to switch off from any sense of urgency and immerse myself in the soothing green of the forest. I find it hard to rush through a wild place because the natural environment is all *potential*, all calling voices. All around are things to eat, to use as natural medicines or to just admire and sit with. In every corner are new plants to be curious about. Is that flash of orange in the bush ripe karamū berries? Why are the leaves of these kawakawa so pocked and lacy and the ones over here untouched? Could today be the day I find some tender kareao tips, the 'bush asparagus' that is so hard to find because of how beloved it is by deer and possums?

I've always lived at a slower speed, dwelling in the present tense while all around me people, life, the world, hurtle forward, intent on tomorrow. I'm the one who drags the pace, way at the back, calling out, 'Hey! Stop! Look! No, *really* look!'

To forage is to slow down enough to be open to the world's mystery. This can be a challenge for those who like certainty and maps with clear destinations.

The forest is the other half of a dialogue, full of unpredictable and ever surprising presences, and answers to questions I didn't know I had at the outset of a walk.

*

In 2017, a new word for autism was officially added to the Māori dictionary: takiwātanga, meaning 'in their own time and space'. The word was devised by civil servant Keri Opai, in consultation with the Māori and autism communities, to create an empowering word from te ao Māori.

I think it captures so well the essence of autism. Magnus lives in a parallel world to ours, not separate. It runs alongside and weaves through our family – not better or worse, just different.

'Magnus is lucky. You two have got a very high tolerance for quirkiness,' Norah, our special-needs advisor, had told us in the early days. 'You've made life very safe for him.'

It was true; we had stretched and stretched our capacity for acceptance until it got near snapping point.

The years we spent coming to terms with Magnus's diagnosis and working through our emotions also seemed to be in their own time and space. At a course about parenting and grief, I learned that memory loss and an altered perception of time are common effects of grieving. It was a relief to hear that I was experiencing normal symptoms and not going crazy, as I sometimes felt I was.

My perception of time changed profoundly then, and has never fully recalibrated. The only moments I don't feel this disorientation are when I'm in the garden or in nature. Since Magnus was diagnosed, it feels like our family has been 'in our own space and time'. In a place that the outer world never fully witnesses and can't fully understand.

*

Last year I was walking in the Pohangina Valley with my family. As usual, I was a long way behind them, wrestling with guilt about slowing them down, ruining their fun. They were flying ahead. I could hear their voices getting fainter as they climbed the ridge to the lookout over the giant tōtara trees in the reserve below.

Three words came into my head and repeated themselves in a plodding rhythm that echoed my trudging steps. *Woman slow walking, woman slow walking, woman slow walking.*

I trudged up the steep steps to the lookout where the boys waited for me. By the time I caught them up, they'd already drained their water bottles and eaten from the stash of cashew nuts and mandarins we'd packed. I sat down on the bench at the lookout and said, 'You guys go ahead. You don't have to wait for me. I'll catch up with you back at the car.' Fraser gave me a kiss and a sad look, then they took off and were soon gone out of sight.

The voice returned. *Your walking is different now. It's time to accept it. There's nothing wrong with going slow. If you let yourself fully become woman slow walking, what could you learn? Who might you be?*

Tears prickled my eyes. Another moment calling for acceptance, making peace with an uninvited challenge, facing what was happening. It was time to release the fantasy that my leg would get better.

I moved along the seat so that the sun's warmth was on my face, rubbed my aching knee. *Woman slow walking.* That was me: not deft or swift or agile, but able to be and to see in all the ways.

I'm the plodding caboose to my family group of three strong men. I gift them twice the exercise they might have had without me because they frequently have to double-back to find me. After many years of saying 'I'm sorry I'm so slow' on every walk, it was time for me to be done with apologising. My role now: back scout, tail-end twitcher, human exclamation point.

I didn't mind that I'd be walking the last stretch alone. When I'm alone I am not slow because I am not compared to anyone else. I'm at the perfect pace ... my own. Alone I can dissolve into the forest for a while. I can feel the pull of the soil beneath my feet with each of my slow steps. Half woman, half tree root.

The plants teach me with their elemental wisdom. *Recharge yourself in the sun. Be unquestioningly generous. Trust that what you need will come to you. And always, always reach towards the light.*

My leg was rested. I stood up and walked back down to the path. As I walked, I looked up to try to identify the trees. I scanned the ground for fungi, for flowers, for wild herbs. A pīwakawaka followed me as my feet scuffed up the forest floor, revealing a banquet of bugs. I wasn't broken or wrong. I just *was*. A mycelial node in a family, a community. Not at the centre but interwoven, in the right place for where I needed to be. Takiwātanga.

A woman slow walking … in forest time.

Appendices

APPENDIX A

A beginner's guide to foraging

Open your eyes

I'm spending the weekend at a beachside cottage with three friends. We've taken ourselves away from our families to write, hang out and recharge. On arrival, we spill out of the car, Alana unlocks the door, and everyone rushes in to check out the house and claim a bed. I am distracted by a small, scraggly herb bed beside the front door. It's a bit unloved but the mint is regenerating, the tips bright green and inviting. I pinch off a handful – it will be the first of many restorative pots of tea.

Curious about the rest of the green surrounds, I walk past the house and into the backyard. On first glance, it appears fairly barren – a typical beach-bach yard. But then I slow down and look more closely. I see abundant red clover flowering in the lawn. Another herb for the teapot. I fill the loose pocket of my dress with pink tufts of red-clover flowers. There's a gnarled old lemon tree in the corner of the yard that's desperate for a prune, but the outer branches are dripping with fruit; I put two lemons in the other pocket. I'm running out of hands, but in front of the back shed I see a large and rambling beach spinach plant – a supplement for dinner. I find a fat stalk in the top of the plant; if I can break it there, I'll be able to take a large bunch with just one pinch of my fingertips. Pockets bulging, one hand full of mint, the other spinach, I go indoors.

Alana laughs. 'Where did that lot come from? There's nothing out there!'

There's always *something* out there. With a forager's curiosity, any stretch of green, however humble, becomes a terrain of possibility and discovery. The main skill of foraging is to sharpen your eyes.

Learning to forage is learning a new way to look.

Many ways to forage

For most people, the first thing that comes to mind with foraging is free wild food! But there are many different approaches to foraging, all with different focuses and nuances. Like with any activity, scratch the surface and you'll find great diversity, worlds within worlds.

In the foraging community in Aotearoa, there are people who forage ingredients for high-end restaurants, people who forage medicinal plants to make skin care and health tinctures, and people who forage plants for fabric dyes. I have a potter friend who forages the riverbanks of the Tararua Range for a wild-sourced clay he likes that has unusual pink blotches once fired. There are mushroom fanatics and seaweed experts. There are plant detectives, people who hunt out old heirloom varieties to save the seeds and bring the plants back from the brink of being lost. There are those who make ice creams from foraged ingredients. In the alcohol market, foraged botanicals are appearing in commercial vodkas and gins.

Then there's the other kinds of urban foraging: dumpster diving, mooching inorganic waste, op-shopping.

It's easy to regard foraging as a quaint middle-class pursuit, nice for those who have the time and resources, or a practice for elite inner-city restaurants so they can add a zero to the price of a plate. But foraging happens across class, social and ethnic backgrounds. Some people are looking for free food as a necessity rather than a hobby.

A nature-centred mindset

Foraging is zero waste and locavore: you transport the food, the rain irrigates the plants, and the only packaging involved is the bag you use. Just as chopping firewood is said to warm you twice, foraged foods feed you twice. Foraging for foods and medicines has the dual benefits of a walk in nature to find the foods, and the goodness and satisfaction of eating them.

I also like to encourage the rebel spirit of foraging. Foraging is slightly transgressive in Western culture – not quite lawless, but at least a bit edgy. To forage you need to be a little cheeky, proactive and tenacious, and doesn't the world need more people like that?

Foraging is not like going food shopping; what you want is not necessarily what you'll get. I might go out with a sense of what's in season and where I might be able to find it, but a large part of the fun is that foraging is unpredictable. To be a committed forager, you have to maintain an attitude of spontaneity and be open to what the terrain wants to offer you that day. When I forage with an agenda, hoping to bring home a good amount of something or find a particular seasonal delicacy, I seem to come home empty-handed. Other times I'll be out for a walk and not even thinking about foraging, when I happen on a cache of wilding fruit, or a dense blackberry patch, or a golden pool of gingko leaves.

You'll know the foraging bug has taken hold of you when every little patch of green life starts to call out to you. Your new foraging eyes will comb the grass for salad greens and medicinal weeds, the bushes for berries and spice seeds, and you'll develop a crick in your neck from gazing up at trees, cruising for fruit.

Foraging is a slow, relational and lifelong journey; there's always more to learn. But just make a start and you'll see how swiftly your skills grow – pattern-sensing, land-reading, plant identification and sense-knowing. There is nothing like the satisfaction of garnering food that hasn't been obtained with money, or even through the labours of cultivating a garden, but through your own explorations, by making yourself into a question that the land can answer.

Foraging gear

The main thing a foraging wardrobe needs is practicality: sturdy shoes, weather-appropriate clothing, harvesting bags and tools, and, most importantly, lots of roomy pockets.

I prefer a light cotton cross-body bag so that my arms are free, the bag won't slip off my shoulder and the opening is wide for ease of collecting. In this larger cotton bag I carry some smaller cotton bags and a sharp pocketknife. Some foragers prefer sturdy kitchen scissors, others use plastic Stanley knives because they are small and light.

Seasoned foragers are generally opportunistic folks. Because I never know when I might stumble across something interesting and edible, I carry pocketknives in all my bags. I have scissors in the glove box, secateurs in the boot, and bags within bags tucked everywhere – endless Russian dolls of bag carrying, just in case.

Then there's processing and preserving your finds – you'll need the usual array of cooking and preserving equipment in your kitchen. It's useful to have some wide, shallow wicker baskets for drying herbs. Fraser found an excellent electric dehydrator for me on Trade Me. I've found most of my kitchen equipment at the op shop.

When to forage

Generally, the optimal time to harvest is a fine day, after the morning dew has dried but before the heat of the afternoon (if it is summer). With greens, always go for new growth where possible, as the older a plant grows, the more dense and tough it becomes. Flowers are best picked before they fully open because they will travel better and will unfurl once in water. A bloom picked at its full expression will droop quickly in a vase.

The guidelines

1. **Always apply commons sense.** Make decisions for the benefit of all human and more-than-human beings in the ecosystem you're exploring. How can you be helpful to that place, in that moment, on that day? (One great way to help any natural environment is to pick up rubbish – especially plastic rubbish. If there is an overwhelming amount of rubbish, report it to the local council so that it gets cleaned up quickly.)

2. **Ask permission where permission is needed.** Don't wander into private property without permission. Check local-council guidelines for foraging in parks and reserves.

3. Be certain about a plant's identification. If you are new to foraging, get a couple of good plant-identification books. A pocket-sized one is good so you can take it on your expeditions.

There are some good plant-identification apps available. PlantNet, iNaturalist and PlantSnap are all free at the time of writing. Don't rely too much on images on the internet, however, unless the website is highly credible. Photographs are often mislabelled. Consider that plants can present quite differently in the northern and southern hemispheres.

Some professional foragers run courses or foraging walks. Or just ask a friend with foraging knowledge to teach you a few plants each time you go for a walk together.

4. Be pollution aware. City soils and urban streams can sometimes be contaminated with heavy metals, pesticides and other chemicals. Avoid foraging from industrial sites or sites where you aren't sure of the recent history.

5. Apply the rule of fourths. When harvesting plants, there's a loose rule of fourths. Leave a quarter for the plant (so it can retain its vitality and reproduce), a quarter for whatever else relies on the plant in the ecosystem (animals, insects, soil regeneration), a quarter for other foragers, and take a quarter for yourself (although you'll often take much less, depending on the plant).

Never take all of a plant. (The exception to this would be an invasive plant, if in harvesting it you are doing conservation work for the wellbeing of the land. Some examples of this would be wilding pines, banana passionfruit vine and gorse.)

6. Slow down, take your time, go deep. If you're starting out as a forager, you're probably hungry to learn as many plants as you can, which is understandable – the enthusiasm of a beginner's mind! However, once you've learned a selection of plants, choose just one or two that particularly appeal to you to go deeper with. Learning the full spectrum of a plant's offerings is a relationship, so try slowing things down to be in that relationship at plant speed rather than human speed. By this I mean, observe the plant through all the seasons, experiment with different ways to eat it or make home remedies from it. Observe how much use you make of what you've foraged, too. Do you enjoy the dishes? The herb teas? Do you enjoy the processing needed when you harvest a lot of seasonal fruit? There's little point in foraging things you don't like to process, eat or drink. Your preferences will form over time as you experiment.

You could start a foraging journal, where you draw the plants or glue in photographs of them and write down your observations. Look out for them whenever you're out walking. Do they start appearing to you in other ways, through art, in books, even in conversation? Plants seem to speak through synchronicity, appearing in all kinds of unusual places once we've begun a relationship with them.

7. Always say thank you. In the moment of harvesting, say thank you to the plant, the tree, the elements, the land you have harvested from, the mana whenua of where you're standing. Gratitude is the secret ingredient in an ecologically sound foraging practice.

The permaculture principles

A nature-informed design system

You don't have to be a gardener to use the permaculture principles – they contain a lot of wisdom that can be used to design any project. Learning them has fortified values I grew up with, re-enlivening them with fresh language, and also given me a solid framework to apply to decision-making in my life. The permaculture principles can be applied to wildcrafting with a kaupapa of care and custodianship.

It's important to acknowledge that many of the permaculture principles are endemic to the world views of Indigenous cultures around the world, and permaculture has borrowed from many of these.

There is much to be said about every one of the principles, but here they are in their barest form. If you're interested in delving further, I've listed some of my favourite permaculture books in Appendix C.

The permaculture principles
1. Observe and interact.
2. Catch and store energy.
3. Obtain a yield.
4. Apply self-regulation and accept feedback.
5. Use and value renewable resources and services.
6. Produce no waste.
7. Design from pattern to details.
8. Integrate rather than segregate.
9. Use small and slow solutions.
10. Use and value diversity.
11. Use edges and value the margins.
12. Creatively use and respond to change.

APPENDIX C

Recommended reading list

Here are some of my favourite books relating to themes in this book.

Foraging and plant identification

Owen and Audrey Bishop, *New Zealand Wild Flowers Handbook*, Hodder & Stoughton, Auckland, 1994.

Andrew Crowe, *A Field Guide to the Native Edible Plants of New Zealand*, Penguin, Auckland, 2004.

Gail Duff, *The Countryside Cookbook: Recipes and remedies*, Doubleday, Sydney, 1982.

Alys Fowler, *The Thrifty Forager: Living off your local landscape*, Kyle Cathie, London, 2011.

Euell Gibbons, *Stalking the Wild Asparagus*, Alan C. Hood & Company, Chambersburg, PA, 1962.

Johanna Knox, *The Forager's Treasury: The essential guide to finding and using wild plants in Aotearoa*, Allen and Unwin, Auckland, 2021.

Richard Mabey, *Food for Free*, Collins, London, 1972.

Sheila Natusch, *Wild Fare for Wilderness Foragers*, Collins, Auckland, 1979.

Murdoch Riley, *Māori Healing Remedies: Rongoā Māori*, Viking Sevenseas, Wellington, 2018.

J. T. Salmon, *The Native Trees of New Zealand*, Reed Methuen, Auckland, 1980.

Julia Sich, 'Julia's Guide to Edible Weeds and Wild Green Smoothies', 2012, juliasedibleweeds.com

Gwen Skinner, *Simply Living: A gatherer's guide to New Zealand's fields, forests and shores*, Reed, Auckland, 1981.

Foraging memoirs

Ava Chin, *Eating Wildly: Foraging for life, love and the perfect meal*, Simon & Schuster, New York, 2014.

Rebecca Lerner, *Dandelion Hunter: Foraging the urban wilderness*, Lyons Press, Guildford, CT, 2013.

Alysia Vasey, *The Yorkshire Forager: A wild food survival story*, Headline, London, 2021.

Plant medicine

Holly Bellebuono, *The Healing Kitchen: Cooking with nourishing herbs for health, wellness, and vitality*, Roost Books, Boulder, 2016.

Isla Burgess and Mary Allan, *A Women's Health and Wellbeing Kete*, Vols I & II, Viriditas Books, 2020.

Dr David Frawley and Dr Vasant Lad, *The Yoga of Herbs: An Ayurvedic guide to herbal medicine*, Lotus Press, Twin Lakes, WI, 2001.

Rosemary Gladstar, *Rosemary Gladstar's Medicinal Herbs: A beginner's guide*, Storey Publishing, North Adams, MA, 2012.

Lucy Jones, *Self-Sufficient Herbalism: A guide to growing, gathering and processing herbs for medicinal use*, Aeon Books, London, 2020.

Kami McBride, *The Herbal Kitchen: Bring lasting health to you and your family with 50 easy-to-find common herbs and over 250 recipes*, Red Wheel, Newbury Port, MA, 2021.

Permaculture

David Holmgren, *RetroSuburbia: The downshifter's guide to a resilient future*, Melliodora, Hepburn Springs, 2018.

Looby Macnamara, *People and Permaculture: Caring and designing for ourselves, each other and the planet*, Permanent Publications, East Meon, 2012.

Rosemary Morrow, *Earth Restorer's Guide to Permaculture*, Melliodora, Hepburn Springs, 2022.

Food and nature connection

Florencia Clifford, *Feeding Orchids to the Slugs: Tales from a Zen kitchen*, Vala Publishers, Bristol, 2012.

Ross Gay, *The Book of Delights*, Algonquin Books of Chapel Hill, Chapel Hill, NC, 2019.

Jay Griffiths, *Wild: An elemental journey*, Penguin, Auckland, 2008.

Philip Heselton, *The Elements of Earth Mysteries*, Element
Books, Rockport, MA, 1991.
Richard Mabey, *Street Flowers,* Kestrel Books,
Harmondsworth, 1976.

Simplicity

John Lane, *Timeless Simplicity: Creative living in a consumer
society*, Green Books, Totnes, 2001.
Annie Raser-Rowland with Adam Grubb, *The Art of Frugal
Hedonism: A guide to spending less while enjoying everything
more*, Melliodora, Hepburn Springs, 2016.

Food localisation and regenerative agriculture

Scott Chaskey, *Seedtime: On the history, husbandry, politics and
promise of seeds*, Rodale, Emmaus, PA, 2014.
Masanobu Fukuoka, *The One-Straw Revolution: An
introduction to natural farming*, Rodale, Emmaus, PA, 1978.
Janisse Ray, *The Seed Underground: A growing revolution to save
food*, Chelsea Green, White River Junction, VT, 2012.
Vicki Robin, *Blessing the Hands That Feed Us: What eating
closer to home can teach us about food, community and our
place on Earth*, Viking, New York, 2014.

Community food in Aotearoa

Jessica Hutchings and Jo Smith (eds), *Te Mahi Oneone Hua
Parakore: A Māori soil sovereignty and wellbeing handbook*,
Freerange Press, Christchurch, 2020.
Emma Johnson (ed.), *Kai and Culture: Food stories from
Aotearoa*, Freerange Press, Christchurch, 2017.

Sophie Merkens, *Grow: Wāhine finding connection through food*, Beatnik Publishing, Auckland, 2022.

Nick Roskruge, *Ko Mahinga o Tōku Māra Kai: Establishing māra kai*, Tāhuri Whenua, Palmerston North, 2021.

Stone Soup Syndicate, A boisterous yet convivial discussion about food and its place in our lives, stonesoupsyndicate.com